THE HORROR PLAYS
ENGLISH RESTOR

Studies in Performance and Early Modern Drama

General Editor's Preface
Helen Ostovich, McMaster University

Performance assumes a string of creative, analytical, and collaborative acts that, in defiance of theatrical ephemerality, live on through records, manuscripts, and printed books. The monographs and essay collections in this series offer original research which addresses theatre histories and performance histories in the context of the sixteenth and seventeenth century life. Of especial interest are studies in which women's activities are a central feature of discussion as financial or technical supporters (patrons, musicians, dancers, seamstresses, wigmakers, or 'gatherers'), if not authors or performers per se. Welcome too are critiques of early modern drama that not only take into account the production values of the plays, but also speculate on how intellectual advances or popular culture affect the theatre.

The series logo, selected by my colleague Mary V. Silcox, derives from Thomas Combe's duodecimo volume, *The Theater of Fine Devices* (London, 1592), Emblem VI, sig. B. The emblem of four masks has a verse which makes claims for the increasing complexity of early modern experience, a complexity that makes interpretation difficult. Hence the corresponding perhaps uneasy rise in sophistication:

> Masks will be more hereafter in request,
> And grow more deare than they did heretofore.

No longer simply signs of performance 'in play and jest', the mask has become the 'double face' worn 'in earnest' even by 'the best' of people, in order to manipulate or profit from the world around them. The books stamped with this design attempt to understand the complications of performance produced on stage and interpreted by the audience, whose experiences outside the theatre may reflect the emblem's argument:

> Most men do use some colour'd shift
> For to conceal their craftie drift.

Centuries after their first presentations, the possible performance choices and meanings they engender still stir the imaginations of actors, audiences, and readers of early plays. The products of scholarly creativity in this series, I hope, will also stir imaginations to new ways of thinking about performance.

The Horror Plays of the English Restoration

ANNE HERMANSON
The Open University, UK

Routledge
Taylor & Francis Group

LONDON AND NEW YORK

First published 2014 by Ashgate Publishing

Published 2016 by Routledge
2 Park Square, Milton Park, Abingdon, Oxon OX14 4RN
605 Third Avenue, New York, NY 10017

First issued in paperback 2021

Routledge is an imprint of the Taylor & Francis Group, an informa business

Publisher's Note
The publisher has gone to great lengths to ensure the quality of this reprint but points out that some imperfections in the original copies may be apparent.

British Library Cataloguing in Publication Data
A catalogue record for this book is available from the British Library

The Library of Congress has cataloged the printed edition as follows:
Hermanson, Anne.
  The horror plays of the English restoration / by Anne Hermanson.
    pages cm.—(Studies in performance and early modern drama)
  Includes bibliographical references and index.
  ISBN 978-1-4724-1552-3 (hardcover : alk. paper)
  1. English drama—Restoration, 1660–1700—History and criticism. 2. Horror plays, English—History and criticism. I. Title.
  PR698.H63H47 2015
  822'.409164—dc23
                                                                              2014019620

ISBN 13: 978-1-03-209885-2 (pbk)
ISBN 13: 978-1-4724-1552-3 (hbk)

Contents

Preface

This has been a long-term project. My interest in the subject began many years ago, early in my academic career, while transcribing Anne Wharton's *Love's Martyr* for an M.A. paper. I was considering the work of female Restoration dramatists, but during an exploration of other serious plays of the period my focus shifted inalterably when I came across *The Rival Queens*. I can remember my surprise and exhilaration – this was progressive and unfettered drama. The more I investigated, the more enamoured I became. As a student of drama and theatre, I did not understand why these radical and disturbing early plays by Settle, Shadwell, Behn, Otway and others were not more widely considered. The critical condemnation intrigued me: even those literary critics who saw value in this theatrical period often seemed to regret that the tragic writers were not Shakespeare or Marlowe – or Dryden.

These early criticisms have now been displaced by a generation of critics who have found value in the Restoration tragedies. But even those who write about these playwrights do so with limited regard to this particular group of tragedies that burst onto the London stage a decade after the Restoration and disappeared ten years later – absorbed into the partisan frenzy which enveloped the theatre at the height of the Exclusion Crisis. Much of the work is extravagant and bombastic, but these very elements are central to our understanding of this group of plays that form an important chapter in the history of English theatre. They are also great fun to read. They take their audience on an exploration of human iniquity, thrusting them into an examination of man's relationship to God, power, justice and evil.

I have been fortunate to have had a great deal of support for this study. I would like to thank Professor Angela Black from the University of Aberdeen who enabled my initial research. My thanks also to Professor Janet Todd, Professor Elaine Hobby and Dr. Thomas Rist, who have generously shared with me their consummate expertise and made invaluable comments on the work. I would also like to thank Erika Gaffney at Ashgate for her continued support – and her willingness to answer all my questions with grace and patience.

I owe a great deal of gratitude to Professor Derek Hughes for his ongoing commitment to this work. I am deeply grateful to him for his encouraging counsel and his generosity.

To my husband and children – Andy, Anthea, Sebastien and Artemis – thank you for unselfishly contributing family time to this project and for cheerily facing the inevitable pressures that researching and writing a book produce.

I would like to dedicate this book to my mother and to the memory of my father.

Anne Hermanson

Frontispiece   Unknown Tuscan school, "Judith and Holofernes,"
17th Century, Oil on canvas, 190 x 133 cm

Chapter 1
Horror and Spectacle

In the central years of the reign of Charles II lies a curious group of English plays. Written and performed in the 1670s, these plays are characterised by a cynical and unrelenting depiction of evil, violence, an insatiable human drive for power, and an explicit absence of providential justice or moral absolutes. While some critics still consider these plays to be part of the heroic genre which became popular during the 1660s, it is now generally acknowledged that they form their own category, as coined by Robert D. Hume: the "horror" or the "blood-and-torture villain" tragedies. Hume was the first critic to classify the horror tragedy as a common type of serious drama, arguing that the horror plays depict "gross brutality" and "the trappings" of the genre include "sex, death, ghost[s] [and] madness," suggesting that "[e]xcept by way of negative examples, contemporary literary theory has little justification for blood-and-torture villain tragedy."[1] Other early proponents of the idea of a horror play are Maximillian E. Novak, who has compared Elkanah Settle's *The Empress of Morocco* to a modern horror movie,[2] and Paul D. Cannan, who calls Nathaniel Lee's play, *The Rival Queens*, "well established in the horror tragedy mode." More recently Janet Todd and Derek Hughes have referred to the "sensational horror tragedy of the 1670s," and Jean I. Marsden has discussed the "cult of horror," tying its prevalence to political turmoil but arguing the movement takes place later in the decade – as a reaction to the Popish Plot and the Exclusion Crisis.[3] Despite recent burgeoning interest, however, there has not been a full investigation into why these deeply unsettling plays were written when they were and why they so fascinated audiences for the brief time that they held the stage.

Although the tumultuous events of the 1670s have produced a great deal of analysis from historians, theatre and literary critics have traditionally chosen to pass by the serious plays written and performed during the early and mid-seventies in order to concentrate instead on the more overtly partisan plays written directly after the chimeric Popish Plot of 1678 and into the subsequent Exclusion Crisis.[4] In order to analyse the unique voice of the so-called horror plays and their precursors, one must go back to the 1670/71 theatrical season, when early signs of the subgenre, such as William Joyner's *The Roman Empress*, emerge. The last classic horror tragedies, Elkanah Settle's *The Female Prelate* and John Crowne's *Thyestes*, produced during the 1679/80 season, form an endpoint to the short history of the horror plays. By this time interest in the genre, by playwrights and audiences, had begun to wane. As the country threatened to founder under internecine strife, shifts in censorship and politics changed the face of the drama. By the 1678/79 season, London's theatres were feeling the sting: the King's company, already dealing with internal disputes, was closed for part of the season.[5] The Duke's company fared better, but only seven new plays are known to have been acted by both companies during this period (if you take the likely production of Edward Ravenscroft's *Titus Andronicus; or, The Rape of Lavinia* in the autumn of 1678 into account). After a precedent set by Lord Chamberlain Arlington, "the Lord Chamberlains took an increasingly large interest in the affairs of the theatre." Between 1680 and 1683, records show "a larger number of censored and suppressed plays than at any other period [...] [and] a majority of the recorded instances of suppression of plays [...] comes as a result of royal command or of the interference of the Lord Chamberlain."[6] Importantly, the beginning of this new decade is also the point at which King Charles's fortunes in his battle with the exclusionists begins to shift and "English monarchical authority [is once again] [...] vigorously asserted."[7] This was no longer a time of hidden anxieties: the outbreak of the two crises associated with popery and arbitrary government forced underlying fears, simmering since the Restoration of Charles II, onto the table. After 1680, the dramatists, responding to a changing environment and reflecting shifting emphasis, became not more political but, rather, more overtly partisan in the politics they espoused. In this new environment, the horror plays vanished from the stage.

The drama of the 1670s reflects and responds to political, social and artistic issues specific to this decade, but it also must be regarded as part of the complete experience of the seventeenth century. The traumatic events of the middle of the century were not resolved with the return of the monarchy. The Act of Indemnity and Oblivion silenced public scrutiny of the civil wars and the execution of Charles I, but underlying, unresolved anxieties were difficult to suppress, and by the mid-1660s the image of the glorious return of the monarchy was increasingly strained. Concerns specific to the 1670s stem from a growing disaffection with Charles and his policies. By the mid-1670s a coalition of interests had allied themselves against the crown. The conversion of Charles's brother James to Catholicism sparked fears of a 'popish' successor and of a return to civil strife. As Charles regularly prorogued parliament and aligned himself with the absolutist Louis XIV, alarm spread that he would repeat his father's deadly errors and attempt to establish an arbitrary government. The recurrent warning cry in contemporary treatises and satire urged people to avoid a return to 1641. Those living through this decade found themselves in a unique position: current unease and fear of arbitrary rule and Catholic succession were inextricably linked to persistent, collective reflection back to these earlier unresolved traumatic experiences. These anxieties drove the focus of, and were influenced by, contemporary literature and drama. Tragic dramatists of the 1670s reshaped and parodied earlier dramatic forms such as the masque, tragicomedy and heroic drama in order to confront very specific issues in crisis at the time.

The themes of these dramatic tragedies and their public staging were critically affected by practical shifts in the world of the theatre. Having only two rival companies with a monopoly over what was produced in the public theatre created a singularly competitive race to draw in the small pool of theatregoers. Both acting companies built state-of-the-art theatres which allowed them to offer to the public spectacular visual productions, once the preserve of the elite. This study will investigate the troubling themes of the horror plays in relation to the specific political, historical and social concerns of the 1670s. But first, it will investigate the practical events that took place on stage to establish how the writers of the horror plays were able to use shifts in the public's perception of theatrical experience to their advantage and the significant role these dramatic pieces played in the evolution of the partisan plays of the Exclusion Crisis.

It has been difficult to come to a critical consensus on the establishment of genres for Restoration serious drama. Many twentieth-century critics saw Restoration drama as a homogeneous, uniform body of work that undergoes a shift from heroic drama in the early Restoration to a more private, sentimental tragedy towards the end of the 1670s.[8] It is now generally accepted in drama and theatre criticism that there was not a monolithic genre, namely 'heroic drama,' dominating the first two decades of serious theatre in the Restoration. The character of the drama was multi-faceted. There was certainly a fashion for rhymed tragedy that was sustained by key playwrights such as John Dryden until well into the 1670s; however, as Derek Hughes argues, "beyond that many distinctions and qualifications need to be made."[9] Although critics are now acknowledging the unique political voice of the plays of the 1670s, by and large there is still a tendency in contemporary criticism to conflate rhymed tragedy with heroic drama. Paulina Kewes, for example, acknowledges the significance of the traumatic events of the civil war on Restoration drama and argues that the drama was highly political throughout the Restoration period; however, she still considers Nathaniel Lee's and Thomas Otway's early plays as rhymed *heroic* dramas. Don-John Dugas speaks of Settle's use of the horror formula in *The Empress of Morocco* but considers the play as an *heroic* spectacular.[10] In even more recent scholarship, Felicity Nussbaum articulates an ongoing attitude that is most damaging to Restoration tragedy when she says, "[w]e are accustomed to think of tragedies such as Lee's bombastic *The Rival Queens* [...] as relics of a genre that, mercifully, came and went quickly, and that soon attracted ridicule."[11]

Some recent critics have gone to the other extreme and developed such narrow categories to describe the various genres at work during the middle years of the Restoration that they tend to confuse rather than clarify our understanding of the drama. J. Douglas Canfield, even though he acknowledges the difficulty in establishing appropriate distinctions between the plays, still puts forward five generic groups: Heroic Romance, Romantic Tragedy, Personal Tragedy, Political Tragedy and Tragical Satire. In the first two, threats to heroic characters are external. In Personal Tragedy, the threats to the "great souls of heroes" are internal. Political Tragedy focuses on threats to states, and Tragical Satire concludes either with poetical justice "that is draconian and virtually apocalyptic" or with none at all.[12] Canfield's generic classifications are too subtle, however, and each genre (exemplified by only a handful of plays) overlaps with the next so that distinctions are difficult to keep in mind. Canfield's main theme is that the plays reflect the struggle of the aristocracy to maintain what they see as their natural right to rule in the face of burgeoning unrest and opposition. This narrow focus, however, deliberately downplays the importance of these very oppositional forces in the dramas. Canfield says "real oppositional ideology [...] [is] at best wildly caricatured, at worst totally absent."[13] As a result, he omits a discussion of the palpable violent, jarring images inherent in the drama of the period and rates it as ideologically static. There is no acknowledgement of a progression of ideas paralleling the dynamic political and social changes which were occurring. By contrast, scholars such as Derek Hughes, Nancy Klein Maguire, Paul Cannan, Robert D. Hume, Jessica Munns and Susan J. Owen suggest that Restoration drama is reflective of rapidly changing societal and political circumstances. Although the approaches and classifications of these critics differ, their redefinitions of Restoration subgenres suggest that the character of the drama continued to evolve and change throughout the period.

In the first decade of Charles II's reign, the theatrical spectacles for the most part were patterned on, and served the same function as, those in pre-civil war days. Nancy Klein Maguire's analysis of the plays of the 1660s distinguishes two subgenres: divided tragicomedy and rhymed heroic plays, both of which share similarities with the masque. She argues that the early playwrights – 'Royalist' aristocrats who had lived under the reigns of both Charles I and Cromwell – appropriated earlier tragicomedy's movement from a threatened to a stable environment, attempting to turn "the 'tragedy' of Charles I into the tragicomedy of Charles I/II." The playwrights

> [...] deliberately set up a state of anxiety whose resolution reinforced the established regime and confirmed the divine right of the Stuarts [...] Dramatizing the tensions resulting from regicide and restoration [...] they attempted to redefine the society by fabricating pious, backward-looking, and repetitious myths of monarchy.

Maguire argues that the use of these genres allowed theatre managers to present "a fictional world distanced from predictable cause-effect relationships where deeply-felt issues could be ignored." Maguire limits her study to plays produced in the sixties, explaining that "[b]y the 1670s, the obsession with regicide and restoration had diminished, and new generic forms appear."[14] Derek Hughes suggests there are three distinguishable stages in the progression of the serious drama through the sixties and seventies: Davenant and Orrery; Dryden, who "deals sceptically with the values, and the political events, that Orrery simply endorses; and the host of new dramatists who take their lead from *The Conquest of Granada* but transform drama to reflect the growing sense of political crisis." In this new drama, problems of uncertain succession predominate and idealism has largely disappeared. In fact, these plays actively subvert the earlier genres: some, such as Lee's *The Tragedy of Nero*, expressing "a comprehensive destruction of the cliches of early Restoration tragicomedy."[15]

The horror plays have very different themes and purpose and entail an outcome dissimilar to the serious drama of the 1660s. The outer trappings of the rhymed heroic plays, such as the exotic settings, the exaggerated characterisation, the bombastic rhetoric and the rhyme itself remain in many cases. But, inside the drama, fundamental ideological shifts are occurring that reflect anxieties specific to the second decade of the Restoration. If, as Allardyce Nicoll tells us, "the tendency of the heroic play had been merely an exaggeration of the rational tragic endeavour – to raise and to generalise human qualities into an almost divine and infallible content,"[16] then there is little in this to characterise the horror tragedies. These plays do not yield sublime depictions of heroic endeavour. In fact, the extreme spectacle of violence in these plays – rape, torture, maimed bodies – undermines the solemnity of tragedy thrusting the action into satire.[17] As Maguire argues, the stylization of the early rhymed heroic plays comes from a specific set of icons: "murdered but saintly kings, self-sacrificing faithful women, king-restoring generals, and disenfranchised true heirs."[18] The horror plays make use of antithetical icons producing degenerate rulers, monstrous women, Machiavellian conspirators and heirs who are unfit for their assigned roles.

There are no 'heroic' heroes in the horror plays of the 1670s. The heroes are deeply flawed: they provide no moral example; they are weak, often cowardly and ultimately ineffectual. The main subjects of these plays are not love and honour; those who seek either are most often shown as ultimately unsuccessful. Family ties (and patriarchal structure generally) are obliterated in the most disturbing way. Lustful tyrants are common to both the heroic and the horror genre; however, the fundamentally conservative depiction of these characters in earlier plays makes way for monarchs who openly contradict pious myths of monarchy, committing the most heinous of crimes and remaining either unrepentant or unpunished. There is no tragicomic movement from threatened to stable environment in the horror plays. Resolution is elusive, and the outcome does not provide any new or fruitful understanding to either the audience or the survivors remaining onstage; nor are the latter in any improved conditions: tyrants have been disposed of in many instances, but there is no clear restoration of order and certainly no sense of renewed faith or hope for the future. Most disturbingly in these plays, no character seems to have learned from the mistakes, and the plays imply there will be a continual repetition of the same errors.

Providential justice – of central importance in earlier Restoration plays – is absent in the horror plays. This is also a key point at which the horror plays distinguish themselves from the bloody Jacobean revenge tragedies. The Jacobean tragedies and the horror plays share many commonalities: violence and dislocation predominate, the meaning of justice and the limits of rebellion are investigated in both.[19] The retributive violence of the revenge plays, however, implies a working providence: ultimately, the world of these plays is shown to be ruled by justice. Where the Jacobean plays concentrate on the lengths to which individuals may go to obtain justice, neither personal nor state justice in the horror plays is seen as attainable – a working providence is nowhere to be found. As Robert Ornstein argues, all of the great Jacobean plays "end with some restoration of order or decency" suggesting "that evil contains the seeds of its own destruction, that because it naturally over reaches it is sterile and self-defeating."[20] G.K. Hunter adds that "[r]evengers are absorbed into the horror of their own obsessed imaginings, but they continue to exist inside a world where justice is remembered as a value. Indeed a central point about revenge on the Elizabethan stage is that it is a perverted form of justice."[21] John Kerrigan notes that "the softening of, and resistance to, providentialism did more than anything else to sap revenge tragedy in England."[22] This is not to suggest that the horror plays, in their post-Hobbes, post-regicide world, are exclusive and that there are no Elizabethan or Jacobean plays that question providential justice. There are always exceptions, and Shakespeare's *King Lear* and Christopher Marlowe's plays share a loss of optimism and are particularly bleak in this respect. The horror plays, written as they were by a group of diverse writers over a contained period of time, are significant, however, in their uncompromising rejection of providential justice. Except in John Crowne's *Thyestes*, the act of revenge is rarely a convincing motivating factor for the violent acts in the horror plays; nor are most of the criminal acts avenged in any retributive way. Even in plays which began their lives as Jacobean revenge tragedies, vengeance is modified or minimised at the hands of the horror dramatists. In John Fletcher's *Valentinian* (1610–14) unjust treatment by a merciless tyrant is the catalyst for revenge and rebellion. In John Wilmot, the Earl of Rochester's revision of the play *Lucina's Rape*, the 'tragic' downfall of Vallentinian and Maximus's revenge are sidelined. The focus of the play is on the destruction of virtue rather than on the punishment of sin. And, although Vallentinian is ultimately killed by his soldiers, Maximus is left a ruined man, no longer believing in moral certainties. Aphra Behn uses the subtitle *The Moor's Revenge* in her play *Abdelazer*: a reworking of Thomas Dekker's *Lust's Dominion*. Although, as with the earlier play, revenge for the death of Abdelazer's father by the Spanish is ostensibly the spur to rebellion in the play, this focus is diluted by Behn's reworking the character of the Queen Mother Isabella whose powerful characterisation weakens Abdelazer's position as worthy rebel and whose motivation for destruction is inconsequential and unjustified. There is no regeneration through violence in the horror plays. As in Seneca's drama, evil villains can commit heinous crimes with impunity (for example, the murderess Roxana in *The Rival Queens*), and they can question the validity of Christian dogma with logic and conviction (as Don John does, for example, in *The Libertine*). The moral degeneration of society depicted in both the revenge plays and the horror plays is linked very clearly to court corruption; however, the horror plays take this a step further. Where the Jacobean plays portray evil, lascivious rulers generally seen to be corrupt individuals, the horror plays produce direct attacks on the office of kingship: almost without exception, those who take on power are unfailingly depicted as corrupt and evil.

Alongside the shifts in theme, dramatists in the early part of the decade made more overt references to a desire for change from the rhymed heroic play. William Joyner is one of the first to ridicule the themes of love and honour and their place in contemporary tragedy. In his preface to *The Roman Empress* (King's 1670), he announces his desire for a movement away from the artificial themes of heroic drama:

Such who expect to have their ears tickled with the gingling Antitheses of Love
and Honor, and such like petty wares, will find themselves deceiv'd. For the
chief intent of Tragedy being to raise Terror and Compassion; I thought a more
masculine and vigorous eloquence and graces more natural, and less affected,
were requisite to inspire such impressions. (The Preface)[23]

Two years later, in his epilogue to *The Fatal Jealousy* (Duke's 1672), in which
Nathaniel Lee had his second acting experience as Captain of the Watch, Henry
Neville Payne emphasises that the audience has just experienced not an heroic play
but, rather, a "tragedy [...] not drest by rules of Art." Payne went on to ridicule
"Love and Honour [as] the two great Wheels, on which all business moves" in
The Morning Ramble (Duke's 1672): "No Tragedy, Comedy, Farse, Demi-Farse,
or Song now adayes, but is full of Love and Honour: Your Coffe-drinking-Crop-
ear'd-Little Banded-Secretary, that pretends not to know more of Ho|nour than it's
Name, will out of abundance of Love be still sighing and groaning for the Honour
of the Nation."[24]

It is significant that the playwrights of the first decade of the Restoration
were mature courtiers who had lived under Charles I and Cromwell. When they
reintroduced the drama at the Restoration, they looked back to old, familiar,
aristocratic forms. Most of them retired from writing at the end of the 1660s, and a
whole new generation of writers exploded onto the scene. These young dramatists,
Thomas Otway (b. 1652), Nathaniel Lee (b. 1651/3) and Elkanah Settle (b. 1648),
were effectively born into a republic: they did not experience life before the civil
wars and interregnum. They were still young at the time of the Restoration and,
although they would have been exposed to the mythology surrounding their recent
history and the changing fortunes of royal power, their writing did not need to
express, as did Orrery's, Dryden's or Davenant's, any atonement for their actions
during Cromwell's rule. These dramatists were, rather, a *product* of this time of
profound change and unease in England; as such, they were deeply involved in
mirroring the repetitious nature of the anxieties that coloured their own early years
and their experiences with conflicting and changing ideologies, often within their
own families.

Nathaniel Lee, for example, was the son of Dr. Richard Lee, the rector of
Hatfield and a man who had held many preferments under Cromwell. The elder
Lee was chaplain to General Monck, but, after the Restoration, he conformed to the
Church of England and renounced many of his former opinions. Thomas Otway's
father was also a rector – of All Hallows, Woolbeding in Sussex. Humphrey Otway,
however, did not support the Commonwealth. He was forced to leave his parish in
the 1650s after being disestablished. According to J.C. Ghosh, Humphrey Otway
seems to have gone north after this, only to return to his Sussex parish at the
Restoration.[25] John Wilmot, Earl of Rochester, also shared with Otway and Lee the
firsthand experience of the opposing religious and political forces tearing England
apart. Rochester was born in April 1647, in Oxfordshire. His mother, Anne, came
from a prominent Puritan family; his father, Henry Wilmot, Baron Wilmot of
Adderbury, was a royalist general under Charles I. After Charles's execution the

Cavalier general became one of the exiled Charles II's chief advisers.[26] When his father died in 1658, however, the young Earl was brought up by his mother and tutored by her chaplain before going on to Cambridge.

Lee and Otway also went on to university. Lee had shown early scholarly promise. He was nominated by his father's patron for admission to Charterhouse School and then attended Trinity College, Cambridge, receiving his B.A. in 1668/69. There is some evidence that Lee continued as a fellow at Cambridge until 1671. Isaac Newton lectured once a week at Cambridge as Lucasian Professor of Mathematics between 1669 and 1671, so it is a fair assumption that Lee would have gained some knowledge of atomism and other new scientific theories which he and other horror dramatists later incorporated into their plays.[27] Otway entered Christ Church, Oxford, in 1669, but his father died in 1671 and, without financial support, Otway was forced to leave Oxford without taking a degree.[28] Elkanah Settle also entered Oxford (Trinity College) and also left without taking a degree. Settle was born in Dunstable in January 1648. Little is known of his early life. In the early 1670s, he held a position at court; later in the decade, he took an active part in the anti-popish agitation, writing for the Whig exclusionists. During and after the Exclusion Crisis, Settle produced virulently anti-Catholic satires, plays and pamphlets. The anti-popery procession of 17 November 1679 was organized by Settle, "who had been hired by Shaftesbury and was subsidized by Shaftesbury's Green Ribbon Club."[29]

Another anti-Catholic propagandist and member of the Green Ribbon Club was Thomas Shadwell (b. 1642?). Before the civil wars, Shadwell's father had inherited substantial property in Norfolk. Because of his support for the king, however, the family was forced to sell a good part of the estate during the interregnum. Shadwell was sent to the King Edward VI Free Grammar School at Bury St. Edmunds, under Thomas Stephens – a royalist supporter. He then went on to Gonville and Caius College in Cambridge, where the royalist master had been ejected and his place taken by William Dell, a chaplain in the parliamentary army.[30] In the 1670s Shadwell was a member of the circle of (Whig) court wits, led by George Villiers, the second Duke of Buckingham, which included, among others, Rochester and William Wycherley.

Although these young dramatists had disparate religious, social and political backgrounds, they all exhibit in their writing an acute dissatisfaction with Charles II's leadership. Together they had an enormous influence on pushing the boundaries of Restoration drama. It is in this brief period (specified by Hume as 1675–77, although I argue it begins earlier and is longer in duration) that Carolean drama "reaches its greatest heights [with] Dryden, Shadwell, Etherege, Wycherley, Lee, and Otway [...] all at or near the peak of their powers."[31] As this younger generation of dramatists began their careers, Dryden's most popular heroic plays, *The Conquest of Granada*, 1 & 2 (King's 1670–71), were being staged. There is little doubt that these new writers were influenced by the heroic genre of the sixties and by Dryden's growing sceptical approach to it. Rather than copy the genre, however, they use it to create a unique dramatic experience.

An important characteristic in the production of the horror plays, and one that is shared with heroic drama through its association with the pre-war court masque, is the use of grand spectacle. The power of spectacle to move people had been a consideration of the Duke's company from the start. William Davenant and his company had developed the use of movable scenery in their first theatre of the Restoration, Lisle's Tennis Court in Lincoln's Inn Fields. Davenant's theatrical project had been to "specialise in the new and expensive operatic form."[32] He had worked with Inigo Jones on his own Caroline extravaganza, *Salmacida Spolia*, and appeared to be interested in using the characteristics of the old court productions to bring the English theatre in line with prevailing theatrical developments in Europe.[33] The company's leading actor, Thomas Betterton, had also been influenced by his own time on the continent and, at Davenant's death in 1668 and with the support of Davenant's widow, Betterton planned the building of a new theatre in which the company could mount even more elaborate productions.

Along with these innovations in theatre staging, there is substantial evidence, from outside the theatres, of a growing public interest in and demand for spectacle at this time. Thus, although some of the elements which characterised the horror plays began to emerge in the theatrical events in the early 1670s, spectacles in which they were put to use – musical productions were particularly fashionable – were often designed for an entirely different outcome: surprise and delight were evoked, rather than the shock and dismay that spectacle in the horror plays produced. In February 1671, for example, there was a grand ballet at court: Lady Mary Bertie wrote that it was so difficult to get room that she had to arrive five hours early. She notes the rich dresses of the Queen and ladies who "danced very finely, and shifted their clothes three times. There was also fine musickes and excellent sing some new song made purpose for it."[34] John Bannister began providing regular musical concerts at his home, 'the Musick School,' and the advertisement of concerts in the London Gazette appeared more frequently as the decade progressed, soon making London "a center of musical entertainments."[35] Performances from foreign troupes were also gaining in popularity. Two French troupes spent lengthy stays in London: one from December 1672 until at least May 1673, the other staying until June 1674. Another troupe of foreign comedians, led by Italian Tiberio Fiorelli (Scaramouchio), arrived by April 1673 and stayed several months, also performing at court and at York House, in front of the King and the Duke of York.[36] According to Allardyce Nicoll, Italian melodrama "contributed to the unreality of the themes and to the development of operatic features in the theatre."[37]

Another pageant that brought entertainment in the form of spectacle to the general public was reintroduced at this time. In October 1671, the first formal pageant for the swearing in of the Lord Mayor of London since the early Restoration years took place. The tradition of the Lord Mayor's shows had ended abruptly 1666, when much of the pageant equipment had been destroyed by the Great Fire. "London's Resurrection to Joy and Triumph" was Thomas Jordan's debut as City poet. Jordan, a Royalist and former actor, went on to produce the Lord Mayor's pageants until the end of Charles's reign. Importantly, Charles II himself began to attend this formal public ceremony in 1671 – and he continued to do so each year until 1678.

The new Dorset Gardens theatre opened in November 1672, and it allowed Betterton to exploit the trend that favoured spectacle, creating theatrical experiences on a scale which previously had not been possible in the public theatre. The theatre featured a mechanical scene-shifting system for elaborate (perspective) scenery, painted shutters, trapdoors and flying machinery for special effects. It also had room to facilitate larger casts and groups of musicians. As exciting new theatrical possibilities were created for the Duke's company, the King's company met with disaster. The company's Theatre Royal in Bridges Street was modern and well equipped. Although the company's manager, Thomas Killigrew, and the older actors were not as committed to the growing fashion for grand spectacle as the Duke's company was, they were able to capture the public imagination (and its patronage) with their extravagant production of *The Conquest of Granada*, which included music by John Bannister and 'very glorious scenes & perspectives.'[38] It was also in this theatre that one of the first horror tragedies, William Joyner's *The Roman Empress*, was produced. Just two months after the Dorset Gardens theatre was built, however, a fire destroyed the Theatre Royal, forcing the King's company to take up residence in the theatre in Lincoln's Inn Fields that the Duke's Company had just vacated. These events created an uneven playing field for the two rival theatre companies which, ultimately, encouraged the further evolution of the horror play. As we shall see, the scarcity of resources available to the King's company (the inadequate venue and the insufficient number of available playwrights) and their resulting loss of patronage to their rivals and foreign troupes proved a catalyst for the company, once their new theatre was built, to stage their own spectaculars steeped in blood.

Before this happened, the Duke's company was taking full advantage of their new theatre and the growing fashion for musical entertainment with increasingly sumptuous productions, particularly after 1673, by which time Dorset Gardens was "fully rigged for machine productions."[39] In February 1673, the first of a series of musical extravaganzas presented by the Duke's company was performed – an updated operatic version of Davenant's *Macbeth* replete with flying witches and Nathaniel Lee as the King of Scotland. Downes suggests that, as with Otway's failed attempt at acting the King in Behn's *The Forc'd Marriage; or, The Jealous Bridegroom* (Duke's 1671), Lee's "Acting Duncan in Macbeth, ruin'd him for an Actor too."[40] It is in this environment that Elkanah Settle's horror play *The Empress of Morocco* was produced by the Duke's company at the new theatre in July 1673, having already been acted at court. Settle's first play to be performed, *Cambyses* (Duke's, most likely in the 1670/71 season), did contain some horror elements and made use of special effects;[41] however, *The Empress of Morocco* took advantage of both the new theatre's facilities and the public appetite for extreme visual display and music: keeping pace with the current fashion for a "promiscuous tendency to musick"[42] in the public theatres and including particularly gruesome visual displays of dead and dying bodies. The play was successful enough to prompt a jealous response from John Dryden, Thomas Shadwell and John Crowne, whose *Notes and Observations on The Empress of Morocco* prompted a tract war with Settle.

The King's company – still foundering at Lincoln's Inn Fields – could only respond to Settle's success with Duffett's burlesque of the same name. This play could have been produced as early as the summer 1673, as the cast includes minor actors; however, evidence suggests it was likely produced in December, at the same time as a repeat production of Settle's play at Dorset Gardens.[43] The paucity of new plays at this time was particularly damaging. *The London Stage* lists nine probable plays performed by the King's company over the 1672/73 season at Lincoln's Inn Fields and at Oxford, although all cannot be dated accurately. Only three of these were new. Several of the prologues and epilogues reflect on the company's hardship. The prologue written for a production of Thomas Middleton's *The Widow* (King's 1672/73?) speaks of "our empty Seats" that "mourn" the audience's absence. The epilogue complains that the company is forced to reproduce old plays instead of writing new material: "For faith 'tis all we can at present make / The Poets and the Players now are poor, / But in our next new house, we'l set you more."[44] A prologue written by Dryden and spoken by Charles Hart for Lodowick Carlell's *Arviragus and Philicia* (King's 1672?), claims the company lies "Languish[ing], and neglected" while the audience keeps "better Company":

> With sickly Actors and an old House too,
> We're match'd with Glorious Theatres and New
> And with our Alehouse Scenes, and Cloaths bareworn,
> Can neither raise Old Plays, nor New adorn.
> If all these ills could not undo us quite,
> A Brisk *French* Troop is grown your dear delight [...].[45]

Public interest in music and spectacle continued to grow. The practice of celebrating Elizabeth I's accession had been revived in the early 1670s, but on 5 November 1673, particularly large crowds attended. An Italian Opera was performed in January 1674 (according to John Evelyn "the first that had been in England of this kind") and a Ballet et Musique at court in February.[46] The King's company's new venue, the Theatre Royal, finally opened on 26 March 1674, and the first play performed was John Fletcher's *The Beggar's Bush*. In his *Prologue Spoken at the Opening of the New House*, Dryden voiced the company's apprehension and its continued frustration at the trends favouring its competitors. He writes disdainfully of the new "mode" for "Pomp," concerned that his audience, who "each Day can Theatres behold, / Like *Nero's Palace*, shining all with Gold," will scorn "Our mean ungilded Stage":

> Great Neibours enviously promote Excess,
> While they impose their Splendor on the less;
> But only Fools, and they of vast Estate,
> Th' extremity of Modes will imitate [...]
> Whilst Scenes, Machines, and empty Opera's reign,
> And for the Pencil you the Pen disdain [...]
> I would not prophesie our Houses Fate;
> But while vain Shows and Scenes you overrate,

'Tis to be feared——
That, as a Fire the former House o'erthrew,
Machines and Tempests will destroy the new.[47]

Ironically, the next production at the theatre was the French Opera *Ariadne; or, The Marriage of Bacchus*, performed by a French company from the Royal Academy of Music.

The Duke's company, meanwhile, continued to realise its investment in musical spectaculars with Thomas Shadwell's operatic version of Davenant's *The Tempest* (Duke's 1674): according to Downes, with new "Scenes, Machines; particularly, one Scene Painted with *Myriads* of *Ariel* Spirits; and another flying away, with a Table Furnisht out with Fruits, Sweet meats, and all sorts of Viands."[48] Charles II loaned the company some singers for the first run of this production from the Chapel Royal.[49] It is likely this production was performed regularly from April until May or June, although it continued to be performed sporadically into November and was reprised in September 1676. It was usual for prices to be raised for the first run of a popular production; however, *The Tempest* was so popular that seat prices remained doubled six months after its opening week.[50] The King's company once again responded to the success with parody: in this case, Duffett's *The Mock-Tempest; or, The Enchanted Castle* (King's 1674). According to Langbaine the parody did its job, drawing "the Town from the Duke's Theatre, who for a considerable time had frequented that admirable reviv'd Comedy call'd *The Tempest*."[51]

Dawn Leacock argues that there is little evidence to support claims that the Duke's company was "responsible for the introduction of spectacular operas in the 1670s."[52] Her evidence is based on a close comparison of the theatre designs and the needs of the plays performed. Although Leacock argues that the use of staging and props in both theatres at this time is comparable, the specific style of the operatic extravaganzas produced by the Duke's company does not have an equivalent in the repertoire of the King's company – unless you consider the recurrent burlesques by Thomas Duffett which were, of course, responding to prototypes from the Duke's company. Other semi-operas followed *The Tempest* and include: John Crowne's *Calisto; or, The Chaste Nimph*, which was performed at court in February 1675 and had several public performances over the winter and involved several members of the Duke's company; and Thomas Shadwell's hugely popular *Psyche*, which opened at Dorset Gardens in February as well and was parodied with Duffett's *Psyche Debauched* at Drury Lane in August. These productions, alongside *The Tempest* and *Macbeth*, were repeatedly produced over the following years, and the last of this group of operatic extravaganzas, Charles Davenant's *Circe*, for which John Bannister wrote the music, opened at Dorset Gardens in May 1677. The company charged double the price, and it brought in so much money that the shareholders were able to declare their highest dividend in two years.[53] So although both theatres aimed to attract audiences and fulfil contemporary expectations with more complex staging and elaborate performances in the new theatres, it was the Duke's company that developed and was successful with this distinct form of operatic spectacular ("a special and short-lived synthesis of music, drama, and spectacle")[54] – based on the fulfilment of their early interest in using continental theatrical practices to *enhance* the English experience as well as on Betterton's ability to understand and satisfy the public's appetite.

The King's company did not have to resort for long to parodies of the Dorset Gardens extravaganzas to bring in the crowds. After the move to the new theatre in Drury Lane, the company had several productive years before internal dissensions became overwhelming and finally led to its amalgamation with the Duke's company in 1682. Even with the problems within the company during this period, important radical theatre was produced that not only brought in audiences but also pushed boundaries and had a significant impact on the plays produced in the rival Dorset Gardens theatre. Along with the improved venue, the King's company's new weapon in its armoury was the young dramatist Nathaniel Lee. Along with Dryden and William Wycherley, the King's company now had a complement of dramatists to provide the fresh, innovative material that they so desperately needed. Lee's first play for the King's company, *The Tragedy of Nero, Emperour of Rome*, opened in May 1674. Clearly influenced by the violent spectacle and the monstrous depictions of evil in Settle's *The Empress of Morocco*, produced five months earlier, *Nero* did not have the overwhelming success of the contemporary musical blockbusters, but there was notable interest in the play: Lee's biographers suggest it was acted several times during the season of its premiere, one suggesting that, for a time, the play created "a kind of Nero cult."[55] It spawned a reproduction of the earlier anonymous play *Piso's Conspiracy* (1624) at Drury Lane in August 1675. The initial performance was attended by the King,[56] and a strong cast included Charles Hart as Nero and, following upon her earlier evil female roles Fulvia and Lyndaraxa, Rebecca Marshall as Poppea. Lee may have failed as an actor, but his recent experience in the Dorset Gardens' operatic production of *Macbeth* had evidently given him insight into the formidable power of spectacle and the thrill that the new technology and the sheer scale of the productions could offer audiences. Along with this new technology, now available to the King's company, came the capacity to stage horror.

Lee's plays from 1674 until 1678, when he moved over to the Duke's company with Dryden, continued to be the most significant response from the King's company to the Dorset Gardens spectaculars. His use of spectacle, however, advanced the development of the horror play in both theatres. Along with Settle's *The Empress of Morocco*, Lee's work set the tone for the plays, manifesting the growing sense of unease with Charles's policies by incorporating into the plays violent spectacle and extravagant supernatural portents. *Nero*'s violent depiction of familial breakdown, the consequences of absolute power and the early expressions of Lucretian agnosticism influenced subsequent plays produced by the Duke's company, such as Shadwell's *The Libertine* (Duke's 1675), produced numerous times from the following spring, and Otway's *Alcibiades* (Duke's 1675) in the autumn. After Lee's reinforcement of the key tenets of the horror play in *Gloriana* (King's 1676), the Duke's company responded with Otway's remarkably popular *Don Carlos* (Duke's 1676) and Aphra Behn's *Abdelazer* (Duke's 1676). These years continued to be difficult for the King's company, riven as they were with internal dissension: Thomas Killigrew was proving to be a poor manager, and the company's debts were high. In February 1676 some of the leading actors stopped acting, and the King, who was "very much displeased," had to step in and order the company "to act and play as formerly."[57] In September the Lord Chamberlain was forced to intervene in an effort to settle disagreements between Killigrew and his son Charles. The following January, Charles tried to force his father to give him leadership of the company, and in February the court agreed.[58] As a result, from the information available for the four years beginning with the opening of the Drury Lane theatre on 26 March 1674, only 26 new plays were produced by the King's company (this is in contrast to 38 new plays that are known to have been produced by the Duke's company). Of these 26 new plays, 16 are comedies (including some of the period's most renowned and influential comedies, such as William Wycherley's *The Country Wife* and *The Plain Dealer*). Of the 10 tragedies, 2 are significant contributions from Dryden (*Aureng-Zebe* and *All for Love*); but 5, half of the new tragedies that we know were performed on the Drury Lane stage in this period, are plays written by Nathaniel Lee. One of the other tragedies, John Banks's *The Rival Kings* (King's 1677), was clearly written and performed as a result of the popularity of Lee's *The Rival Queens* (King's 1677) performed three months earlier. Subsequent horror plays at Drury Lane also show evidence of Lee's influence: among them, Edward Ravenscroft's *Titus Andronicus* (1678), John Crowne's *The Ambitious Statesman* (1679) and *Thyestes* (1680) and Elkanah Settle's *The Female Prelate* (1680).

These tragic dramatists, making use of the new technology and investing in the public's desire for theatrical spectacular, offered audiences what they wanted. In a similar way to the operatic extravaganzas produced at Dorset Gardens, Lee and the other horror dramatists made use of the new technology and the power of grand spectacle in their tragedies to move audiences and inspire awe, but they did not merely employ it for visual excitement. Modern critics in particular have derided the stage spectacle of the 1670s as gratuitous – as no more than a gimmick. Elkanah Settle has been one of the playwrights most frequently criticised on the subject. Hume describes 'the recipe' in Settle's *The Empress of Morocco*: "to blood, thunder, rhyme, and rant, add villainous intrigue, the spectacular execution [of the criminal], an elaborate masque, and a fine battle scene." For Hume, Settle's "exuberance and [...] deliberately absurd exaggerations put his play in the silly thriller realm."[59] Anne Righter (Barton) opines that, behind the 'rant' and stage scenery, the plays of this period were "essentially frivolous."[60] Critics are correct in saying that the spectacle depicted in the 1670s is empty and meaningless, but not for the reasons normally posited. Its *raison d'être* is to reflect contemporary dislocation.

Spectacle, as used in the horror plays, can be interpreted to suggest that a disparity exists between its perceived and actual meanings – between the external ceremony or show and what, if anything, it represents. For example, in *The Tragedy of Nero* (Kings, 1674), the image conjured up of the triumphal procession of the conqueror Galba, sweeping into Rome to rid the city of the degenerate Nero, might encourage the idea of English strength and mastery in battle; whereas, in fact, the English had just been defeated in a war with the Dutch, and Charles was in the throes of forging deep financial, cultural and covert religious bonds with England's archenemy France. Similarly, the cathartic effects of graphically violent stage spectacles, which could be tolerated by the audience when understood as a justified payback for horrible crimes, were unexpectedly shocking when, instead, the spectacles were flagrant displays of brutality or showed bold perpetrators remaining unrepentant or unpunished. Theatrical spectacle in the 1670s can also be interpreted as a parody of the solemn stage ceremony from the recent past; a suggestion that the grand spectacles of the masques and other ceremonials are only smoke and mirrors – ostentation used to hide something essentially empty or meaningless. Certainly it could be seen as an ironic comment that dazzling façades, which at one time produced wonder and reverence for king and God, cease to impress when the belief systems that they represented cannot necessarily be revived; and the desire of church and crown to bring back and embrace pre-Restoration ceremony will not, of itself, rekindle faith.

Re-establishing ceremony as a manifestation of the king's power was one of the Restoration architects' primary weapons in the struggle to legitimate Charles II's authority as a monarch. Church and state have historically linked spectacle and ceremony. Ceremony lends spectacle formality and a degree of decorum, and spectacle strengthens the meaning of ceremony with its visual impact. Charles's first public spectacle as king was his day-long ceremonial procession through London to Whitehall to take up the mantle that his father had left him 11 years earlier in a bizarrely parallel final procession through London to his place of execution. With elation and some exaggeration, John Evelyn describes the pomp and circumstance surrounding Charles's triumphant procession of May 1660, after, in Evelyn's words, a "sad, & long Exile":

> This was also his Birthday, and with a Triumph of above 20000 horse & foote, [Evelyn exaggerates] brandishing their swords and shouting with unexpressable joy: The wayes straw'd with flowers,the bells ringing, the streetes hung with Tapissry, fountaines running with wine: The Mayor, Aldermen, all the Companies in their liver<ie>s, Chaines of Gold, banners; Lords & nobles, Cloth of Silver, gold & vellvet every body clad in, the windos & balconies all set with Ladys, Trumpets, Musick, & <myriads> of people flocking the streetes & was as far as *Rochester*, so as they were 7 houres in passing the Citty, even from 2 in the afternoone 'til nine at night [...].[61]

Such a lavish and sustained public spectacle, with its display of military might, celebratory bell-ringing and important people in their finery paying homage, cast Charles as a hero returning home after a victorious battle. This majestic cavalcade could also link the triumphal entry of Charles into London with the triumphal entry of Jesus into Jerusalem (John 12:12). In any case, the event gave notice that the splendour of the court was about to replace the asceticism, encouraged by Presbyterianism, of the interregnum. Early Restoration civic pageantry, such as the Lord Mayor's Shows, also gave notice of government policy to the people, emblematically illustrating "how peace, prosperity, and order were all inextricably linked with the restoration of monarchy."[62]

Anglicanism, of royal genesis, once again became the state religion; the Church of England, with all its attendant elaborate ceremony and rigid hierarchy, was re-established as the state church. The transparency of non-conformist worship was replaced by the traditional scrim of vestments, mitres and processions, before which congregations became not so much participants as audience. Charles also immediately reinstated the ancient ceremony of touching for the King's Evil – a custom established as early as the thirteenth century in English courts. Although it was the sacred nature of the king's touch that was supposed to heal his scrofulous subjects, at least one medieval historian suggests that royal touching for the king's evil was "not a manifestation of [the king's] holiness but of regality."[63] Even as it confirmed the monarch's political stature, however, this ceremony also made the important link between royal and divine authority.

Nancy Maguire argues that these entertainments celebrating the return of Charles II "come closest to the pure form of the court masque."[64] Lois Potter articulates the intimate relationship between monarchy and spectacle in early Jacobean and Caroline masques:

> One of the reasons why spectacle is so much a part of monarchy is that the visual without the verbal always retains a sense of mystery [...] In masques and triumphs, for instance, the figure of supreme authority is never the one who speaks; the audience hears only personifications of his or her attributes. When, in addition, the machinery of the spectacle is hidden, the various miracles involved in the change of scene can be attributed to the presence of the silent, wonder-working monarch.[65]

As already noted, vestiges of the Caroline masque were incorporated into the rhymed heroic plays and the divided tragicomedies in the early Restoration theatre. Characteristics such as the masque's loftiness of tone and general heroic attitude, the use of verse and music, the exotic settings and the grand battle scenes, were present in most cases to celebrate the glory of the monarch. Early Restoration tragicomedy and the pre-war masques share other characteristics: both are "artificial, stylized, and peopled with ideological counters rather than with psychologically viable characters."

> Extending the idealized masque order to the audience, the performers and the audience (the ideal and the real) commingle in the Revels. The climactic centrepiece for the dances in the audience, the Revels patched up the divisions coded into the masque and antimasque oppositions. Embodying the laws of the society, the king, by his very appearance, overrode the anxiety aroused by the disorderly antimasque.[66]

Ceremony as a foundation of the monarchic order is transformed into chaos in the horror plays. In *Lucina's Rape or the Tragedy of Vallentinian* (written c. 1675/76)

Rochester comprehensively parodies the celebration of the divinely appointed glory of the monarch; in fact, the monarch in Rochester's play does anything but dispel the antimasque and restore order. As masquers prepare for a performance in honour of the emperor, they are encouraged by his courtiers to sing and dance more loudly, in order to muffle the screams of a woman being raped *by the* emperor. Rather than "embodying the laws of the society" or God, and resolving the state of anxiety, Rochester's monarch, under the cover of a masque, emblematises the essential anxiety and chaos connected with the antimasque. Elkanah Settle's *The Empress of Morocco* (Duke's 1673) includes a masque of the rape of Eurydice. What might appear at first sight to be simply a vehicle for gratuitous spectacle, Settle's play-within-a-play has another purpose as well: it parodies the main intent of a court masque, where the monarch as spectator receives obeisance. Settle's young king is weak – under the influence of his evil mother and unable to rule effectively. He does not understand his role as king. Rather than spectating as he should, the young king upsets the decorum of the masque and takes an active part in it, under the cover of a disguise. His wife, believing him to be someone else, murders him. Because he is unrecognisable, the king dies ignominiously behind the façade of a spectacle that is meant to apotheosise him. There is an interesting link here to William Davenant's *Salmacida Spolia*, which is distinctive in that it is the only Caroline masque in which the king, Charles I, and the queen themselves performed. As Charles I prepared for the next parliamentary session after 11 years of personal rule, the masque's intended message was pacifist. It was ineffectual, however; and the inversion of the masque's decorum led to disaster. The next session was the Short Parliament: *Salmacida Spolia* was the last court masque performed before the outbreak of civil war.

Similarly, lack of faith in king and church is at the heart of other visual spectacles in the horror plays, in the form of supernatural portents, depictions of Hell, ghosts and triumphal marches. Dire future events and impending doom are often prefigured by dramatic and impressive depictions of the heavens: rainbows, dark clouds, showers or hail. As much as these visual spectacles are meant to engender awe, the playwrights minimise their impact when the central characters are found to be incapable of interpreting the signs. In *The Empress of Morocco*, the hero, Muly Hamet, dismisses the warnings: to his detriment he belittles the importance of what his friend calls the portent of "some Dire Event" (IV.ii).[67] In *The Rival Queens* (King's 1677), Alexander the Great's denial of potent omens leads to his death. In *The Roman Empress* (King's 1670), the emperor Valentius's inability to interpret his dreams leads to fatal consequences, including the death of his son. Vivid visions of the supernatural, which should be expected to stir primordial fear in the pagan characters, are shown to be no more successful. When the prodigies light up the sky in Lee and Dryden's *Oedipus* (Duke's 1678), the court regards them with fear and amazement. Oedipus, in contrast, shows no dread. Even when he sees his name emblazoned across the sky, he self-righteously denies that doom awaits him, because his conscience is clear. When Tiresias interprets the omens and insists they are for Oedipus, Oedipus consigns the prophet to the ranks of other lying priests. The playwrights utilise theatrical innovations to enhance their depiction of masque-like spectacle. Yet the expected emotional responses of awe or dread to such supernatural manifestations are dulled by the playwrights through their characters' lack of belief in, or ignorance of, the significance of the phantasms. The fact that the omens in most cases prove accurate is simply ironic; it does not suggest the playwrights believe that omens or superstitious portents are real or valid. As one critic suggests, when speaking of Settle's play, "behind the threatening clouds and the fragile promise of the rainbow the heavens are empty."[68]

The same might be said of Hell in the horror plays. Depictions of spirits and of Hell have been part of theatre spectacle in England since the medieval morality play. In the horror plays, however, Hell – this ultimate place of punishment – has lost its power to terrify. In Shadwell's *The Libertine* (Duke's 1675), Don John's life of depravity finally catches up with him. When he is faced with a ghastly parade of the ghosts of his victims in front of the gaping mouth of Hell, Don John sees it as nothing more than a deceptive mirage created to frighten people into obedience. Even as he goes to his inevitable death, he ridicules Hell and defiantly considers its existence no more than superstitious nonsense.

The spectacles of violent death and torture are further defining features of the horror plays, and both are exhibited more graphically in this genre than had been the case in the theatre since Jacobean times. The playwrights regularly depict body parts, execution and bloodshed. The English theatre of the time is known for its brutality. For contemporary critics such as Rymer and Settle, the graphic savagery is what distinguishes it from the theatre of the French and the ancient Greeks, where incidents of murder and mutilation took place offstage and were announced rather than seen. In the horror plays, violence is not only seen; it is described and dwelt upon, and the verbal enhances the visual horror. In John Crowne's *Thyestes* (Kings 1680), Aerope fatally wounds Thyestes after he ravishes her and estranges her from her husband. As she stabs him Aerope cries,"[t]hus, thus, thus." Then, punctuating her actions with anguished words, she continues to stab him – again and again and again:

> This for the loss of my dear Husband's love:
> This for the loss of my dear daughter's life
> This for the ruin of my honest name
> This for my Life I am about to lose. (V p54)[69]

When the Protestant Admiral is executed in Nathaniel Lee's *The Massacre of Paris* (written 1679), verbal descriptions of the act of murder accompany and accentuate the horror. The Duke of Guise tells his soldiers to "fling" the Admiral's body to the court:

> Expose his Carcass to the Peoples mercy,
> Drag him away, and hurl him from the
> Window: See all his Bastards strangled on the spot;
>   [...] burn his Statue, haste:
> There's a Commission granted for the deed;
> Nay, kill, as if 'twere Sport to see 'em bleed. (V.iv.54–62)[70]

When a new scene opens, the audience is exposed to the Admiral's body burning. Guise conjures up further horrific imagery through his reflexions:

> I saw the Master Villain dragg'd along
> To Execution, by the Common People,
> Who from the Shoulders tore the mangled Head,
> Cut off his Hands, and at Mountfaucon hung him,
> Half burning, by one Leg upon the Gallows. (V.v.4–8)

When bodies are shown on stage, they are not just shown dead but are shown deliberately mutilated; and the accompanying words emphasise the fact. In Crowne's *Thyestes* (King's 1680), Atreus triumphantly tortures Thyestes with the knowledge that he has drunk the blood of his own son. And then, to inflict further torment, Atreus declares: "Here shew the Father the Son's remains." The Temple is opened, and Philisthenes lies bleeding. Thyestes gasps, "Oh! my Philisthenes! my mangled Son!" (V p51). Even violent words alone can conjure ghastly images. In *Caesar Borgia* (Duke's 1679), Borgia, reading a forged letter to Bellamira from Palante, tears up the letter in a jealous rage and mouths words of self-mutilation: "I could mangle, tear up my own Breast, / Drag forth my heart that holds her bleeding Image," He then adds a vicious postscript: "And dash it in her face" (IV.i.200–203).[71] These merciless verbal and visual assaults produce plays of almost pornographic intensity. That is to say, after the first jolt, there is another and often another until the audience is forced from a sense of shock into feelings of abhorrence. This is in contrast to many of the Jacobean revenge tragedies, where, although the death toll can be as large, there is little emotion aroused in the audience. In Cyril Tourneur's *The Revenger's Tragedy*, for example, four men seated at a table are stabbed to death by four other men. According to the stage directions, the revengers "steal out their swords, and these four kill the four at the table, at their chairs. It thunders." There is no buildup to a frenzy of violence, and the revenger, Vindice, refers only to the blessing of providence: "No power is angry when the lustful die: / When thunder claps, heaven likes the tragedy" (V.iii.49–50).[72] In this 'staged' scene of revenge, the murders are emotionless and static: the deed is done quickly and efficiently without further verbal assault. Neither the murderers nor their victims react in any detailed emotional way to the event.

Contemporaneous propaganda – particularly the anti-Catholic propaganda – is imbued with the same violent imagery as the horror plays. If we examine tracts reprinted in the period, such as Samuel Clarke's *General Martyrology* or John Foxe's *Acts and Monuments*, for example, the detailed persecution of Protestants is bloody and frightful. In *General Martyrology* inhumane tortures perpetrated by the Catholics are described in relentless succession, in order to elicit a similar response of abhorrence in the reader. There are graphic 'eyewitness' accounts (occasionally accompanied with crude drawings) of various massacres of the innocent: in this case, the Protestant Massacre at Piemont in 1655:

The Soldiers of Bagnols cut off first the Nose, then the Fingers, and lastly the Hands of a very old, and decrepid Woman, and so left her languishing in this woful condition, not having so much as a Hand to feed her self with, till she died.

They also took many little Children, and tender Infants, and flung them down the steep Rocks, whereby they were dashed to pieces.

[…] Anna Daughter to Giovanni Charboniere of La Torre had a long Stake thrust into her Privities by some of the Soldiers, who each man in his turn carried her upon their shoulders till they were weary, and then stuck the end of the Stake into the ground, and so left her hanging in the air […].[73]

The visual and verbal violence in the horror plays, and its evocation of passionate response, is also reminiscent of Seneca. In Seneca's *Phaedra*, for example, the Messenger narrates in vivid and horrifying detail the gradual disintegration of Hippolytus's body. He tells Theseus that after Hippolytus's horses bolted,

> Hippolytus fell, entangled
> and struggling in the reins to get himself free
> […] He bounced on the ground, was dragged,
> trying to miss the rocks, but helpless, bruised,
> batterered, terribly bloodied […]
>   The horses plunging and running,
> dragging the body behind them, or what remained
> that hadn't caught on the thorns, bushes, rocks,
> and brambles.

When the horses finally stop, the Messenger continues, "We walked as in a nightmare, / to gather up the bits of his broken body / that we could find for the funeral pyre […]." As the ghastly narration draws to a close, a further shock awaits as the servants enter "bearing a box with the pieces of Hippolytus in it" (1078–1110).[74]

In Seneca's *Oedipus* there is a similar list built up of nauseating images, one more hideous than the last. A heifer is sacrificed so the seer Tiresias can interpret the reasons for Thebes's punishment by the gods. Since Tiresias is blind, his daughter Manto must verbalise what she sees in the sacrifice. Her detailed description of the butchered animal moves relentlessly from a depiction of the entrails, which "are not gently shaking, but with a violence […] splashed with fresh blood. / The heart lies deep within; / rot and infection run through every vein;" to the monstrous discovery that inside the "virgin animal" two fetuses grow "deformed, unnatural." Then, even more appallingly, the agonised heifer moves: "With a bawling moan / it tries to urge its twitching limbs along" (359–81). This assault on the senses is not mindless rant, it is deliberate hyperbole to evoke passionate reaction.

Seneca's violent emotional plays mock "Athenian taste and decorum" in the same way the horror dramatists mock Caroline and early Carolean propriety and deference.[75] Modern critics have accused Seneca of many the same failings of which Lee, Settle and others have been accused. One of Seneca's translators, Dana Gioia, argues that modern critics denigrate Seneca's work by unfairly comparing it to realist drama: "Seneca's plays make little dramatic sense judged by the assumptions of realist drama [...] as [such] Seneca's plays appear bombastic, lurid, schematic." Gioia lists the "standard legal charges leveled against the ancient Iberian." These charges are strikingly similar to those made against the horror dramatists:

1. Seneca is derivative and decadent;
2. Seneca is rhetorical rather than dramatic;
3. Seneca's sensibility is lurid and violent. Seneca's chief innovation on his Greek models was to make them more graphic in their violence;
4. Seneca is technically incompetent as a dramatist: his plays are shapeless displays of rhetoric and horror;
5. Seneca's vision is ultimately not tragic, only terrifying: there is no catharsis in Seneca, no pity and awe – just horror.[76]

Much has been written about Seneca's influence on the Renaissance; however, his influence on Restoration playwrights is not as often acknowledged. The middle of the seventeenth century saw a tremendous increase in English translations of Seneca's plays: there were more translations after 1648 than there had been in Renaissance England. *Medea* (1648), the *Troades* (1679) and *Phaedra* (published with the others in 1701) were translated by Sir Edward Sherburn; Edmund Prestwich translated *Phaedra* in 1651; Samuel Pordage translated the *Troads* in 1660. Excerpts of *Thyestes* were translated by Abraham Cowley, Sir Matthew Hale and Andrew Marvell and published in 1668, 1676 and 1681. Rochester translated the chorus of the second act of the *Troads* in 1674 (published 1680); in the same year, John Wright translated *Thyestes*, and in 1686 John Talbot published the *Troads*. Aside from the numerous translations, *Senecae Trageodiae cum notis*, J.F. Gronovius's edition, which is generally considered to be the best text of Seneca's tragedies published in the century, was printed in Leyden in 1661.[77]

There are, of course, the horror dramas as well: Dryden and Lee's *Oedipus* (Duke's 1678) and John Crowne's *Thyestes* (King's 1680), both based on Seneca's plays. Senecan traits can also be found inside individual plays. Caligula's ghost in *Nero* resembles the ghosts in *Thyestes* and *Agamemnon* (or their reincarnation in Sulla's ghost in Jonson's *Catiline*, which was produced by the King's company at Bridge's Street several times in the 1668/9 season). Lee's later plays provide further evidence. The hero in *Theodosius* (Duke's 1680), on meeting his old friend Varanes, recalls their acting together in Seneca's *Hercules Furens*:

When on the Stage to the admiring Court
We strove to represent Alcides Fury,
In all that raging Heat, and pomp of madness,
With which the stately Seneca adorn'd him;
So lively drawn, and painted with such horror,
That we were forc'd to give it o'er, so lowd
The Virgins shriek'd, so fast they dy'd away. (I.i.257–63) [78]

As Derek Hughes has pointed out, Brutus' concluding speech in *Lucius Junius Brutus* is a close translation of the speech in Seneca's *Hercules Furens* which Hercules delivers immediately before going mad and killing his children.[79] John Banks's *Cyrus the Great*, not performed until 1695 but written before *The Unhappy Favourite* (King's 1681), contains an attempt to reassemble a mangled corpse, as in Seneca's *Phaedra*. Panthea, the daughter of the Queen of Scythia, is discovered "weeping o're the mangled Body of Abradatas, whose Limbs she had seemingly fix'd to his Body," crying, "These Hands and Feet which the sharp Scythes / Mow'd from thy lovely Body, I have try'd / A thousand times to joyn 'em with my Kisses, / But 'tis in vain" (Act 5, p53).[80]

Writing amid the chaos and corruption of Nero's Rome, "Seneca's plays test our assumptions about the limits of the cruelty men and women can visit upon one another. Or worse, he asks whether there are any such limits."[81] The horror playwights, in the turmoil of 1670s England, seem to have been affected by a Senecan despair. Like Seneca, they seek responses very different than pity and fear. They create characters and events so outrageous and despicable that their audiences are bound to react with horror – with moral repugnance – to the apostate and perverted anti-heroes. The outrage of these criminal acts is heightened to horror because the perpetrators of the crimes are those to whom love, respect and loyalty is usually due. Robert Hume observes of this period that "audience predilection for gore and horror has been underplayed by a lot of critics [...] [and] this bent defies contemporary critical prescriptions and ill accords with later hypotheses about 'neoclassicism.'" More simply: "regardless of theory and noble prescriptions, sex, horror, and spectacle flourish."[82] This implies that the playwrights are simply pandering to their audience's desire for gross titillation. I would argue that the gruesome, irreverent spectacle and its attendant extravagant language are, rather, an attempt to break through audience passivity and rouse passionate response. Like Seneca, the horror dramatists question received ideas and ask "how to endure a world in which there is no justice, no safety from tyrants, no guarantees – political or divine – of human dignity."[83]

The spectacle of staged violence in these plays defies expectations – it throws into relief the very real violence that was part of everyday life and that was often legitimised with ceremony. One such ceremony, which sought to extol the divine nature of the king's justice and was closely tied with dramatic spectacle in the early modern period, was state-sponsored torture and death. Early modern historians agree that because of the relative instability of the governments involved, public punishment at the Restoration, "is to be understood not only as a judicial, but also as a political ritual. It belongs even in minor cases, to the ceremonies by which power is manifested."[84] The success of the system depended for its effectiveness on evoking several responses from the populace: horror at the iniquity of the perpetrators, terror at their ghastly fate and amazement at the king's forbearance in saving some of the condemned from death. The horror playwrights parody the solemn rites of public torture and death. For them the ritual of death works to subvert the reassertion of the institutional messages of obedience and conformity.

The theatrical equivalency of the playhouse and the scaffold has been well researched. One recent study by Molly Easo Smith describes the theatre-like setting at a hanging in London: "[a]t Tyburn, seats were available for those who could pay, and rooms could be hired in houses overlooking the scene; the majority of spectators, however, stood in a semi-circle around the event, while hawkers sold fruits and pies, and ballads and pamphlets detailing the various crimes committed by the man being hanged."[85] In London, the formal course of events included a ceremonial procession to the place of execution. The accused (often with his or her coffin) would be drawn on a sled from Newgate, through the heart of London, to the gallows at Tyburn: "[t]he route of the hanging procession crossed the busiest axis of the town at Smithfield, passed through one of the most heavily populated districts in St Giles' and St Andrew's, Holborn, and followed the most-trafficked road, Tyburn Road, to the gallows."[86] All the city's churches would ring their bells. Public executions were popular, and huge crowds would attend. Samuel Pepys watched Colonel James Turner hanged for burglary in 1664, after which Pepys noted "[i]t was believed there was at least 12 or 14000 people in the street."[87] When Stephen Eaton and several others were executed for murder in 1669, "the streets were thronged with Spectators, and at Tyburn they were in such numbers that the Carts could not get up to the place of Execution, the Prisoners being led thither on foot."[88]

Like theatrical productions, public executions were well planned and acted-out events. Early modern historian Pieter Spierenberg says regulation was central: "in one way or another the stage [was] set [...] Executions were dramatized in order to serve as a sort of morality play. The stagers, of course, were the magistrates. The social drama should reflect their view."[89] In both forms of drama, the audience – the voyeuristic spectator – was central. Michel Foucault suggests that, "[i]n the ceremonies of the public execution, the main character was the people, whose real and immediate presence was required for the performance."[90] Certainly audiences attending both theatrical tragedies and public punishments had particular expectations. The context of ceremony and ritual created a procedure that was familiar. There could be odd moments of spontaneity – such as a last-minute reprieve – but most often, events were expected to unfold in a predictable way. Ultimately, those characters found guilty of serious transgressions would be punished for their crimes with death – sometimes a long, drawn out affair. And, as is the same for tragedy, the audience response at public executions was key to the success of the 'production.'

The expected 'role' of a condemned felon at a public punishment was to confess guilt and express repentance. According to J.A. Sharpe, condemned criminals on the scaffold did not merely accept their fates:

> They were the willing and central participants in a theatre of punishment, which offered not merely a spectacle, but also a reinforcement of certain values [...] they were helping to assert the legitimacy of the power which had brought them to their sad end [...].[91]

Their confessions were formalised and expressed as a farewell or 'last dying' speech. The penitent end to a 'just' sentence was expected to edify the audience. In his last dying speech, as reported in *A Murderer Punished; and Pardoned*, the convicted murderer Thomas Savage says he has "come to dye a cursed and ignominious Death, and I most justly deserve it." Savage is then quoted as asking his audience to take heed and learn an important lesson from his degeneration into sin and wickedness:

> I would have you all that look upon me, take warning by me: the first sin I began with, was Sabbath-breaking, thereby I got acquaintance with bad company and so we went to the Ale-house, from the Ale-house to the bawdy-house: there I was perswaded to rob my Master, as also to murther this poor innocent creature, for which I am come to this shameful end.[92]

After the account of Savage's speech, prayer and execution, the pamphlet turns to the account of Hannah Blay's execution. Blay is the "bawd" who was convicted of being an accessory to the murder. Compared to the extensive account of Savage's penitence, the account of Blay's imprisonment and execution is short – one page long. Blay never speaks directly; rather, her words or actions are reported to us. We are told that during her time in prison she was "rude [...] debauched [...] seldom sober." She tried to coerce Savage by making him drunk "and endeavoured very much to draw him off from his Repentance, by driving his old trade of sin and wickedness." It is clear that her case gets such little print space (and is only an 'Addition' to the 12th edition) because "she ended her wicked life by a shameful death, without the least sign of sorow or repentance."[93]

Given the well-rehearsed procedures, audience reaction to public executions was predictable. The expectations of the audience watching horror plays, however, featuring tortured innocents and unrepentant villains, were rudely undermined. In *The Empress of Morocco* (Duke's 1673), for example, the most despicable character is the queen mother Laula, who sets up the murder of her own husband and son, among others. If Elkanah Settle followed state or traditional stage justice in his play, there would be retribution: at the very least, Laula would be punished for her monstrous deeds. In the bloody Jacobean revenge plays, there is most often some form of retribution against the villain: for example, the evil Flamineo in John Webster's *The White Devil* is taken away "to prison, and to torture" (V.vi.296); and, the revengers Hippolito and Vindice are taken "to speedy execution" in *The Revenger's Tragedy*.

After some form of retribution, an audience could feel satisfied that the horror of an evil character's actions would somehow be expiated by their 'good' death. In the horror plays, however, there is little if any moral closure or edification. Against all the audience's assumptions that sin will be punished, characters such as Laula are not made examples of: they die without remorse. Laula defies the powers that be and dies by the method and at the time of her own choosing. Nor does Laula repent of the numerous murders of which she is guilty. And, unlike Hannah Blay's compromised dissent, Laula's dissent is heard loud and clear. She tells the audience she is "too Innocent to Dye" (V). She dies defiant: she curses her faithless lover to share her doom in Hell, and the single thing she despairs of is not having had enough sons to kill. Another female villain, the evil queen Deidamia in Thomas Otway's *Alcibiades* (Duke's 1675), kills herself with similar defiance. Exhibiting neither remorse nor repentance, her last dying speech simply allows her to glory in her dissent:

> Think you that I will dye by formal law?
> No, when I'm dead be thus my fame supply'd:
> She liv'd a murd'ress, and a murd'ress dy'd. [*stabs her self*]
> Justice would but my happiness retard:
> Thus I descend below to a reward. (V.506–10)[94]

The regicides in both *The Empress of Morocco* (Duke's 1673) and Aphra Behn's *Abdelazer* (Duke's 1676) are killed off at the end of the plays. Their final speeches, however, also show an utter lack of repentance for their crimes, coupled with an undiminished strength of conviction in their causes. In *The Libertine* (Duke's 1675) and *Lucina's Rape* (1675/6), evil characters similarly disdain those who try to make them show remorse for their crimes. In *Lucina's Rape* the Emperor Valentinian tells his victim's husband that if Lucina were raised from the grave he would rape her again. He then makes it clear that he will gain immortality in death, but not through any Christian belief. "Altars shall be rais'd / To my great Name; while your more vile inscriptions / Time rots and mould'ring Clay is all your portion" (V.v.250–52).[95]

The validity of certain aspects of Christian theology also comes under satirical scrutiny through the horror dramatists' use of last dying speeches. The church, which played a large role in the struggle to maintain order, supported the use of these speeches in criminal executions in order to exert ideological control: "to demonstrate the inadvisability of transgressing God's laws as well as those of the secular power."[96] In the 1670s, more and more pulpit sermons were dedicated to attacking atheism. The playwrights took advantage of the clergy's fear of losing the battle and produced theatrical dramas marked by the absence of justly deserved punishment and quite devoid of penitence. They just as avidly questioned coerced contrition, showing its weaknesses by exposing the meaninglessness of the 'show' of repentance.

A key motif running through all of these plays is that the playwrights give a voice – often in the form of a 'dying speech' – to those who are least likely to merit it; and the legacy of their words outlasts them. Where Charles (and the church) chose to silence dissent as sedition in print and on the scaffold, regardless of the guilt or innocence of the victims, the horror playwrights regularly chose to amplify the voices of the guilty and silence the voices of the innocent. Pardoning the innocent is as integral a part of state and providential justice as punishing the guilty. The perception of Charles as a merciful monarch, wise enough to fathom and deal justly with guilt or innocence, was an important tool in fortifying the legitimacy and strength of the crown. But mercy is drained of its inherent

meaning in the horror plays. Almost without exception, the innocent are given
no recourse to mercy – most often it is they who are tortured and killed – while
the guilty escape formal retribution. An interesting contrast can be shown in
execution scenes from John Crowne's *The Ambitious Statesman* (King's 1679)
and Cyril Tournier's Jacobean play *The Atheist's Tragedy* (c. 1610). In Tourneur's
play, the evil D'Amville plots to kill his nephew Charlemont: he arranges the
arrest of Charlemont and Charlemont's former fiancée Castabella on false charges
of adultery and the innocent lovers are condemned to die. As they prepare for
execution, D'Amville announces to the judges and to his nephew, "I'le be thy
executioner my selfe [...] You shall see how eas'ly / I can put you out of paine"
(V.ii.225–6, 238–9).[97] When he raises the axe, however, he "strikes out his owne
braines" (V.ii.239). As he dies, D'Amville admits to his crimes and accepts the
justice of his punishment: "yond power that strucke me knew / The Judgement I
deserv'd; and gave it" (V.ii.263–4). The judge frees the innocent lovers:

> With the hands
> Of Joy and Justice I thus set you free.
> The power of that eternal providence,
> Which overthrew his projects in their pride
> Hath made your griefes the instruments to raise
> Your blessings to a greater height then ever. (V.ii.267–72)

Charlemont's response is, "Only to Heav'n I attribute the work, / Whose gracious
motives made me still forbear / To be mine own revenger. Now I see / That
patience is the honest man's revenge" (V.ii.273–6). In Crowne's drama, the
innocent Protestant hero, the Duke of Vendosme, is deceived and tortured by his
own father: it is Vendosme who is exposed to the audience, "wrack't [with his
lover] Louize dead by him." His evil father, in contrast, is offered life; but, in his
final speech, he *chooses* death:

> My glory [...]
> Is out, now send me t' eternal darkness ! [...]
> Be sure you get to heaven, for if your piety
> Shou'd crack, and let you fall to Hell where I am,
> I'll plague you worse than all the devils there. (V.p238)[98]

The horror dramatists make complex use of the similarities between the playhouse
theatre and the theatre of punishment in order to de-sanctify, by parody, the basis
for ideological control. Unlike state-sanctioned death under Charles's rule, death
in the theatre of the 1670s is seldom formal and public; it is more often than not
random, private and casually brutal. It does not make for the assertion of obedience
and conformity: there are many tortured, dead bodies and dismembered body parts
littering the stage in the horror plays, but they belong to innocent victims. Aside
from the examples already given, there are others: the hero Britannicus's horrific
death by poisoning in *The Tragedy of Nero* (King's 1674), Caesar Borgia's young
son emerging on stage with his eyes gouged out (Duke's 1679), the mutilated

body of Lavinia in Edward Ravenscroft's *Titus Andronicus* (King's 1679) and preparations for the burning at the stake of the innocent Duke of Saxony at the end of Settle's *The Female Prelate* (King's 1680).

The lack of moral closure, tied as it is in these plays to a sense of injustice, is de-stabilising. When looking at the speeches of political re-establishment at the final scenes of Shakespeare's *Hamlet* and *Macbeth*, Stephen Booth argues,

> [t]he tragedies put their audiences' minds through a turmoil of conflicting systems of value. Fortinbras and Malcolm return order to the stage; they do not resolve the conflicts in the mind of the onlooker, but they do reestablish order in one of the threatened systems. The completion of the story, the completion of the artistic whole, and the resolution of the *particular* conflict of the play puts a frame to the audience's experience of intellectual turmoil and makes it bearable.[99]

Tragic storylines and graphic depictions of violence can be made bearable for an audience if evil acts are acknowledged, expectations are fulfilled and moral order is re-established. In the horror plays, there are no frames, there is no moral closure: innocent people are murdered and the audience is helplessly party to the evil machinations of the villains. This causes an upheaval of the emotions that cannot properly be dealt with or reconciled, because of the malefactors' overwhelming lack of remorse and repentance – even consciousness of guilt. An audience can accept and even, perhaps, enjoy an execution when it knows the criminal is guilty of a serious crime but, having made his peace with God and king, dies a good death. When this element of the drama is undermined, as it is in the horror plays, the spectacle of death can offer neither meaning nor edification to an audience.

A particularly striking example of spectacle bereft of justice, exigency or edification is in the final act of *Oedipus* (Duke's 1678). The theatre audience is exposed to a 'discovery' of Oedipus's wife and mother Jocasta, "held by her Women, and stabb'd in many places of her bosom, her hair dishevel'd." The graphic spectacle of a mother bleeding from her breast is made more horrifying when the audience discovers that Jocasta has also murdered her innocent children: we are told her daughters [i]n twisted Gold [...] hang / On the Bed Royal; and her little Sons / Stabb'd through the breasts [lie] upon the bloody Pillows" (V.i.406–8).[100] The imprint of these violent images is intensified when it is clear that Jocasta is not even cognisant of her sacrilege; she continues to deny she has committed a sin in executing her children, and her only consideration is her obsessive sexual desire for the man with whom she committed incest.

At the Restoration, ceremony and spectacle were restored to reconnect with and keep alive monarchical traditions that were broken by the civil wars and the interregnum. In the theatre as in life, spectacle gains meaning from ceremony, and ceremony is the public face of religious and political doctrine. If these doctrines begin to lose their validity, spectacles become mere show. One implication to be drawn from the playwrights' use of lavish but empty spectacles on the mid-Restoration stage is that the spectacles inherent in the contemporary state and religious ceremonies are likewise in danger of becoming devoid of meaning. These plays, therefore, are the opposite of the morality play. The playwrights use horror as an element of misrule; they become Masters of the Revels, fashioning their drama to unmask the 'show' that Charles is simultaneously producing.

Endnotes

[1]   Robert D. Hume, *The Development of English Drama in the Late Seventeenth Century* (Oxford: Clarendon, 1976) 199–202, 290.

[2]   Maximillian E. Novak, ed., *The Empress of Morocco and Its Critics* (Los Angeles: U of California P, 1968) vii.

[3]   Paul D. Cannan, "New Directions in Serious Drama on the London Stage, 1675–1678" *PQ* 73 (1994): 227. Cannan does argue, however, that this mode is a separate experimentation within a broadly heroic genre; Derek Hughes and Janet Todd, "Tragedy and tragicomedy" *The Cambridge Companion to Aphra Behn* (Cambridge: CUP, 2004) 89; Jean Marsden, "Spectacle, Horror and Pathos," *The Cambridge Companion to English Restoration Theatre*, ed. Deborah Payne Fisk (Cambridge: CUP, 2000) 175.

[4]   In her influential study, Susan J. Owen argues for crucial links between the politics and the theatre during the Exclusion Crisis, but the political nature of the serious plays leading up to this period is often disregarded. *Restoration Theatre and Crisis* (Oxford: Clarendon, 1996).

[5]   Leslie Hotson, *The Commonwealth and Restoration Stage* (Cambridge: Harvard UP, 1928) 262.

[6]   Arthur F. White, "Office of the Revels and Dramatic Censorship during the Restoration Period" *Western Reserve University Bulletin* 34 (1931): 14–15. Henry Herbert, who had been Master of the Revels for the Jacobeans, returned to the post in the first year of the Restoration. Thomas Killigrew took over the role from Herbert's death in 1673 until 1677. Arthur White contends that, "judging from available records [this period] was singularly free from interference so far as drama was concerned." White goes on to argue that it is "quite beside the point to lay the blame for the moral laxity of the Restoration drama, as has been done, on the shoulders of Tom Killigrew because he failed to curb the tendencies of the age during his term of office" (30, 12). It is notable, however, that so much passed the censor during the period of Killigrew's stewardship, in both the tragic and the comic theatre of the time.

[7]   John Spurr, *England in the 1670s* (Oxford: Blackwell, 2000) 288.

[8]   Laura Brown, for example, argues heroic action is the predominant form of serious drama in the Restoration until 1677, when another form – affective tragedy – takes over and "drains the heroic play of evaluative efficacy and meaning, and substitutes the affective response of pity for the judgmental one of admiration" (*English Dramatic Form 1660–1760* [New Haven and London: Yale UP, 1981] 69). Anne Righter (Barton) groups together as heroic all the serious drama between the years of 1660 and 1685. She goes on to argue that the first part of the period is dominated by rhyming plays which are gradually replaced by the blank-verse tragedy of pathos: "In both, the furious gestures of the heroes, the rant and the declarations of passion are literary and hollow" ("Heroic Tragedy" *Restoration Theatre* [London: Edward Arnold, 1965] 135). Christopher J. Wheatley broadly describes heroic drama as "serious plays written in rhyming couplets, popular between 1663 and 1676" ("Tragedy" *The Cambridge Companion to English Restoration Theatre*, ed. Fisk

[Cambridge: CUP, 2000] 75). Even though Allardyce Nicoll acknowledges the 'school of horrors' model, he suggests that the heroic play had acknowledged reign in the theatres until 1677. Here Nicoll is clearly focusing on Dryden's output and his change to blank verse in *All for Love* at the end of 1677. Nicoll does not look at Lee, Otway or Settle when discussing 'other types' of tragedy between 1660 and 1677 and considers Lee's plays under the genre of Rimed Heroic Tragedy (*A History of English Drama 1660–1900*, vol. 1 [Cambridge: CUP, 1923, rev. 1952]).

⁹   Derek Hughes, "Heroic Drama and Tragicomedy," *A Companion to Restoration Drama*, ed. Susan J. Owen (Oxford: Blackwell, 2001) 202.

¹⁰   Paulina Kewes, "Otway, Lee and the Restoration History Play," *A Companion to Restoration Drama*, ed. Owen 355; Don-John Dugas, "Elkanah Settle, John Crowne and Nahum Tate," *A Companion to Restoration Drama*, ed. Owen 380.

¹¹   Felicity Nussbaum "'Real, Beautiful Women': Actresses and *The Rival Queens*" *Eighteenth-Century Life* 32:2 (Spring 2008): 142.

¹²   J. Douglas Canfield, *Heroes and States* (Lexington: UP of Kentucky, 2000) 3.

¹³   Canfield 199.

¹⁴   Nancy Klein Maguire, *Regicide and Restoration* (Cambridge: CUP, 1992) 39, 93, 124, 218 and 220.

¹⁵   Hughes 208–10.

¹⁶   Nicoll, *History of English Drama* 135.

¹⁷   Laura Lunger Knoppers makes a similar point in her discussion of Milton's *Paradise Regained* when contrasting the solemn Focauldian tragedy of Charles I's execution with the brutal horror of the regicides' debasement during their execution: "the spectacle of the grotesque body falls below tragedy into satire, even farce' (*Historicizing Milton: Spectacle, Power, and Poetry in Restoration England* [Athens/London: U of Georgia P, 53]).

¹⁸   Maguire 94–5.

¹⁹   This is an issue that struggling democracies continue to question in parts of the world today, most recently in Egypt: when can a legally elected government be thrown out by a coup?

²⁰   Robert Ornstein, *The Moral Vision of Jacobean Tragedy* (Westport, Conn.: Greenwood P, 1975) 274.

²¹   G.K. Hunter, "Seneca and English Tragedy," *Seneca*, ed. C.D.N. Costa (London and Boston: Routledge & Kegan Paul, 1974) 176.

²²   John Kerrigan, "Revenge Tragedy Revisited: Politics, Providence and Drama, 1649–1683" *The Seventeenth Century* 12:2 (1997): 222.

²³   William Joyner, *The Roman Empress* (London, 1671). All references to Joyner's play are hereafter cited parenthetically in the text.

²⁴   Henry Nevil Payne, *The Fatal Jealousy*, London 1673: The Epilogue; *The Morning Ramble*, London 1673. Act 4, p 54.

²⁵   *The Works of Thomas Otway*, ed. J.C. Ghosh, vol. 1 (Oxford: Clarendon, 1968) 3–4.

²⁶   *The Complete Poems of John Wilmot, Earl of Rochester*, ed. David M. Vieth (New Haven and London: Yale UP, 1968) xviii–xix.

²⁷   J.M. Armistead, "Nathaniel Lee," *Oxford Dictionary of National Biography* (Oxford: OUP, 2004); A.L. McLeod "Nathaniel Lee's Birth Date" *MLN* 69:3 (1954): 167–70.

²⁸   Jessica Munns, *Restoration Politics and Drama* (Newark: U of Delaware P, 1995) 21.

²⁹   Michael G. Finlayson, *Historians, Puritanism and the English Revolution* (Toronto: Toronto UP, 1983) 154.

[30] Albert S. Borgman, *Thomas Shadwell* (New York: Benjamin Blom, 1969) 8–12.

[31] Hume, *Development of English Drama* 269.

[32] Hotson, 219, 228.

[33] Edward A. Langhans, "The Theatre," *The Cambridge Companion to English Restoration Theatre*, ed. Fisk 3.

[34] W.E. Van Lennep, E. Avery and A. Scouten, eds., *The London Stage 1660–1800*, Part 1 (Carbondale, Ill.: Southern Illinois UP, 1965–68) 180.

[35] *The London Stage* 197, 202.

[36] *The London Stage* 191, 205.

[37] Nicoll, *History of English Drama* 95.

[38] John Evelyn, quoted in *The London Stage*, 180.

[39] Judith Milhous, "The Multimedia Spectacular on the Restoration Stage," *British Theatre and the Other Arts, 1660–1800,* ed. Shirley Strum Kenny (London and Toronto: Associated UPs, 1984) 42.

[40] John Downes, *Roscius Anglicanus*, ed. J. Milhous and Robert D. Hume (London: The Society for Theatre Research, 1987) 72–3.

[41] Don-John Dugas discusses Settle's skills as a set designer in *A Companion to Restoration Drama*, ed. Owen 378–95.

[42] Roger North, when referring to *The Empress of Morocco. The London Stage*, ed. Van Lennep et al. 206.

[43] *The London Stage*, ed. Van Lennep et al. 212–3. The play was printed three times in the seventeenth century and made Settle one of the most well known playwrights of the generation.

[44] *London drollery, or, The wits academy, by W.H.* (London, 1673) 11–12.

[45] "Prologue to *Arviragus Reviv'd*: Spoken by Mr. Hart," *Miscellany Poems* (London 1684).

[46] *The London Stage*, ed. Van Lennep et al. 213.

[47] "A Prologue Spoken at the Opening of the NEW HOUSE," *Miscellany Poems* 286–9.

[48] Downes, *Roscius Anglicanus* 73–4.

[49] Milhous, "The Multimedia Spectacular on the Restoration Stage" 46.

[50] Nicoll, *History of English Drama* 348.

[51] Quoted in *The London Stage*, ed. Van Lennep et al. 224.

[52] Dawn Leacock, "Computer Analysis of Restoration Staging, II" *Theatre Notebook* 47:3 (1993): 155.

[53] See Judith Milhous, "The Duke's Company's Profits, 1675–1677" *Theatre Notebook* 32 (1978): 76–88.

[54] Milhous, "The Multimedia Spectacular on the Restoration Stage" 62.

[55] Lee, *The Works of Nathaniel Lee*, ed. Thomas B. Stroup and Arthur L. Cooke (New Brunswick, N.J.: Scarecrow, 1955), 1:21; Roswell Gay Ham, *Otway and Lee* (New Haven: Yale UP, 1931) 50. Ham likens this cult of Nero to the flourishing cult of libertinism in 1674–76, arguing that Lee's play was libertinism's "completest dramatic expression." He also suggests that parts of John Oldham's 1676 "Ode" (printed as "The Satyr against Vertue" in *The Works of Mr. John Oldham* (London, 1684)) was influenced by *Nero* as an expression of libertinism: "Yet greater was that mighty Emperor; / (As greater crime befitted his high Pow'r) / Who sacrific'd a City to a Jest" (105–6).

[56] Downes, *Roscius Anglicanus* 80, editor's note 249.

57 L.C. 7/1, p. 5, quoted in Nicoll, *History of English Drama*, 325n.

58 Hotson 260–261.

59 Hume, *Development of English Drama* 288.

60 Righter [Barton] 135.

61 John Evelyn, *The Diary of John Evelyn*, ed. E.S. de Beer, vol. 3 (Oxford: OUP, 1955) 246.

62 John Patrick Montano, "The Quest for Consensus: The Lord Mayor's Day Shows in the 1670s," *Culture and Society in the Stuart Restoration*, ed. Gerald MacLean (Cambridge: CUP, 1995) 31–2.

63 Frank Barlow, "The King's Evil" *The English Historical Review* 95:374 (January 1980): 25–6.

64 Maguire, *Regicide and Restoration* 84.

65 Lois Potter, *Secret Rites and Secret Writing* (Cambridge: CUP, 1989) 157.

66 Maguire, *Regicide and Restoration* 51, 84.

67 *The Empress of Morocco, A Tragedy with Sculptures* (London, 1673). All references to Settle's play are hereafter cited parenthetically in the text.

68 Philip Parsons, "Restoration Tragedy as Total Theatre," *Restoration Literature*, ed. Harold Love (London: Methuen, 1972) 53.

69 *The Dramatic Works of John Crowne*, ed. James Maidment, 4 vols. (New York: Blom, repr. 1967). All further references to *Thyestes* are from the Maidment edition, vol. 2, and are hereafter cited parenthetically in the text.

70 *The Works of Nathaniel Lee*, ed. Stroup and Cooke. All further references to *The Massacre of Paris* are from Stroup and Cooke's edition, vol. 2, and are hereafter cited parenthetically in the text.

71 *The Works of Nathaniel Lee*, ed. Stroup and Cooke. All further references to *Caesar Borgia* are from Stroup and Cooke's edition, vol. 2, and are hereafter cited parenthetically in the text.

72 *Three Jacobean Tragedies*, ed. Gamini Salgado (Harmondsworth: Penguin, 1965). References to *The Revenger's Tragedy* and John Webster's *The White Devil* are from the Penguin edition and are hereafter cited parenthetically in the text.

73 Samuel Clarke, *A general martyrologie*, 3rd edition (London, 1677) 301. Clarke's work also appeared in 1640 and in 1651, other periods of intense civil stress.

74 *Seneca: The Tragedies*, ed. David R. Slavitt (Baltimore: Johns Hopkins UP, 1995). All references to *Phaedra* and *Oedipus*, trans. Rachel Hadas, are from Slavitt's edition, vol. 1 and vol. 2 respectively, and are hereafter cited parenthetically in the text.

75 Dana Gioia, *Seneca: The Tragedies* 2, xxxvi.

76 Gioia xxxvi and ix.

77 Don Share, ed. *Seneca in English* (London: Penguin, 1998); G.K. Hunter, "Seneca and English Tragedy," *Seneca*, ed. D.N. Costa 194.

78 *The Works of Nathaniel Lee*, ed. Stroup and Cooke. All further references to *Theodosius: or, The force of love* are from Stroup and Cooke's edition, vol. 2, and are hereafter cited parenthetically in the text.

79 Derek Hughes, *English Drama 1660–1700* (Oxford: Clarendon, 1996) 294.

80 John Banks, *Cyrus the Great* (London 1696). This discussion on Senecan elements within the plays was generated by correspondence I had on the subject with Professor Hughes.

[81]   Slavitt, *Seneca: The Tragedies* 1, ix.

[82]   Hume, *Development of English Drama* 199 and 269. I do not agree with Hume's linking of gore with horror. Horror can certainly be present without gore and vice versa.

[83]   Gioia xxviii.

[84]   Michel Foucault, *Discipline and Punish*, trans. Alan Sheridan (New York: Vintage, 1979) 47.

[85]   Molly Easo Smith "The Theatre and the Scaffold: Death as Spectacle in The Spanish Tragedy," *Revenge Tragedy*, ed. Stevie Simkin (Basingstoke: Palgrave, 2001) 72. A more recent study on the subject includes the essays in James Robert Allard and Mathew R. Martin, eds., *Staging Pain, 1580–1800* (Farnham: Ashgate, 2009).

[86]   Peter Linebaugh, "The Tyburn Riot Against the Surgeons," *Albion's Fatal Tree*, ed. Douglas Hay, Peter Linebaugh et al. (New York: Pantheon, 1975) 67.

[87]   Samuel Pepys, *The Diary of Samuel Pepys*, ed. Robert Latham and William Matthews, 11 vols. (London: G. Bell and Sons 1970–83) 5:23.

[88]   Anon, *An Exact Narrative of the bloody murder ... committed by Stephen Eaton* (London, 1669) 8. This pamphlet was licensed by Roger L'Estrange.

[89]   Pieter Spierenburg, *The Spectacle of Suffering* (Cambridge: CUP, 1984) 43.

[90]   Foucault, *Discipline and Punish* 57.

[91]   J.A. Sharpe, "'Last Dying Speeches': Religion, Ideology and Public Execution in Seventeenth-Century England" *Past and Present* 107 (May 1985) 156.

[92]   Robert Franklin, *A Murderer Punished; and Pardoned, or, A True Relation of the Wicked Life, and Shameful-Happy Death of Thomas Savage* 12th ed. (London, 1669) 38–9.

[93]   *A Murderer Punished* 48.

[94]   Ghosh, *The Works of Thomas Otway*. All references to *Alcibiades* are from Ghosh's edition, vol. 1, and are hereafter cited parenthetically in the text.

[95]   Rather than the 1685 quarto, I am using the manuscript version of Rochester's play entitled *Lucina's Rape or the Tragedy of Vallentinian* reproduced in *The Works of John Wilmot*, ed. Harold Love (Oxford: OUP, 1999). All references to the play are hereafter cited parenthetically in the text.

[96]   J.A. Sharpe, *Crime in Early Modern England 1550–1750*, 2nd ed. (London and New York: Longman, 1999) 96.

[97]   *Four Revenge Tragedies*, ed. Katharine Eisaman Maus (Oxford: OUP, 1995). All references to Cyril Tourneur's *The Atheist's Tragedy* are from Maus's edition and are hereafter cited parenthetically in the text.

[98]   Maidment, *The Dramatic Works of John Crowne*. All further references to *The Ambitious Statesman* are from the Maidment edition, vol. 3, and are hereafter cited parenthetically in the text.

[99]   Stephen Booth, *An Essay on Shakespeare's Sonnets* (New Haven and London: Yale UP, 1969) 131.

[100] *The Works of Nathaniel Lee*, ed. Stroup and Cooke. All references to *Oedipus* are from Stroup and Cooke's edition, vol. 1, and are hereafter cited parenthetically in the text.

Chapter 2
Memory, Re-enactment and Trauma

In Elkanah Settle's *Love and Revenge* (Duke's 1674), the lascivious king Clotair dispatches the object of his lust (who also happens to be his brother's fiancée) to the dungeon after she rejects his advances. When he visits her, Clotair's ardor is once again aroused, and he turns on his 'Slave' Burbon, deriding him for carrying out his orders:

> How, obey me Villain! Obedience
> To a command so barb'rous and so monstrous,
> Deserves more than an enraged King can utter,
> Or torments act: What if you had been commanded
> To Whore your Sister, Stab your Father, Ravish
> Your Mother, Curse your God, or Kill your King?
> Dog, would you have obey'd and done all this? (Act 3, p36)[1]

The sensational taboos – these barb'rous and monstrous acts – that Clotair vocalises here are elemental features of the horror plays. Essential violations of a social order that was put in place to protect individuals and their communities, they are repeatedly re-enacted in the horror plays. Communities, depicted as fractured and chaotic in these plays, have no recourse to moral, political or social certainties, allowing perverse individuals to transgress boundaries freely – often with little or no meaningful retribution.

In investigating the extent to which these macabre tragedies engaged with contemporary discourse on social, political, religious and philosophical issues, this study contends that the genre of horror gains its popularity at times of social dislocation. It reflects deep schisms in society, and English society – a decade after the Restoration – remained profoundly unsettled and in a (delayed) state of shock from years of social upheaval and civil conflict. The horror plays reflect a traumatised society by troping recurrent, deep-seated and unresolved anxieties – the same anxieties that came close to producing renewed civil strife in the late 1670s. They engaged profoundly with contemporary discourse by abreacting the conspiratorial climate of suspicion and fear. As a result, they were conspicuously involved with, and had a major impact on, the frenetic events of this decade, which ended in crisis.

As historians continually remind us, the politically unsettling threats of popery and arbitrary government that led to crisis in England in the late 1670s did not arise out of a vacuum. These issues were, in fact, intrinsically tied to a recurring and ongoing pattern of anxiety and paranoia that had haunted the English public psyche since the aftermath of the Reformation. Overwhelmingly, the anxieties in the decade of the 1670s projected a fear of internal upheaval – a return to civil war. The growth of these fears can be traced clearly in the literature of the time.

The horror plays respond to earlier drama and panegyric, picking up on certain themes, responding ironically to others: ultimately steering the trajectory of tragic drama into the heart of the Exclusion Crisis and beyond.

There is no question that the problems the Restoration architects faced were enormous. The restoration of a monarchy was unprecedented, and the publicly sanctioned execution of Charles I had permanently shifted the structure of kingly authority. Jonathan Sawday argues that rather than paradoxically trying to summon up the past in order to consciously forget it, Charles II and his supporters made a decision to bridge the 20-year gap by "ignoring the discontinuity, and substituting, in its stead, an alternative and comforting dream – the collective myth of the divine nature of the monarch. Thus, in the alternative model of remembrance, the father-figure killed in 1649 by the English people [...] re-emerges unsullied in 1660."[2] At the moment of the Restoration, symbols and iconography in the country reverted back 20 years. As Charles was preparing to enter London, the statue of his father was replaced in the Guildhall yard. On the same day, an order was passed for "the arms of the commonwealth [...] to be 'taken down in all the courts of justice, and other publick places [...] and all the king's arms set up in their room.' A further order was promulgated [...] which led to the navy's colours, flags, and standards being replaced with those of 1648."[3] The ship in which Charles sailed to England, the *Naseby* (named for the Battle of Naseby – the defeat of the royalist cause in 1645) was quickly renamed *The Royal Charles*.

The office of kingship was no longer associated, as it was in King James's reign, with the absolutist Yahweh of the Old Testament. The restored king is now closely linked with the forgiving and peaceful son of God – and with his father, Charles I. Since his execution, Charles I had been linked numerous times to the martyred Christ. In the frontispiece to the *Eikon Basilike*, written after his execution, Charles is adorned with his crown of thorns. Inside the book he is depicted as the shepherd, a father to his people and the husband of his kingdom.

In the panegyric of the early Restoration, the two kings are invariably linked ("Charls from Charls must be greatest of that name"),[4] and a seamlessness is suggested between their two reigns. Cromwell and the wars appear only as a temporary blip. Most commonly, the dark afflictions of the interregnum are synonymous with a nightmarish unreality. In the poem *A Second Charles*, the mistake of the civil war and interregnum period is represented as night: in darkness it is difficult to distinguish the real from the imagined. It is also a time of nightmares. "Black and dark was our morning Star, / As darksome night or far blacker." Cromwell and the wars can only be perceived through a phantasmagorical lens, which distorts reality and questions the very existence of the events. The real world is seen by the honest light of the day, which allows no *trompes d'oeil*. Charles's restoration subsumes and cancels out the darkness that came before: "now our bright morning doth arise / And golden hopes doth paint our skies" (6–7, 13–14).[5] In John Dryden's *Astraea Redux*, the "sullen Intervall of Warre" is likened to a dark storm: "when black Clouds draw down the lab'ring Skies, / Ere yet abroad the winged Thunder flies / An horrid Stillness first invades the ear, /

And in that silence Wee the Tempest fear" (5–8).[6] As with nightmares, storms are chaotic but temporary, and with the new day and Charles's rightful restoration, "[t]hose clouds that overcast your Morne shall fly / Dispell'd to farthest corners of the sky" (294–5).[7] During the dark chaos in *Astraea Redux*, providence is nowhere to be seen: "Heaven […] seem'd regardless of our Fate […]" (13). In the light of day, however, God's intervention and "vengeance" return dramatically with the shifting of allegiance by "MONCK whom Providence design'd to loose / Those real bonds false freedom did impose" (151–2). Dryden's poem further reinforces the mythology of the divine monarch already begun in the Restoration process. Christ-like Charles II, as his father had been, is now the husband of the kingdom. He absolves his wife's guilt for straying while he was away. England, finally reunited with her true spouse, is Charles's "virgin love." Because the country is reborn, it can do the impossible – return to its uncorrupted, virginal state – "As you meet it, the Land approacheth you. / The Land returns, and in the white it wears / The marks of penitence and sorrow bears" (253–5).

Early Restoration drama is similar in theme to the early poetry. The plays generally celebrate the re-establishment of legitimate rule (in other words, the restoration of the Stuarts), mainly for the purposes of royalist propaganda and often for the playwright's own ends (in the case of the Earl of Orrery, to expiate his guilt for his service under Cromwell). When a play deals directly with Cromwell, as for example in *The Unfortunate Usurper* (1663), *The Usurper* (1664), or *Andronicus Comnenius* (1664), he is seen as an anomaly: a tyrant who must be overthrown and killed for his sins. Edward Howard's *The Usurper*, in fact, enacts Cromwell's death repeatedly. Although it has an obvious affiliation with contemporary panegyric, early Restoration drama is also deeply associated with political pamphleteering. The theatre had been silent for nearly 20 years. During this time its polemic role had been taken over by the pamphlet satirists. At the Restoration, as the vigorous pamphleteering of the past two decades decreased and the theatres opened up, it was time for the dramatists to speak again. Nicholas Jose articulates the interdependence of the two genres: "[b]oth before and after the Restoration controversialists cast their versions of contemporary history into the form of plays. These unacted tract plays share the vigorous satirical energy of the pamphlet writing of the 1640s and 1650s, presenting an extreme, simplistic, but effective burlesque of the issues of the day."[8]

Soon after Charles II was crowned, however, traditional fears of Catholicism and absolutism rapidly resurfaced in parliament and in public. Jonathan Scott argues that the Restoration of Charles II succeeded too well, "for it restored not only the structures of early Stuart government, but subsequently its fears, divisions and crises.[9] In the first few years of Charles's reign, the new Cavalier parliament created legislation strongly attached to its Royalist and Anglican roots. It passed the Corporation Act (1661), which stipulated that municipal office-holders take the Anglican sacrament and renounce the Presbyterian Covenant; it also restored bishops to the upper house. The following year the Licensing Act made it illegal to print anything heretical, seditious or schismatical, or any doctrine or opinion contrary to the Christian faith or the doctrine and discipline of the Church of England. The Act of Uniformity, established in the same year, required all clergymen and teachers to conform to the liturgy of the Church of England as prescribed by the Book of Common Prayer. Tensions between the king and the parliament, however, were emerging. After the Act of Uniformity was passed, the king attempted to excuse Catholics and Protestant dissenters because, he said, among other things, the 'old religion' had shown loyalty to his father. In 1663, parliament spoke to the king of the growing "jealousy and apprehension [...] [of] your good Subjects [...] that Popish Religion may much increase in this Kingdom [...]."[10]

Inherent anxieties and fears about Catholicism were made manifest in the wake of the Great Fire of London in 1666. The public was quick to apportion blame. While the fire still burned, Samuel Pepys wrote in his diary of the "discourses now begun that there is plot in it and that the French had done it [...]."[11] Gilbert Burnet tells us "[t]he papists were generally charged with it."[12] Although the government claimed the fire was not part of a conspiracy, a commons committee found that the Catholics were responsible, and a French "papist" was eventually hanged for starting the fire. In October 1666, the House of Commons resolved to ask the king for a proclamation banishing all priests and Jesuits and to implement the anti-recusant laws. On 27 October 1666, Andrew Marvell wrote to Hull's Mayor Richard Franke saying that "[m]any informations are daily brought in to the two Committees about the Fire of London & the insolence of Papists."[13]

The mid-1660s also saw the extremely unpopular and unsuccessful Second Dutch War. As the war progressed, concerns grew over England's military failures. The joyful panegyric of the early Restoration made way for the growing uncertainty about the ability of Charles's regime to make England safe. In the poetry and drama of the mid to late 1660s, key figures surrounding the king, and in particular his ministers, are blamed for administrative mismanagement leading to political and naval disasters. In *Second Advice to a Painter* (1666), which satirises the English naval campaigns of the Dutch War, Andrew Marvell addresses Charles directly:

> Imperial Prince, King of the seas and isles, Dear object of our joys and Heaven's smiles: What boots it that thy light does gild our days And we lie basking in thy milder rays, While swarms of insects, from thy warmth begun, Our land devour and intercept our sun? (345–50)[14]

Those around the king disable him and create havoc, particularly in war where "kings are [...] but cards" (368): instruments of their ministers. In *The Last Instructions to a Painter* (written in 1667 but not published until 1689), Marvell continues to treat Charles with respect but attacks, among others, Charles's mistress the Countess of Castlemaine, Sir William Coventry and the Earl of Arlington. It is this scheming inner circle that has an evil influence on the (still innocent) king:

> Bold and accurs'd are they that all this while Have strove to isle our Monarch from his isle, And to improve themselves, on false pretence, About the common Prince have rais'd a fence; The kingdom from the crown distinct would see And peel the bark to burn at last the tree. (967–72)

By the end of the first decade of Charles's reign, overt royalist statements in the serious drama have all but disappeared – even from the work of old exponents such as Orrery – but issues surrounding kingship and legitimate rule have not, and tensions are evident in the plays. In 1667, Charles, under pressure to find a scapegoat for his diminishing popularity, impeached his close advisor and Lord Chancellor since the Restoration, the Earl of Clarendon. Sir Robert Howard's *The Great Favourite* was performed in 1668 shortly after Clarendon's impeachment. This play shares the structure of the earlier Restoration plays in that a tyrant is deposed and a monarch is restored; however, a shift has taken place. The evil, ambitious tyrant is no longer a representative of Cromwell but is a key figure in the king's court. The king himself is not attacked directly, but the court is attacked through the depiction of the king's chief counsellor as corrupt.[15] Orrery's *Mustapha* (1665) is another play which depicts an unscrupulous counsellor and draws attention to the issue of succession.

Charles's extramarital affairs were compounding already considerable anxiety. Only a handful of years after the Restoration, playwrights were already tacitly censorious of Charles's sexual excesses. Edmund Waller's revision of John Fletcher's *The Maid's Tragedy* (1664?) exposes the playwrights' already ambivalent response to Charles II's sex life. The anonymous and unperformed *Irena* (1664) is also implicitly critical. Even though Sultan Mohomet eventually saves himself and his throne by relinquishing Irena, his debilitating infatuation with an unavailable woman at the expense of his ability to govern effectively, clearly implicates Charles. Orrery's *The Black Prince* (1666) also depicts an infatuated ruler. In this case, the object of his obsession leads him to a sexual rivalry with his son, prefiguring another of the key motifs of the horror plays of the next decade.

Charles's lascivious lifestyle was also seen as threatening the succession. In 1669, the queen miscarried, and it became clear that Charles's marriage to Catherine of Braganza would not produce the much-desired successor to the throne. Parliament tried to convince Charles to divorce. By 1667, there had already been talk in parliament of Charles's eldest son being made legitimate. The following year, according to Gilbert Burnet, "[t]he duke of Buckingham pressed the king to own a marriage with the duke of Monmouth's mother [...] When the party saw they could make nothing of the business of the duke of Monmouth, they tried next by what methods they could get rid of the queen; that so the king might marry another wife."[16] Charles refused to divorce his queen, but he continued to produce children with his numerous mistresses. According to many historians, this latter part of the 1660s and the early 1670s was also a watershed in Charles's government: between 1669 and 1672, changes occurred (at court and in government policy) from which there was no going back. From this time forward, Charles was on the defensive: "the trust between crown and parliament, never perfect, had broken down."[17] This period sees the genesis of the horror play where the celebration of restored authority is replaced by an interrogation of the moral and political value of monarchy and the nature of power. The earlier Cromwellian and Machiavellian tyrants have made way for a new threat to political stability and good government – the king himself.

William Joyner's *The Roman Empress* (King's 1670) provides an early prototype for the horror plays in its investigation of these issues. The play extends the theme of merited rule in several significant ways. Here, scheming courtiers and the influence of an evil female affect the emperor's ability to rule equitably. Whereas in earlier plays, such as *Irena* and *The Black Prince*, the compromised characters are able to see the error of their ways, regaining order and honour, nothing is seen as recoverable in Joyner's play. Although he is not a cruel or evil ruler, Valentius allows any number of injustices in his court as a result of his lack of insight. When the evil empress Fulvia fails in her attempt to seduce Valentius's faithful general (and unknown son) Florus, she accuses Florus of rape. Unable to distinguish between truth and dissimulation and weakened by his infatuation with Fulvia, Valentius believes her and executes his son. His errors are too serious to recall: several innocent and honourable characters (including the heroes and the lovers) die as a result of his incompetence. In a pathetic last attempt to account for his errors of judgement, Valentius's character is reduced further when he blames others for the string of injustices, and ensuing chaos, before killing himself: "How long have I this viper in my bosom, / Never suspected for a poisonous creature [...] O my reputation / Betrayd by those, in whose hands 'twas committed, / As in the safest custodie" (Act 5, p59).

Direct attacks on the king in poetry and satire are evident from this point on. Andrew Marvell's *Further Advice to a Painter*, written in 1671, signals a "change in Marvell's attitude" toward the king.[18] In this poem Marvell blames the king for the state of the nation: he accuses Charles of devoting his time to his mistress Nell Gwynne instead of running the country and, like Joyner, makes analogies between Charles's court and Roman corruption and excess, comparing Charles with the Roman tyrant Commodus. As their fathers look on "[w]eeping to see their sons degenerate," Charles and Commodus "tir'd with the work of state [...] / Do to their more belov'd delights repair, / One to his pathic, the other to his play'r" (4–10). *The History of the Insipids* (1674) is unrelenting in its assault on kings and on kingship:

> Of kings curs'd be the power and name,
> Let all the earth henceforth abhor 'em;
> Monsters which knaves sacred proclaim
> And then like slaves fall down before 'em.
> What can there be in kings divine?
> The most are wolves, goats, sheep, or swine. (157–62)

A Dialogue between the Two Horses (1676) violently attacks Charles II and Charles I, comparing both kings to the degenerate Roman tyrants Sardanapalus and Nero.

> Though the father and son be different rods,
> Between the two scourges we find little odds.
> Both infamous stand in three kingdoms' votes:
> This for picking our pockets, that for cutting our throats. (127–30)

Nathaniel Lee makes forceful use of the intertextual analogies of Charles with Roman despots in his first theatrical endeavour, *The Tragedy of Nero* (King's 1674). Although it is likely Lee was still at Cambridge when *The Roman Empress* was performed, he may have read the play, printed in 1671. The two plays share similarities: both are Senecan in nature (Lee goes further, incorporating the character of Seneca in his drama as well as a Senecan ghost), and both address issues of Epicurean materialism. Nero and his licentious court clearly reflect Charles and the Restoration counterpart, but *Nero* displays a more extreme example of Roman decadence than Joyner's play does. Images of madness and disease pervade the play – themes that are picked up in several of Lee's subsequent plays, including *Gloriana, The Rival Queens* and *Mithridates.*[19] *Nero* overtly questions ideas of absolutism and sovereignty and begins Lee's long-term investigation into the nature of power. This emperor neglects the affairs of state in his pursuit of pleasure, but his impulsive, cruel nature places his depiction beyond evil. Employing madness as a metaphor for absolute power, Lee depicts a ruler in the process of moral and mental degeneration during which he inexorably becomes a tyrant.

Henry Neville Payne's *The Siege of Constantinople* (Duke's 1674) was produced several months after *Nero*. A number of key ideas in *The Roman Empress* and *Nero* are developed in this play, which also provides clear responses to current affairs. Though not as extreme as Lee's play in its depiction of despotism, Payne's play is set in the context of the Roman Empire and depicts an absolute ruler unable to recognise duplicity in his own court. There are no female distractions for the emperor of Constantinople – he is simply not competent to rule effectively. The character of the emperor (Charles) is undermined in early scenes which juxtapose his ignorance with his brother Thomazo's (James) perspicacity, "genius" (Act 2, p25)[20] and military prowess. In the final scenes, he is juxtaposed with the just and virtuous Turkish Sultan. Interestingly, in the subplot Payne returns to the well-known story of Irene – with a twist. Irene is replaced by the evil chancellor's malicious daughter Calista. The Sultan's sagacity enables him to discern Calista's malevolence, and he is able to delude everyone; pretending to be captive to the imposter's beauty, he abruptly cuts off her head in front of a full assembly, demonstrating "how much he valu'd / True Glory above Beauty" (Act 5, p82). The emperor is unable to demonstrate such assured and defensible action. Although he says he believes in the importance of counsel, he tells his advisers: "I give account / To none but Heav'n for any thing I do" (Act 3, p48). He goes on to make choices that ultimately allow his city to fall in the Turkish siege. When asked by Thomazo about the progress of discussions with the Senate on the upcoming war, the emperor simply replies, "Their obstinacy forc'd me to dismiss them" (Act 4, p66). Just before his ignominious death, the lasting image Payne provides of the emperor is of a pathetic figure of ridicule, begging for money in an attempt to pay his soldiers to fight.

By the time *Nero* was produced, Charles's relationship with the cavalier parliament was deeply unsettled. Early in the seventies, Charles had made moves to free himself financially from parliament by forging strong bonds with Europe's new Catholic superpower – Louis XIV's France. Louis himself was widely regarded as the greatest enemy of European Protestantism, and, as an absolutist monarch, his influence on Charles was feared. In *An Account of the Growth of Popery and Arbitrary Government*, Andrew Marvell sums up the public's hatred of the French king, describing him as "the Master of Absolute Dominion, the Presumptive Monarch of Christendom, the declared Champion of Popery, and the hereditary, natural, inveterate Enemy of our King and Nation."[21] In 1670, Charles publicly aligned himself and his country to France and Louis through an agreement between the two monarchs – the Treaty of Dover – which pledged to introduce toleration for Catholics in England. In a parallel secret treaty, Charles was promised further financial support from France if he joined with them in attacking the Dutch, declared his own conversion to Catholicism and worked to convert his subjects – with the use of French troops, if necessary.

In March 1672, while parliament was prorogued and only days after the beginning of the Third Dutch War, Charles published the Declaration of Indulgence, which sought support from the heterodox religious groups who had been excluded from the Restoration settlement. Although it officially opened up possibilities of liberty for Protestant dissenters, it excited fears that its real aim was to secure toleration for Catholics. So, just as James I and Charles I had seemed to neglect the Protestant cause in 1621 and 1641, a similar pattern was re-emerging with Charles II in the early 1670s. Bishop Gilbert Burnet wrote of the dawning realisation of the English people:

> The proceedings of the former year [1672] had opened all mens eyes. The king's own religion was suspected, as his brother's was declared: and the whole conduct shewed a design to govern by the French model. A French general was brought over to command our armies [...] [A]n army is a very unacceptable thing to the English nation, so it came to be the more odious, when commanded by a General sent over from France.[22]

Charles, however, kept to his pledge to Louis by engaging in the planned Anglo-French attack against the Dutch. He also silenced parliament by proroguing it for the duration of 1672. Literature began responding to Charles's regular 'silencing' of parliament. The anonymous *On the Prorogation* (1671) asks, "Have we our country plagu'd, our trust betray'd, / Giv'n polls, loans, subsidies, and royal aid, / [...] Crush'd poor Fanatics and broke through all laws / [...] to be thus fobb'd at last? (3–9).

By 1674, there were no fewer than ten bills in progress in the Commons to reduce the power of the crown. George Villiers, Duke of Buckingham, and Anthony Ashley Cooper, Earl of Shaftesbury, moved into permanent opposition to the court. In an attempt to suppress hostile opinion in London, Charles issued a proclamation ordering the closure of all coffee-houses. As the opposition party worked at dissolving parliament, Charles regularly prorogued it. Parliament did not meet once in 1676. Andrew Marvell's *The Statue at Charing Cross* (1675) and *A Dialogue Between the Two Horses* (1676) both respond to the long prorogation of 1675–77. Characteristic of these satires, the anonymous *The Royal Buss* (1675) sources Charles's decisions to prorogue parliament with his enfeeblement at the hands of his mistress Louise de Keroualle:

> when the Parliament would no more
> Raise taxes to maintain the whore,
> When they would not abide the awe
> Of standing force instead of law,
> When law, religion, propery
> They'd fence 'gainst will and Popery
> ....
> Then Carwell, that incestuous punk,
> Made our most gracious Sovereign drunk
> ....
> And so, red hot with wine and whore,
> He kick'd the Parliament out of door. (37–42, 65–6, 69–70)

As an extension of their investigation into the pathology of evil and the repercussions of arbitrary rule, the horror plays also interrogate the act of silencing voices. In Nathaniel Lee's *The Rival Queens* (written during the long prorogation and produced in March 1677), the covenant between the absolute king and his subjects has broken down. Writing *The Tragedy of Nero, Gloriana* and *The Rival Queens* during periods of time when parliament was silenced, Lee depicts the vacuity of words. Subjects must be silent unless they agree to tell their ruler what he wants to hear. As a result, words have little relationship to truth. Silenced voices are also a predominant trait of other horror plays, including Rochester's *Lucina's Rape* and Shadwell's *The Libertine*. As with Lee's tragedies, in these plays oaths are meaningless and cries go unheard.

Fearing the threats of absolutism and Catholicism with Charles's strengthening relationship with France, it is not surprising that recourse was made to past events which for the public signalled the triumph of Protestantism, such as the practice of celebrating Elizabeth's accession, which was revived in the early 1670s. New material printed in this period regularly reflects back on historical events in the Protestant propaganda calendar. The author of *The Burning of the Whore of Babylon* indicates how tradition kept the past alive:

> [...] notwithstanding the *Romanists* have made it their business to quench the fire of the *Gunpowder-Treason*, in the thoughts of the present Generation, yet with all their Artifices, they have not been able to do it, but the memory of that never to be forgotten day, is carefully transmitted from the Elder to the Younger, so that the Child, as well as the Man of years considers it [...] nor is there any degree of men in the Kingdom that have not [...] testified their abhorrency of the *Papist* Principles and practices.[23]

A glance at only a handful of titles can illustrate the focus of much of the propaganda of the early to mid-seventies: Samuel Clarke's *A True and Full Narrative of those two never to be forgotten Deliverances* (1671) (here Clarke refers to 1588 and the Powder Plot); Pierre du Moulin's *The Papal Tyranny as it was Executed over England for some Ages* (1674); *The Histories of the Gunpowder-Treason and the Massacre at Paris: Together with a Discourse concerning the Original of the Powder Plot ...* (1676). The sense of continuity with the past is also seen in work such as Anthony Egane's *The Book of Rates now used in the Sin Custom-house of the Church of Rome* (1673), where Egane tries to convince the reader that he must lay open this "Warehouse" and publish the "Merchandise of the Popish-Market [...] it being only to let the world see that the abuses that were long since discovered in the Popes Dispensations, are yet still in being."[24]

Thomas Shipman's *Henry the Third of France Stabb'd by a Fryer* (Duke's 1672) is an early theatrical piece of anti-Catholic propaganda which also relies on the fear and relevance of past events. There is a detailed description of the St. Bartholomew's Day massacre and of the Spanish Armada. According to Shipman's French king, "[t]he bravery of these English are so great / It is no shame that us so oft they beat" (IV.i). Queen Elizabeth is described as "That British Heroine [...] valiant and wise [...] [t]he World shall never, nor has ever seen / A braver Nation, or a braver Queen" (IV.i).[25]

Charles withdrew the Declaration of Indulgence in March 1673 and was made to enforce the recusancy laws with the Test Act, which required all office-holders under the crown to take the Anglican sacrament and make a declaration against transubstantiation. His brother's non-compliance to the Act – James gave up his office as Lord High Admiral in June – alerted the public to his conversion to Catholicism. In September James married the Catholic princess Mary of Modena. She was the daughter of an Italian client of France, whose dowry was provided by Louis XIV. This new match was widely regarded "as another stage in England's betrayal to Rome."[26] There were protests in parliament about the marriage. Gilbert Burnet wrote that "[t]he House of Commons resolved [...] to make an address to the King, to stop the Princess of Modena's coming to England, till she should change her religion."[27] There were once again calls in parliament for Charles to divorce and remarry, but no petition was effective, and it became apparent that the offspring of this Catholic union would ultimately succeed to the throne. Charles's new mistress, Louise de Keroualle – a 'present' from Louis XIV – was created a duchess in 1673 and was in a position of great power at court. She was also a French Catholic. On 5 November 1673, there were more bonfires and more popes burnt in effigy than there had been for 30 years.[28] Between 1673 and 1674, a huge number of anti-Catholic works appeared, and earlier Protestant texts such as Lord Burghley's *The Execution of Justice in England*, John Foxe's *Acts and Monuments* and Samuel Clarke's *General Martyrology* were reprinted. The last two in particular concentrate on the gruesome details of bloody persecutions of Protestants. Clarke's book even includes more recent historical accounts, such as the horrific Irish massacres of 1641.

Within a month of James's non-compliance with the Test Act, Elkanah Settle's violent and bloody *The Empress of Morocco* (Duke's 1673) was staged. It is with this play that depictions of Catholicism shift significantly. The past continues to play an important role, but rather than reflect on past events, such as the St. Bartholomew Day massacre, as Shipman's play and other anti-Catholic propaganda does, Settle personifies the Catholic church with a character that is an amalgamation of despised and dangerous Catholic female icons (and queen mothers) such as Catherine de'Medici and Charles's own mother, Henrietta Maria. Settle produces a notorious example of an evil queen mother – monstrous, eroticised and power-hungry, she abuses her position in an attempt to subvert the legitimate right of succession. This theme is picked up later with another evil queen mother in Aphra Behn's *Abdelazer; or The Moor's Revenge* (Duke's 1676). Settle's most renowned depiction of female monstrosity as a representation of the Catholic menace is Joan in *The Female Prelate* (King's 1680), whose 'unnatural' desires for ambition and glory impel her to pursue the popedom.

The female principle in these plays, subversive and unnatural as it is, causes untold chaos. There are important precursors to these later depictions. In *The Roman Empress* (King's 1670), an incipient version of the monstrous female can be seen in the character of Fulvia – a queen whose evil machinations and lust for her son-in-law are the catalysts for the destruction of all the principal characters in the play. Once again, using a well-known historical character associated with evil, Joyner bases the character on Phaedra, "a Pagan woman who for the atrocity of these crimes is known in History" (Preface). There is evidence that Joyner's characterisation caused some consternation: in his Preface to the printed version of the play, he speaks of the "exceptions" which had been taken "at the wickedness I shew in her person." His study of female wickedness, however, is more Shakespearean in tone. When Fulvia's machinations are revealed, the stalwart Honorius responds:

> The earth doth many monsters generate;
> So does the sea; yet nothing can produce
> So mischievous in nature, as a woman,
> Pursuing her revenge, and scorning honor.
> Mankind should have been propagated from
> Some other origine, and not from this;
> The fatal source, the occasion, and cause
> Of all his miseries, and servitude. (Act 4, p52)

The presence of the evil female force here, and the added taboo of her explicitly incestuous lust, remains important, however, in its representation of primal violations of social order. And what is particularly significant is that this murderous woman escapes at the end of the play with impunity. Dryden's *The Conquest of Granada* (King's 1670/71) is heroic in form and theme, however, an interesting early precursor to the monstrous female is evident in the internal workings of this play as well: the cruel and ambitious Lydaraxa was played by Rebecca Marshall, who had played the incestuous Fulvia several months earlier. Many of the tragedies in this period include particularly vicious female characterisations, including Poppea in *Nero*, also played by Rebecca Marshall, who went on to play

Roxana in *The Rival Queens*; Fredigond in *Love and Revenge*; and Diedemia in *Alcibiades*, played by Mary Lee, who also played the evil Isabella in *Abdelazer*.

Concerns over Charles's ability to keep his focus on his duties continued unabated into the middle of the decade. In a sermon preached before the king, the Bishop of Chester spoke forcefully about the "mortal [...] infection" of Sin and his concerns for (the King's) salvation:

> Men must first be forced and fired out of themselves, or else they will never come to Christ: [...] Our Commission and Instructions are to tell you, that if you would be saved from suffering, you must also be saved from sinning; your Lives and your Lusts cannot both be preserv'd: nor will it be sufficient that you forsake some of your sins; but, the whole body of them must be destroyed [...]
>
> You must Crucifie the Old Man, and Mortifie every Iniquity which now reigneth in you; so, that unless you leave the Lap of Dalilah, and be Divorced from your Herodias, you cannot be saved.[29]

John Lacy's *Satire* (1677) mocks early Restoration panegyric by undermining the iconography of the Royal Oak. The prince, "[p]reserv'd by wonder in the oak" (1), fails to fulfil any expectations of him as a man or as a king. Charles II emerges as a leader who cannot focus on the business of governing because of his obsessive lechery.

> C---t is the mansion house where thou dost swell,
> There thou art fix'd as tortoise is to shell,
> Whose head peeps out a little now and then
> To take the air and then creeps in again.
> Strong are thy lusts, in c---t th'art always diving,
> And I dare swear thou pray'st to die a-swiving.
> How poorly squander'st thou thy seed away,
> Which should get kings for nations to obey! (13–20)

Lacy returns to the story of Irene and the Sultan. He goes further than the earlier play *Irena* does, however, by suggesting that Charles follow the legendary actions of the Sultan Mahomet,

> Who, whilst transported with his mistress' charms,
> And never pleas'd but in her lovely arms,
> Yet when his janizaries wish'd her dead,
> With his own hand cut off Irene's head.
> Make such a practice of thyself as this,
> Then shalt thou once more taste of happiness:
> Each one will love thee, and the Parliament
> Will their unkind and cruel votes repent [...]. (77–84)

Converging with the censorious probing of religious and political institutions expressed in the literature of this period was a powerful but equally subversive form of scepticism. It questioned preconceived ideas of moral absolutes, divine justice and providence and, as a result, could be seen further to undermine the validity of Charles's return to power as a 'divinely-appointed' monarch. The scepticism was most commonly referred to as atheism.

To be an atheist, one did not need to deny the existence of God but merely to deny the existence of divine intervention, or a 'divine economy of rewards and punishments, in heaven and hell.'[30] Atheism was regarded as 'irreligion in the sense of a more or less extreme attack on orthodox Christianity from a cynical [...] viewpoint.'[31] The denial of the existence of God, or even the view that there was a God but that He was uninvolved in human affairs, raised furious objections not only from religious groups but also from the political establishment – in particular, the monarchists. If there was no divine intervention, there was no Divine Right of Kings – no legitimate hereditary basis for Charles's power and no providence inherent in his return to the throne. The Anglican clergy were so concerned that the bishops met to discuss the issue in January 1675. According to their conclusions,

> ... nothing is more necessary than the suppressing of atheism, profaneness and open and professed wickedness, without the amendment or punishment of which nothing can avail to the preservation of a Church which God has threatened for such sins, unrepented and unpunished, to destroy.[32]

Putting aside its sectarian differences, the religious establishment joined forces against the threat of this "Fraternity and Combination of wicked and apostate Powers, spread up and down the World, which envy the happiness of Mankind, and seek by all imaginable ways to undo them."[33] In the spring a broadsheet, *The Voice of the Nation*, appealed to parliament "for their just severity to repress [...] the growing Disease of Domineering Atheism." The broadsheet quotes a "Right Reverend Bishop lately promoted to Heaven" who supported the idea that "Atheism ought to be punished capitally, as of most pernicious consequence to Government."[34]

Parliament drew up draft bills on atheism in 1666/67, 1677/78 and 1697. Of these, the only one to criminalise atheism was the draft act of Parliament of 1677/78. It was written up for ("the better punishing of those crying sins of atheism and blasphemy"):

> If any person, *being of the age of 16 years or more* not being visibly and apparently distracted out of his wits by sickness or natural infirmity, or not a mere natural fool, void of common sense, shall, *after the day whereon the Royal Assent shall be given to*, by word or by writing deny that there is a God [...] [that person] shall be committed to prison.[35]

Of the three decades in which draft bills were considered, atheism was clearly viewed as particularly threatening in the 1670s.

Scholars and writers coming of age in the early years of the Restoration had benefited from the explosion of knowledge brought about by the discoveries in advanced mathematics of Kepler, Galileo, Boyle, Descartes, Pascal, Fermat,

Hobbes, Spinoza, Newton and Leibniz. These discoveries led to attempts to integrate new scientific knowledge into existing philosophical and religious thought. It was becoming apparent to some that man could interpret and systematise the laws of nature. Atomism, which was gaining scientific acceptance, posited that everything that exists is physical – the world is made up of tiny atomic particles randomly moving through space. In the Restoration, the re-assessment of this form of materialism spawned renewed interest in the ancient atomists Epicurus and Lucretius, who taught that both the body and the soul were material, thus mortal. The philosophers also explicitly negated divine presence or divine intervention in men's lives by arguing that the random motion and arbitrary colliding of atoms established that the world was created by chance, not by design. Thomas Hobbes, who was at Charles's court in the early 1670s and who had acquired a new prominence in the Restoration, shared this materialist, non-teleological view of nature, and he was generally singled out by contemporaries as the instigator of this neo-Epicurean movement.

Many of the young playwrights and wits associated with the so-called 'libertines' of Charles II's court combined selected elements of both Hobbesian and Epicurean philosophies to create their own 'libertine' ethic. For example, in Epicurus's teachings the goal of human life is happiness. This goal can be realised primarily through the absence of mental disturbance. A key disturbance, according to Epicurus, is fear of the afterlife. Epicurean atomic theory attempted to dispel the anxiety and help man obtain tranquillity by teaching that the mind is only a group of atoms that disperses upon death: thus, there is no life after death. The libertines and rakes at court took up Epicurus's identification of happiness with pleasure and with satisfying one's desires. What they chose not to take into account, however, was his belief that virtues, such as courage and moderation, are necessary to obtain happiness; and they signally ignored his recommendation that leading a virtuous, moderately ascetic life was the best means of securing this pleasure.

In a similar way, the supporters of a libertine ethic propounded parodic versions of Hobbes's theories on free will and on the state of nature. For Hobbes, the condition of Man, or the 'state of nature' (famously "nasty, brutish, and short") is "a condition of Warre of every one against every one; in which case every one is governed by his own Reason […] in such a condition, every man has a Right to every thing; even to one anothers body" (14:91).[36] It is the state man is driven to without the restraints of law and authority. Samuel Mintz argues that some critics, misreading Hobbes's doctrine, interpreted it as "a practical guide to conduct":

> It was believed by a number of critics that the 'state of nature' represented Hobbes' view of what human conduct *ought* to be. It announced a programme for libertinism. It told men that unbridled lust, greed, stealth, and force were their right 'by nature,' and hence that such conduct was entirely 'justifiable,' and was limited only by the need for self preservation.[37]

Both proponents and critics of libertinism in the Restoration ignored the fact that Hobbes did not agree with licence or absolute egoism; his Commonwealth was envisioned for the very purpose of freeing men from the fearsome state of nature. Hobbes's ethical relativism – his belief that there are no moral absolutes, that man's actions are predetermined and that he has no free will – was similarly misread by many of his contemporaries. It was taken by some to mean that men had no moral responsibility for their actions and could do as they pleased, with impunity, because their natures, not the individuals themselves, were at fault.

Although the clergy looked to Hobbes as a cause for the spread of immorality and atheistic principles when the indecent behaviour of courtiers and wits became a national scandal, it seems more likely that the wits and playwrights of the mid-Restoration were open to religious and moral scepticism at this particular time, when, as a result of the experiences of the past 30 years, political certainties and moral absolutes were openly questioned. Certainly Hobbes's negative view of human nature – in which "the greatest part of Mankind" are "pursuers of Wealth, Command, or sensuall Pleasure" (99) – was exploited. The result in the literature was the depiction of extreme characters in extreme situations: "a cynical and brutalized view of human nature unrelieved by Hobbes' remedy for it."[38]

The horror dramatists use expressions of materialism to expose underlying scepticism about the validity of Christian dogma and the existence of moral absolutes. In early horror plays, such as Joyner's *The Roman Empress* (King's 1670), Epicurean and Hobbesian ideas are broached. The Epicurean Honorius is principled in name and action, and he is the voice of reason in this play, often contrasting with the increasingly hysterical absolute ruler Valentius. When Valentius asks Honorius if he does not believe "some celestial pow'rs above / Direct the course of our affairs?" Honorius replies, "No […] / They rest secure, happy not thinking on them, / Nor us, such little crawlers here on earth" (Act 3, p28). The lack of resolution in Fulvia's escape without punishment at the end of the play is an important hallmark of the horror plays. Others, such as Lee in *The Rival Queens* (King's 1677), follow Joyner's lead, and evil goes unpunished in the play (in this case, the malevolent Roxana escapes). Hobbesian ideas, however, are not as fully woven into the fabric of the drama as they are with the plays of the mid-1670s, when the cult of Libertinism is at its height. Lee's *Nero* (King's 1674), Thomas Shadwell's *The Libertine* (Duke's 1675) and the Earl of Rochester's *Lucina's Rape* (written 1675/76) go further than the earlier play in irrefutably discounting the existence of providence and a sentient supernatural force willing or able to listen to human supplication. In these plays virtue is ridiculed and evil doers remain defiant: if they are punished they show no repentance or remorse. They do not fear the repercussions of their actions, because Hell and providence are shown to be fantasies. Many contemporary plays exhibit the influence of the horror plays in their depiction of loss, societal dislocation and lack of hope and in their rejection of providence. Thirty years after the production of his two-part *Destruction of Jerusalem* (King's 1677), for example, John Crowne reflected back and apologised for his earlier portrayal of atheism: "I have, in my *Jerusalems*, made too beautifull an Image of an Atheist; and Atheism appears too reason / able and lovely' (The Epistle to the Reader).[39]

Towards the end of the decade, major shifts in Charles's court party augmented concerns over standing armies and ideas of arbitrary power. Thomas Osborne, Earl of Danby, had risen quickly to prominence in the government during the mid to late 1670s, creating a 'Court' party in support of the king against growing opposition. Danby's policies demanded loyalty to church and king (in the sense of exclusive Anglicanism and unrestrained monarchy) and equated religious dissent with rebellion. Danby was hostile to Catholicism and tried to allay fears of a popish successor to the English crown. Many, however, feared his authoritarian tendencies, which were widely viewed as a revived Laudianism. As had been the case in Bishop Laud's time, fears of arbitrary government were once again rife. Gilbert Burnet is one of many who connects Danby to Laud: "such was the corruption and poverty of that party, that, had it not been that French and popish counsels were so visible in the whole course of our affairs, [Danby] had very probably gained them to have raised the king's power, and to have extirpated the dissenters, and to have brought things very near to the state they were in, in king Charles I.'s time, before the war."[40] Suspicions were further augmented when Danby raised an army larger than the one raised for the Third Dutch war. In early 1678, opposition pushed for a Militia Bill – an attempt to disband the standing army. This bill was rejected by Charles on the grounds that it encroached upon his prerogative by removing the militia from his control.

The horror plays of this period increasingly focus on ideas of corruption through metaphors of incest and familial internecine strife. As an extension of the evil mother motif, the dysfunctional familial relationships in these plays situate the source of distress in the domestic realm rather than the foreign. The danger is within, and the betrayals are personal. The monstrous taboo of incest is a device in the earlier horror plays to signal a violation of the social order: in *The Roman Empress*, Fulvia falls in love with her stepson; in *Nero* Poppea tries to seduce her brother and Nero's incest with his mother is revealed. As the decade progresses, however, the incest theme shifts to incorporate another level of meaning further fracturing the notion of the family: the role of the father as trustworthy patriarch is entirely devastated. Father-son relationships take up a central position, and they are fraught with distrust and rivalry. In Thomas Otway's *Alcibiades* (Duke's 1675), for example, the Fulvia-like queen/mother-figure lusts after the hero/son Alcibiades; but in a more disturbing addition, the king/father-figure orders the death of his 'chosen' son Alcibiades and lusts after Alcibiades's betrothed. Elkanah Settle's *Ibrahim* (Duke's 1676) makes use of this trope. Produced six months after *Alcibiades*, the play is an example of the ways in which other contemporary plays were influenced by the themes of the horror plays. As in *Alcibiades*, the great Solyman falls in love with his chosen son's lover and articulates his ruination:

> I'm grown so alter'd, and deform'd a thing;
> In *Solyman* you'l scarce find out your King.
> An impious and devouring flame has raiz'd
> All in me that was good, all that was great defac'd. (Act 2, p19)[41]

In a violent extension of the father-son rivalry, Lee's *Mithridates* (King's 1678) depicts the father/king raping and marrying his son's betrothed; he also orders the death of one son and unknowingly poisons another. In Otway's *Don Carlos* (Duke's 1676), the father, King Philip of Spain, forcibly marries his son's fiancée and then orders the death of them both. The theme is revisited in Nathaniel Lee and John Dryden's reworking of *Oedipus* (Duke's 1678) where the son kills the father and marries the mother and in John Crowne's *Thyestes* (King's 1680), where two royal brothers clash violently and a father is made to eat his own son. The result of the corrupt and unnatural relationships in the royal family is a community in disarray – like the cyclical pattern of incest, society is caught in a tragic reinforcing cycle of corruption and defeat. Contemporary fears of a divided nation are made manifest as notions of alienation and loss predominate in the plays. Not only are fathers the destructive force but also true heirs are exiled or unknown. The dislocation of this core element of hereditary succession – those within the social order that should lead and protect handing on power to enlightened, competent offspring – is not resolved in these plays. Arbitrary rulers and eroticised queens, the heads of family and state, hand down their degenerate power to heirs who are too emasculated to effect change.

As already argued, the fears of arbitrary power and the loss of belief in absolutes as they were articulated in the horror plays had a profound impact on other forms of drama. Just as the changing theatrical facilities and fashions (and the public desire for spectacle) affected the way in which the horror plays were conceptualised and staged, there is evidence of a reciprocal effect. Charles Davenant's *Circe* (Duke's 1677) was the last of the semi-operatic spectaculars to be staged until Dryden's *Albion and Albanius* in 1685. The earlier semi-operas either took tragicomedy (*The Tempest*) or tragedy (*Macbeth, Psyche*) as their basis; but with each, an overriding sense of hope ultimately surmounts any strife. William Davenant's *Macbeth* (King's 1673) was altered from its 1663 version to accommodate theatrical advances at Dorset Gardens, but Davenant's original thematic notions remain intact. At the end of the play, as the regicides were at the Restoration, Macbeth's body is to be displayed, "to shew to future Ages what to those is due / Who other Right, by Lawless Power pursue." Macduff looks to providence as an essential guide for their deliverance from Macbeth, asking that "kind Fortune" crowns Malcolm's reign "[a]s it has Crown'd your Armies with Success" (Act 6, p66).[42] Davenant's play reflects its genesis in 1663, conjuring images similar to those in early Restoration poetry: Macbeth's usurpation is seen as a blip, his vice will make Malcolm's "Virtue shine more Bright, / As a Fair Day succeeds a Stormy Night" (Act 5, p66). *Psyche* (Duke's 1674) was performed the following year. Performed the month before Lee's *Nero* and only four months after the later productions of *The Empress of Morocco*, this semi-opera still focuses on optimism. Love and light (Love/Heaven) ultimately triumph over darkness (Death/Hell). Psyche is released from Hell, but just as it appears she will die, the *deus ex machina* in the form of Jupiter descends to offer hope and immortality to her to share with her beloved Cupid, claiming, "T'almighty Love the Universe must bow" (Act 5, p65).[43] With Charles Davenant's *Circe*, however, produced three years later and after the horror plays had long established themselves as models of spectacle, these themes change significantly. Circe's husband Thoas, King of Scythia, becomes enamoured of the young exile Iphigenia. He and his stepson Ithacus become rivals for her love. Thoas is too consumed by his lust to rule effectively, and when his lascivious advances are rejected, he plans rape. Circe shares key similarities to the evil queens of the horror plays: this "lustful" (Act II, sc 4, p21) and "bloody" (Act II, sc 3, p19)[44] queen shatters her natural bonds with her husband and her son: "If any kindness of the Mother rest, / It shall be quickly banisht from my breast," and is consumed by desire for Orestes: "Let lust, and rage, humanity succeed, / Rather than [Orestes] all human kind shall bleed" (Act III, sc 6, p29). The gentle and kind Osmina seeks love from Circe's son Ithacus, but it is unrequited. She is powerless in a nation divided by internecine conflict: "Here cruel discord, noise, and bus'ness reign" (Act 5, sc 4, p49). In the end all of these characters are destroyed. Only two principal characters, Iphigenia and Pylades, survive the devastation. Here there is little hope, and darkness ultimately triumphs over light and love.

As the 1670s drew to a close, evaluations on contemporary events became more closely linked with a reflection back to the events of the middle of the century. Charles's repeated prorogation of parliament in 1675–77 led to comparisons with his father's personal rule in the 1630s. In *A Letter from a Person of Quality*, attributed to Shaftesbury, the writer attacks Danby's policies:

> [...] it is the first time in the World, that ever it was thought adviseable after fifteen years of the highest Peace, Quiet, and Obedience, that ever was in any Countrey, that there should be a pretense taken up, and a reviving of former miscarriages, especially after so many Promises, and Declarations, as well as Acts of Oblivion [...] the design is to declare us first into another Government more Absolute, and Arbitrary, then the Oath of Allegiance, or old Law knew, and then make us swear unto it, as it is so established: And less then this the Bishops could not offer in requital for the Crown for parting with its Supremacy, and suffering them to be sworn to equal with it self. Archbishop Laud was the first Founder of this Device; in his Canons of 1640, you shall find an Oath very like this, and a Declatory Canon preceding that Monarchy is of divine Right.[45]

The royalist apologist Marchamont Nedham responded to this letter by painting Shaftesbury and his group as the evil instigators, identifying them with the "Old Faction" of 1641. He also stokes the flames of paranoia by comparing the present situation to that period of unprecedented chaos:

> [...] there can be no Man that ever felt the sad Consequents of the Year, or remembers the Sea of Blood that then we swam in, and many Years after; with the Plunderings, Free-Quarters, and Desolations that followed on every side [...] but must reckon himself bound in Conscience and Prudence, to bid his Friends in the Country and City too, to learn, by considering the dark Contrivances past [...] how to understand the present, and prevent a being gull'd in the future.[46]

Andrew Marvell's *An Account of the Growth of Popery and Arbitrary Government*, published in 1677, continues the attack on Danby and the arbitrary tendencies of the court. Marvell also underlines the apparent iteration of the events that had led to the civil wars. He blames the court, however, for repeating dangerous mistakes, claiming that as early as 1673 the court party was threatening "the Nation was running again into Fourty One." It was "by these means," Marvell argues, that the court "designed to have raised a Civil War."[47]

The notorious court propagandist and pamphleteer Roger L'Estrange responded to Marvell's attack. L'Estrange was renowned as a vehement apologist of the monarchy and had been appointed Surveyor of printing and printing presses in 1663. This royal grant conferred on him the sole privilege of writing, printing and publishing mercuries, advertisements, and other books of 'public intelligence.' He was also given the power to search for and seize unlicensed books and papers. According to N.H. Keeble, "[it] was [L'Estrange's] animus and zeal which made censorship and press control during the Restoration period so much more vindictive and so much more partisan than anything experienced before […] for it was L'Estrange who saw to it that no offender was left unpursued and that, though detection and trial might not necessarily attend unlawful writing and printing, these would always be undertaken in circumstances of apprehension and fearful risk."[48] L'Estrange announces *An Account of the Growth of Knavery* as a response both to "the author of "A letter from a Parliamentman to his Friend in the Country" and to "the Author of An Accompt of the Growth of Popery." With consummate guile he merges images of the block and the cross and taints parliament with treachery to both King and God:

> you may not take the Libels here in question for Originals, let me assure you that these Notable Pieces are neither better, nor worse, than the Old Declarations of 40, and 41 only Turn'd, and New Trimm'd […] This is not the first time that we have heard of Words Smoother than Oyl, which yet are very Swords. It is the very Stile that brought the Late King to the Block; and the Saviour of the World was betray'd by a Hail Master, and a Kiss. It is the very Crown of the Parallel betwixt 77, and 41.

For L'Estrange, as for many English men and women of the period, history is cyclical: the relevance of the past to the present is significant because the past inevitably repeats itself. L'Estrange argues that people must learn from former mistakes so as not to repeat them endlessly:

> Do we not strike Fire the same way Now, that we did Then? And may not a Spark in the Gun-Room do as much Mischief This Year, as it did Thirty, or Forty years ago? Are not the People as much Tinder now, as they were Formerly? and as apt to take Ill Impressions? What if the same Method should work the same Confusion over again? or in Truth, what is there else to be expected? For the same Cause, acting at Liberty, must eternally produce the same Effect.[49]

As evidence suggests, a great deal of the population (whether or not they lived through it) could not fully resolve the events of the 1640s, and there was no desire to repeat them. People were, in Jonathan Scott's phrase, "prisoners of memory" – haunted by images of civil war and an executed king and fearful of a repetition of social and political upheaval.[50] It was not only the politicians and the propagandists who were making cogent connections with the past; references to the civil war period continue to surface regularly in other literature. When he writes about the events of 1673, Gilbert Burnet refers back to the earlier civil turmoil as if it were recently undergone: "A nation weary of a long civil war was not easily brought into jealousies and fears, which were the seeds of distraction, and might end in new confusions and troubles."[51] In a 1676 sermon, Robert South speaks of "the late Times of Confusion, in which the Heights and Refinements of Religion were professed in conjunction with the Practice of the most Execrable Villainies that were ever acted upon the Earth."[52]

Many historians of the period argue there was a public or a shared memory of the events of the civil war and interregnum period that governed both Restoration thought and politics. According to Jonathan Scott, the political culture of the Restoration had suffered "a traumatic *collective* experience with which it was necessary to come to terms."[53] Steven Zwicker suggests that the designation of the Restoration as a period is problematic, as it obscures important continuities across the middle decades of the century, "undervaluing the specter of civil war and social turbulence and political experimentation that must have haunted many of those who carried living memories of the 1640s and 1650s into the 1660s and 1670s."[54] As indicated earlier, in *The Burning of the Whore of Babylon* there was a tradition of preserving beliefs and mythologies through generations; memories of recurrent anxieties were kept alive through the use of specific motifs and metaphors. So even for those who did not live through it, there were constant psychological reminders of the period of chaos in repetitive reference and metaphorical recollection. As Jay Winter has argued, even in the modern period there has been a recourse to traditional motifs in the 'search for an appropriate language of loss [...] and [...] mourning' after large collective tragedies.[55] The English not only had to live through a war – they lived through a *civil* war, fought in their own backyard, where families and neighbours, who had lived together in peace, betrayed and killed each other. They saw God's representative on earth lose his head and watched or participated in the setting up of a republic. As Jonathan Scott argues:

> It fell to the second half of the century to become comprehensively haunted by the first. It was the magnitude of what it had experienced that drove the nation first to seek exit in repetition; and then back into the arms of the same fears again. In short the Restoration is not a "normal" period, for we are dealing in it with a traumatized patient [...] susceptible to both nostalgia [...] and nightmares ...[56]

Modern clinical definitions of post-traumatic stress disorder suggest there is a common response to being confronted with "a catastrophic stressor event that involves actual or threatened death [...] or a threat to the physical integrity of self or others." That response is "fear, helplessness, or horror."[57] Research shows that post-traumatic stress disorder can "persist for at least 50 years after a conflict" and that representative criteria for those diagnosed with the disorder include "[r]e-experiencing the trauma by recurrent, intrusive, distressing recollections of the stressor [and] [p]ersistent efforts at avoidance of the memories and numbing of general responsiveness [...] with emotional blunting."[58] This may appear contradictory – re-experiencing the trauma but simultaneously avoiding the memories. In psychoanalysis, according to Paul Connerton, there is a distinction "between two contrasting ways of bringing the past into the present: acting out and remembering." Acting out occurs when the subject, "in the grip of unconscious wishes and fantasies, relives these in the present with an impression of immediacy which is heightened by [their] refusal or inability to acknowledge their origin and, therefore, their repetitive character." Acting out, he says, is evidence of the compulsion to repeat:

> It is as a result of this compulsion [...] that [subjects] deliberately place themselves in distressing situations: in this way repeating an old experience. But in compulsive repetition the agents *fail to remember the prototype of their present actions*. On the contrary, they have the strong impression that the situations in which they are 'caught up' are fully determined by the circumstances of the moment. *The compulsion to repeat has replaced the capacity to remember.*[59]

Dominick LaCapra argues that working through trauma (in processes such as mourning) can counteract the force of acting out and the repetition compulsion.[60] The English, however, were never given the opportunity to mourn: to analyse fully the events of the 1640s and 1650s. The causes that led to civil war, the destruction of the monarchy and the creation of a republic were never addressed publicly; rather, the source of people's anxieties and trauma was forced underground during the process of Restoration, which, according to trauma theory, compels a repetitive recalling of past experiences. As Paul Connerton puts it, "[t]o construct a barrier between the new beginning and the old tyranny is to recollect the old tyranny [...] The more total the aspirations of the new regime, the more imperiously will it introduce an era of forced forgetting."[61]

An incredible act of forgetting was necessary to rebuild England as a monarchy after the Restoration of Charles II. One of the most striking elements of the Restoration process was the belief, by its architects, that it was possible to suspend public memory, to excise certain moments or events and present a strengthened view of monarchy: "the political theatre of the restoration process [was] to imply continuity where there had been interruption, and confidence where there was none."[62] The return of the Stuart monarchy was negotiated by *The Declaration of Breda*, in which Charles promised to give a general pardon to all those (with the exception of the regicides) who had acted against the crown for the past 20 years: "we desiring and ordaining that henceforth all notes of discord, separation and difference of parties be utterly abolished among all our subjects, whom we invite and conjure to a perfect union among themselves, under our protection [...]."[63] This led to the aptly named *Act of Indemnity and Oblivion* which legislated the promised amnesty. The same paradox of simultaneously forgetting and remembering is set up for Charles II and his supporters, as Jonathan Sawday elucidates:

> All actions taken by every member of the nation (save for those excepted from
> the Act) between 1 January 1638 and 24 June 1660 were to be cast, as the Act
> put it, 'in utter oblivion.' The past twenty-two years were, by Act of Parliament,
> deemed not to have taken place [...] But on the other hand, we have to be
> aware of the counter-pressure to remember and re-call the past which is equally
> encoded within its clauses. Thus, whilst the king 'forgets' the wrongs done to his
> royal father, he must also 'remember' them in order to offer a pardon.[64]

When trauma theory is applied to literature, the two contradictory elements
of the traumatic experience include the traumatic event itself and also "a kind of
memory of the event, in the form of a perpetual troping of it by the [...] severely
split [...] psyche." Geoffrey Hartman suggests that "[o]n the level of poetics, literal
and figurative may correspond to these two types of cognition."[65] If, as LaCapra
argues, "hyperbole enacts stylistically the fact that one is affected by excess and
trauma" and the common desire for full unity or community is figured as lost or
lacking through traumatic experience, then the recurring figurative depiction of
loss, alienation and exile and, indeed, the violent overstatement in the horror plays
can take on important meaning.[66]

The tragicomedies and heroic plays of the early 1660s reflected on very recent
events through the repetition of the usurpation/restoration trope. For obvious
reasons, the crown actively promoted plays from Roger Boyle, William Davenant
and others in which restored authority is the desired end. But the disruptive break
in experience which is caused by trauma has belated effects.[67] The optimism at the
Restoration which had foreseen a return to peace, security and prosperity under
a constitutional monarchy had drained away, leaving behind a general wariness
and consternation. The king, like his father before him had been, was depicted in
contemporary satire as an object of mistrust. As he regularly silenced parliament,
many believed he was working to re-establish arbitrary government. And his
alliances with French Catholics were threatening, in the public mind at least, to
hold England hostage to foreign power and a foreign religion, ominously recalling
the events that had led to the downfall of his father and to civil war.

In the post-civil war, post-Hobbes and post-Restoration world of seventeenth-
century England, the voices of the horror dramatists are unparalleled in their
relentless depiction of a breakdown of what were seemingly infrangible moral,
political, religious and philosophical certainties. This is a drama that reflects
the circumstances and the passions of the 1670s. As current political and social
uncertainty escalated with growing insecurity about Charles's motives and his ability
to govern, unresolved, deep-seated anxieties were also rising uncontrollably to the
surface. The profoundly popular horror plays abreact the climate of fear, anxiety,
scepticism and forced forgetting in images of monstrosity, diseases of the mind
and body, repellent sexual aberrations and unrepentant agnosticism. The depiction
of these violent transgressions in these plays constructs a cycle of corruption and
defeat that is replayed again and again – with no discernible resolution.

The following chapters will examine these metaphors in order to illustrate how
the horror playwrights, under the scrutiny of the censor and the Master of Revels,

were able to express anxiety about a return to civil strife and fears of unlimited sovereign power, by peopling their plays with legendary personages – some real, some imagined – associated in the public mind with villainy. And how they were able to examine with scepticism the source of that power, its relationship to justice and its congruity with the moral obligation of the population – vital considerations in the fraught years leading up to the Exclusion Crisis.

Endnotes

[1]   Elkanah Settle, *Love and Revenge: a tragedy acted at the Duke's Theatre* (London, 1675).

[2]   Jonathan Sawday, "Re-writing a Revolution: History, Symbol, and Text in the Restoration" *Seventeenth Century* 7 (1992): 186.

[3]   Sawday 185.

[4]   John Collop, *Itur Saytiricum* (London, 1660) 8.

[5]   Gerald MacLean, ed., "A Second Charles," *The Return of the King* Electronic Text Center, U of Virginia Library, 17 November 2003 http://wyllie.lib.virginia.edu:8086/perl/toccernew?id=MacKing.xml&images=images/modeng&data=/texts/english/modeng/parsed&tag=public&part=all.

[6]   John Dryden, *The Works of John Dryden*, ed. H.T. Swedenberg, Jr., et al., 20 vols. (Berkeley and Los Angeles: U of California P, 1956–2000). All references to *Astraea Redux* are from the California edition, vol. 1 and are hereafter cited parenthetically in the text.

[7]   Another example is in *The Ghost of Charles the Great King and Martyr*. The ghost of Charles I comes during a nightmare when "The Sun was set, and *Prosperpine* [sic] had hurld / *Lethean Poppy* o're the silent World" (1–2). *The Return of the King*, Electronic Text Center, U of Virginia, 17 November 2003.

[8]   Nicholas Jose, *Ideas of the Restoration in English Literature* (Cambridge, Mass.: Harvard UP, 1984) 125.

[9]   Jonathan Scott, *Algernon Sidney and the Restoration Crisis* (Cambridge: CUP, 1991) 8.

[10]   Quoted in Jonathan Scott, *England's Troubles* (Cambridge: CUP, 2000) 170.

[11]   *The Diary of Samuel Pepys* 7:275.

[12]   Gilbert Burnet, *Bishop Burnet's history of his own time*, 2nd ed., vol. 1 (Oxford, 1833) 422.

[13]   Andrew Marvell, *The Poems and Letters of Andrew Marvell*, ed. H.M. Margoliouth, vol. 2 (Oxford: Clarendon, 1971) 43.

[14]   Unless otherwise stated, this and the following satires are taken from vol. 1 of George deF Lord et al., eds., *Poems on Affairs of State* (New Haven and London: Yale UP, 1963) and are hereafter cited parenthetically in the text as *POAS*.

[15]   Nicholas Jose presents a cogent argument of this key shift of emphasis in the first decade of the Restoration in *Ideas of the Restoration* 138–40.

[16]   Burnet, *Bishop Burnet's history of his own time* 1:479.

[17]   Scott, *England's Troubles* 93.

[18]   *POAS* 1:163.

[19]   In "Otway, Lee and the Restoration History Play," Paulina Kewes argues that mid-Restoration plays use history as a political guide to critique tyranny: centring on the literary association of Charles II with Roman despots. Kewes contrasts Lee's representation of imperial despotism with pre-civil war depictions of Roman tyranny, arguing that although Jonson, May, Massinger and Richards's Roman plays were written at a time of growing political tension, their drama refrained "from personal satire or immediate topicality"; however, "by the time Nathaniel Lee came to dramatize the fate of Nero [...] the connections between Stuart monarchs and Roman tyrants had been long established and long exploited to devastating effect by the opponents of the Crown" (Owen, *A Companion to Restoration Drama*, 357–8).

[20]   Henry Neville Payne, *The Siege of Constantinople* (London 1675).

[21]   Andrew Marvell, *An Account of the Growth of Popery and Arbitrary Government* (Amsterdam, 1677) 16.

[22]   Burnet, *Bishop Burnet's history of his own time* 2:2–3.

[23]   Anon, *The Burning of the Whore of Babylon* 1–2.

[24]   Anthony Egane, *The Book of Rates* (London, 1673) A2.

[25]   Thomas Shipman, *Henry III of France, Stabb'd by a Fryer, with the Fall of the Guise* (London, 1672) 43–4.

[26]   Ronald Hutton, *Charles the Second* (Oxford: Clarendon, 1989) 309.

[27]   Burnet, *Bishop Burnet's history of his own time* 2:31.

[28]   John Miller, *Popery and Politics in England 1660–1688* (Cambridge: CUP, 1973) 106, 131.

[29]   Thomas Cartwright, Bishop of Chester, *A Sermon preached before the king at Whitehall, January 9, 1675/6* (London, 1676) 25–7.

[30]   David Wootton, "Unbelief in Early Modern Europe" *History Workshop Journal* 20 (1985): 86. Quoted in Nigel Smith, "Atheism and Radical Speculation," *Atheism from the Reformation to the Enlightenment*, ed. Michael Hunter and David Wootton (Oxford: OUP, 1992) 134.

[31]   Michael Hunter, "The Problem of 'Atheism' in Early Modern England" *Transactions of the Royal Historical Society*, 5th ser., 35 (1986): 136. Quoted in Nigel Smith, "Atheism and Radical Speculation" *Atheism from the Reformation to the Enlightenment*, ed. Hunter and Wootton 134.

[32]   *Calendar of State Papers Domestic: Charles II, 1673–5*: 548–9. Quoted in Spurr 69.

[33]   William Cave, *A sermon preached before the King at Whitehall, January 22, 1675/6* (London, 1676) 2.

[34]   Anon., *The Voice of the Nation* (London 1675); Spurr 69.

[35]   *House of Lords Calendar 1677–8*. Ninth Report of ... Historical Manuscripts, Appendix, part 2 (London, 1884) 98. Quoted in David Berman *A History of Atheism in Britain: From Hobbes to Russell* 48–9. As Berman notes, the words in italics were added after the original draft; the words in parentheses were subsequently deleted.

[36]   Thomas Hobbes, *Leviathan*, ed. Richard Tuck (Cambridge: CUP, 1996). All further references to *Leviathan* are from Tuck's edition and are hereafter cited parenthetically in the text.

[37]   Samuel I. Mintz, *The Hunting of Leviathan* (Cambridge: CUP, 1962) 32.

[38]   Mintz 134–40.

[39]   John Crowne, *Caligula: a tragedy, as it is acted at the Theatre Royal, by His Majesty's servants* (London 1698).

[40]   Burnet, *Bishop Burnet's history of his own time* 2:92–3.

[41]   Elkanah Settle, *Ibrahim the illustrious Bassa: a tragedy* (London, 1677).

[42]   William Davenant, *Macbeth: a tragedy: with all the alterations, amendments, additions, and new songs* (London, 1674).

[43]   Thomas Shadwell, *Psyche: a tragedy* (London, 1675).

[44]   Charles Davenant, *Circe: a tragedy as it is acted at His Royal Highness the Duke of York's Theatre* (London, 1677).

[45]   *A Letter from a Person of Quality* (London, 1675) 29, 32.

[46]   Marchamont Nedham, *A Pacquet of Advices and Animadversions Sent From London to the Men of Shaftesbury* (London, 1676) 1.

[47]   Marvell, *Growth of Popery* 56.

[48]   N.H. Keeble, *The Literary Culture of Non-Conformity* (Leicester: Leicester UP, 1987) 105.

[49]   Roger L'Estrange, *An Account of the Growth of Knavery* (London, 1678) 8, 33, 24.

[50]   Jonathan Scott, *Algernon Sidney and the English Republic 1623–1677* (Cambridge: CUP, 1988) 2.

[51]   Burnet, *Bishop Burnet's history of his own time* 2:1.

[52]   Robert South, "A Sermon Preached at Westminster-Abbey 1676," *Twelve Sermons Preached upon Several Occasions* (London, 1692) 438–9.

[53]   Scott, *England's Troubles* 163.

[54]   Stephen Zwicker, "Is There Such a Thing as Restoration Literature?" *Huntington Library Quarterly* 69:3 (September 2006): 447–8.

[55]   Jay Winter, *Sites of Memory, Sites of Mourning* (Cambridge: CUP, 1995) 5. Quoted in Scott, *England's Troubles* 163.

[56]   Scott, *Algernon Sidney* 9.

[57]   Roger Gabriel and A. Neal, "Post-traumatic stress disorder" *British Medical Journal* 9 February 2002: 340, British Medical Association, 8 March 2002. http://bmj.com/cgi/content/full/324/7333/340? lookupType= volpage?eaf.

[58]   Gabriel and Neal 341. Authors of another report in the *BMJ* state that "Post-combat syndromes have arisen after all major wars over the past century, and we can predict that they will continue to appear after future conflicts" and that "each new post-combat syndrome should not be interpreted as a unique or novel illness but as part of an understandable pattern of normal responses to the physical and psychological stress of war" (Edgar Jones et al., "Post-combat syndromes from the Boer war ..." *BMJ* 9 February 2002: 321, BMA, 8 March 2002. http://bmj.com/cgi/content/full/ 324/7333/ 321?eaf.

[59]   [My italics.] Paul Connerton, *How Societies Remember* (Cambridge: CUP, 1989) 25.

[60]   Dominick LaCapra, *Writing History, Writing Trauma* (Baltimore: Johns Hopkins UP, 2001) 23.

[61]   Connerton 10.

[62]   Scott, *England's Troubles* 173.

[63]   *The Declaration of Breda* printed in Carl Stephenson and Frederick George Marcham, eds., *Sources of English Constitutional History* (New York and London: Harper & Row, 1937) 533.

[64]   Sawday 185.

[65]   Geoffrey H. Hartman, "On Traumatic Knowledge and Literary Studies" *New Literary History* 26 (1995): 537.

[66]   LaCapra 35, 60.

[67]   LaCapra 41.

Chapter 3
Monstrous Women:
Aphra Behn's *Abdelazer; or, The Moor's Revenge* and Elkanah Settle's *The Empress of Morocco*

Evil women fascinate. They attract and repulse in a pornographic way, much like freaks of nature at a sideshow. In literature, and in life, the *bad* women are as well remembered and often more infamous than their male counterparts.[1] At the Restoration, the mimetic representation of female evil on stage underwent a startling change with the advent of the actress, who was seen as a sexual and amoral being: a seductive conflation of physical beauty and moral baseness. The sexualised female body, present on stage, took away once and for all the safety in male impersonations of women. When the façade disappeared, the audience was face to face with the creature herself – in all her potential sexuality and wickedness.

As the Restoration tragedies became increasingly violent in the 1670s, the evil female characters were increasingly portrayed as monsters, "blur[ring] boundaries, transgressing, violating, polluting and mixing what ought to be kept apart."[2] During the civil war and interregnum periods, Catholics, Cavaliers, Levellers and regicides all had the epithet 'monstrous' attached to them;[3] however, in polemical tracts and in Western literature, "male monsters and antiheroes [...] [are] not considered to stand for the masculine as a whole, or even for the destructive side of the masculine energies."[4] In contrast, female monsters are most often represented as the female principle. Susan C. Straub argues that the crime literature of seventeenth-century England "presents women felons (and by extension all women) as threatening and monstrous." Further, by preying on cultural anxieties about motherhood and "depicting violence as deriving from maternal duty, the popular press makes all mothers suspect."[5] In dramatic and other literature, monstrous women are routinely characterised as completely and innately immoral: they need a rigid patriarchal system to control their lustful instincts. In Elkanah Settle's famous depiction of female monstrosity, *The Female Prelate* (King's 1680), for example, Joanna Anglica is a woman who disguises herself as a man. The adjectives used to describe her equally *evil* roles as John and Joan are striking. As *John* she is described as "That canker'd Fiend" and "that ungrateful Monster" (I.ii); as *Joan* the character is described through derogatory, sexual language: "that lust-burnt Hag," a "Loath'd Sorceress, a filthy rank Adulteress" (V.i).[6]

The theatrical depiction of such monstrous women had current as well as fairly recent historical counterparts, the memories of whom it suited the religious and political establishments to keep before the public. Religious writers took examples of female wickedness from the Bible to give impetus to their homiletic writings. When powerful women do evil deeds, it authenticates and reaffirms the basis of fear and the need for repression. "All wickedness is but little to the wickedness of a woman" (Ecclesiasticus 25:19). John Knox's 1558 pamphlet *The First Blast of the Trumpet Against the Monstrous Regiment of Women* was republished twice in the seventeenth century. In it Knox lists example after example of "the imperfections of women [...] their naturall weaknes, and inordinat appetites." According to Knox, some women,

> haue burned with such inordinat lust, that for the quenching of the same, they haue betrayed to strangiers their countrie and citie: and some to haue bene so desirous of dominion, that for the obteining of the same, they haue murthered the children of their owne sonnes. Yea and some haue killed with crueltie their owne husbandes and children.[7]

That such sentiments had not changed in more than 100 years may be evidenced by Robert South's *A Sermon Preached at Christ-Church, Oxon* in 1675. In his sermon South implies the evil deeds of powerful women reverberate:

> Did not [...] Agrippina [...] cry out to the Assassinate sent by her Son to Murder her, to direct his Sword to her belly, as being the only Criminal for having brought forth such a Monster of Ingratitude into the world?[8]

South says there is nothing that can transcend "the Ingratitude, and Cruelty of Nero, but the Ingratitude and Cruelty of an Imperious Woman." He uses the example of Tullia, the daughter of the king of Rome, who,

> having marryed Tarquinius Superbus, and put him first upon killing her father, and then invading his Throne, came through the Street where the Body of her Father lay newly Murdred and wallowing in his Blood, She commanded her Trembling Coach-man to drive her Chariot and Horses over the Body of her King, and Father triumphantly, in the face of all Rome, looking upon her with Astonishment and Detestation. Such was the Tenderness, Gratitude, Filial Affection, and good Nature of this weaker Vessel.[9]

In the horror plays, the contaminating presence of the monstrous female in the dynastic unit is seen as an omen of severe social dislocation, akin to images of monstrosity and monstrous births in sixteenth- and seventeenth-century political rhetoric. Laura Lunger Knoppers argues that monsters "carry the weight of political, social, sexual, or religious aberration or transgression."[10] Monsters and monstrous births in the early modern period were generally perceived of as providential signs from God of his displeasure: a portent or a warning. David Cressy suggests that, given the common trope of the 'body politic,' "it is not surprising that writers of broadsheets and pamphlets presented these fleshly violations as signs of a world turned upside down." Cressy suggests that pamphleteers who published stories on these monstrosities ensured that the events were perceived as significant disruptions of the predictable life cycle:

Regular patterns were a sign of good order, all right with the world. Irregular
occurrences indicated disturbance, possibly to the good – like the appearance of
a new star over Bethlehem – but more likely baneful, a disruption to the great
chain of being [...] Disorder in nature was one of the most fearful things one
could imagine.[11]

The arousal of fear and hatred of monstrous women was also part of a political
agenda designed to deny women any access to positions of power. According to
The First Blast of the Trumpet, "[t]o promote a woman to beare rule, superioritie,
dominion or empire aboue any realme, nation, or citie, is repugnant to nature."
The emphasis in Knox's pamphlet is on the *monstrous* women currently holding
positions of power in Europe:

> The lawe doth [...] pronounce womankinde to be the most auaricious (which is a
> vice that is intolerable in those that shulde rule or minister iustice). And Aristotle
> [...] doth plainly affirme, that wher soeuer women beare dominion, there must
> nedes the people be disordered, liuing and abounding in all intemperancie,
> geuen to pride, excesse, and vanitie. And finallie in the end, that they must nedes
> come to confusion and ruine.[12]

When Knox published his pamphlet in 1558, there were four female monarchs
who were effectively controlling a large part of Europe and were hostile to the
Protestant faith. The most notorious of these were Catherine de'Medici and Mary
Tudor. In England, 'Bloody' Mary earned her epithet as a result of her persecution
of hundreds of Protestant heretics. The Marian martyrs received lasting fame in
John Foxe's *Book of Martyrs*, which was republished twice in the seventeenth
century and kept Mary's villainy alive for centuries afterwards. Bruce Thomas
Boehrer argues that Mary's threat was also aligned to her "polluted" blood. Her
unpopular marriage to Philip II of Spain provoked an outcry "because of the threat
it posed to the perceived integrity of the English royal bloodline." At least one
contemporary tract "figures this threat as intrinsic to the queen herself whose
English identity has been polluted by her Spanish ancestry" – in other words,
the blood of her Spanish mother. Boehrer suggests that feminine inheritance is
associated with debasement of lineage:

> Henry's authentic royal blood has been replaced, in Mary, by a foreign substitute
> [...] Mary in particular, and female sovereignty in general [is presented] as
> dangerous, corrupting the royal family and subverting the systems of difference
> and inheritance upon which a healthy social order depends for its continuity.[13]

Catherine de'Medici was equally notorious. As the queen mother of France, she
had allegedly played a key role in instigating the St. Bartholomew's Day Massacre
of Protestants in 1572. Protestant propaganda after the massacre focussed on
Catherine as the villain and created her black legend as the wicked queen. The
most scurrilous of the propaganda against Catherine was the anonymous *Discours
merveilleux de la vie, actions et deportemens de Catherine de Medicis, Royne
mere*. It was published in ten separate editions in 1575 and 1576 (several of these

were in English), reprinted in 1660, 1663 and 1666 and continued to be popular in France and abroad in both the seventeenth and eighteenth centuries.[14] In the introduction of the *Discours*, the author says he does not want to soil his hands and make himself sick by dealing with a matter that is so villainous and reeking, but, because Catherine still has power as regent ("un titre audacieusement usurpé"), the writer feels he must expose this woman who holds France under her paws. The Massacre is seen as Catherine's greatest coup – an attempt, in fact, to kill off all of France's nobility. Robert M. Kingdon's study highlights that even after the massacre the author pronounces that Catherine,

> surpassed all her own previous villainy in her mad drive for power, turning against not only the entire French nobility but also her own sons. She is so depraved that she lacks even the normal mother's concern for her own flesh and blood. Her son the king, Charles IX, who had meekly followed her bidding, began to show signs of independence, entering into negotiations with the Montmorencies. Immediately his health declined and the doctors warned he would not live much longer.

Poisoning is alleged. The biography propagates Catherine's so-called "Black Legend," claiming that her murderous impulses stretched far back and that she initially poisoned her brother-in-law, the Dauphin, so her husband could be king. Finally, the *Discours* makes a broader attack on the government of women in France, comparing Catherine with Brunhild, queen of the Franks from 567 to 613, demonstrating, as Kingdon asserts, "that at every point Catherine has surpassed in villainy this greatest of all villainesses in the history of France [...] The comparison [...] ends with Brunhild's barbarous death as she was dragged by a horse after appropriate torture – to which there is unfortunately no equivalent yet in Catherine's career."[15]

During the Restoration, the wickedness and brutality of these monarchs was fresh in people's minds: rekindled by the anxieties and propaganda surrounding the ascendancy of Charles's Catholic mistresses, in particular Louise de Karouille, who was created a duchess in 1673, and the marriage of James to the Catholic princess Mary of Modena that same year. Not only were these earlier anti-Catholic/misogynistic tracts republished at this time but also Protestant propaganda continued to reaffirm and connect with the prejudices of the past by publishing new tracts, such as *The History of the Bloody Massacres of the Protestants in France in the Year of our Lord, 1572*, published in 1674 and republished two years later as *The Histories of the Gunpowder-Treason and the Massacre at Paris: Together with a Discourse concerning the Original of the Powder Plot*.

Two playwrights who made perceptive and imaginative use of society's fascination with the monstrous woman, in her guises of wife, mother and queen, were Elkanah Settle and Aphra Behn. Settle's *The Empress of Morocco* (Duke's 1673) and Behn's *Abdelazer; or The Moor's Revenge* (Duke's 1676) contain two of the most notorious theatrical examples of evil queen mothers. The plots of the two plays are almost identical: the evil queen is willing to have her husband and children murdered in order to place her lover on the throne. When he has reached his goal, the lover betrays the queen by falling in love with a chaste younger woman. The queen kills this rival before she herself dies. The motive for the evil actions of Settle's queen mother, Laula, is to retain illicit power through her lover, Crimalhaz. The motive of Behn's queen mother, Isabella, is initially to support the ambitions of her lover, Abdelazer; but gradually she is corrupted by personal ambition and revels in her illicit power. Whereas Laula uses sex as a tool and her gender as a disguise to deceive and retain control, Isabella is held in thrall by her sexuality and is seduced and diminished by it. In both plays this deadly mixture of female sexuality, ambition and power leads to wholesale destruction.

Settle sets his play in Morocco to enable him to display a brutal and immoral court. As N.I. Matar tells us, in the seventeenth century,

> Islam was consistently being vilified in polemical writings: from theologians to millenarians [...] there was a continuous attack on Islam as an evil religion which would be destroyed by God [...] The Muslim had succeeded Satan as the embodiment of the anti-Christ. To turn to Satan or to Islam was tantamount to the same atheistic sin.[16]

In his dedication to *The Empress of Morocco*, Settle says he owed the story to the Earl of Norwich's embassy to Africa.[17] A description of part of this trip was published by one of the men travelling with the earl. In it he describes the barbarity of the Moors: "Strangers, especially Christians, do run so many hazards when they enter into the Land [...] it being one of the Articles of the Moore's Faith, that he that sheds Christian Blood in their Ramedam, merits Heaven, and purchases the Eternal Favour of God with this Sacrifice." He also stirs patriotic interest with his reference to English slaves "taken in English Bottoms by the Pyrates of this place [...] We gave them all the assistance our Purses or Favour could afford, and put them in some hopes to obtain their Freedom [...] a joyful news to those poor wretches, that had left all hopes of returning home to their beloved Soil."[18]

By setting his play in a court of 'infidels,' Settle plays to his audience's received notion of the Moors as bloodthirsty barbarians. As already commented upon, modern critics have often taken Settle to task over his excessive use of violent spectacle. In particular, they point to the final scene of *The Empress of Morocco* when "Crimalhaz appears cast down on the Gaunches, being hung on a Wall set with spikes of Iron." Settle's depictions of cruelty, however, are consistent with contemporary accounts. He recreates on the stage John Burbury's chronicle, in his travels to Constantinople, of Moorish barbarity: "without the Town was a Gaunch, or double Gallows, full of Hooks, on which Malefactors were thrown headlong down, and as they were caught, had either a quicker, or a lingering death."[19]

Settle anticipates audience expectations by setting Crimalhaz up as the apparent villain – the 'outsider' to the royal family, the would-be usurper of the crown. The real villain, Laula, is an insider and is able to be as outrageous and destructive as she likes. When the hero Muly Hamet discovers Crimalhaz in Laula's chambers, his initial reaction is a desire to protect her:

Ha! Does she thus for her dead Husband weep?
Oh fond and amorous Queen! Has Lust such Charms,
Can make her flie to an Adulterers Arms? [...]
For lest I should my Queen's disgrace proclaim,
I'll right her wrongs, but I'll conceal her shame. (III.i)

Because Laula is a woman, Muly Hamet is not surprised that she is too helpless to resist an Adulterers Arms. He sees her as not responsible for her actions, as needing protection from her own weakness. No one suspects any evil of Laula, because she is a woman, a queen and a mother. Neither the 'hero' nor any other of the characters identifies her as the true destructive force. The audience, however, knows there is no external threat; Settle encourages their apperception of Laula as the enemy within.

Aphra Behn sets her play in a Christian court, where the outsider – Abdelazer – is a Moor. *Abdelazer* is an adaptation of the inferior Jacobean tragedy *Lust's Dominion; or the Lascivious Queen*. In her adaptation, Behn removes the association of evil with a particular race or gender: Abdelazer is not evil because he is a Moor; the queen mother is not evil because she is a woman. The 'white' queen mother is associated with the devil; the Moorish Osmin is likened to an "Angel." The villains in *Abdelazer* are vulnerable to manipulation because of their lust and their thirst for illicit power. Behn's changes are significant enough that the two lead characters re-emerge as almost unrecognisable. In *Lust's Dominion*, the "Black Devill" (II.iii.34)[20] Eleazar is clearly the evil force, leading the weak queen mother astray. His skin colour is regularly associated with his evil actions; to Prince Philip, Eleazar has "damnation dy'd upon his flesh" (V.ii.20). Eleazar is vengeful and his motivation for excessive destruction is not clear.

Cardinal you die, if the King bid me live;
Philip you die for railing at me: proud Lords you die,
That with Mendoza cry'd, Banish the Moor.
And you my loving Liege, you're best sit fast;
If all these live not, you must die at last (I.ii.240–44) [...]
from discontent grows treason. (II.ii.57)

Behn diminishes the stereotypical association of black with evil and concentrates instead on Abdelazer's motivation for revenge after being stripped of his heritage (something that is only briefly mentioned in *Lust's Dominion*). Abdelazer must re-create himself as a villain "[r]eform[ing] each faculty that is not Ill" (I.i.187).[21] Behn also manages to engender some audience sympathy for Abdelazer by several references to the grief occasioned by his father's cruel death at the hands of the Spanish and his own fall from royal to slave status:[22]

My Father, Great Abdela, with his Life
Lost too his Crown: both most unjustly ravisht
By Tyrant Philip [...]
How many wounds his valiant breast receiv'd,
Ere he wou'd yield to part with Life and Empire:
Methinks I see him cover'd o're with bloud,

Fainting amidst those numbers he had conquer'd;
I was but young, yet old enough to grieve,
Though not revenge, or to defie my Fetters. (I.i.167–75)

Behn's feelings about conquest and slavery are implied in her other work, particularly *Oronooko*. A group that is overthrown by another group is effectively conquered: it loses its right to govern, its people becoming slaves to the victors. Although Behn depicts his dispossession with sympathy, Abdelazer's tragedy is that his relentless campaign to regain honour and power cannot and (by the rules of Natural Law) should not enable him to arrogate the Spanish throne. By rights, he is entitled to regain his crown only by conquering the Spanish outright – not by guile. For Behn, the lawful right of succession must be upheld to ensure the stability of society. Abdelazer works insidiously; thus he must fail.

While Behn offers a relatively balanced interpretation of Abdelazer, the Moor in her play, she also creates a calculating, intelligent and independent queen mother. In *Lust's Dominion* the queen mother is weak and malleable; she is only ever an instrument for the Moor's villainy: unquestioning, she allows herself to be constantly degraded and controlled. She is, by her own reckoning, a "silly" woman who has allowed her spirit "beyond the limit of a womans mind" (V.vi). She is even absolved of her complicity in the crimes (much as a child would be) at the end of the play when she repents. Behn's Isabella of Spain is no longer a passive victim. Instead, Behn's characterisation and language specifically reflect on the baseness and depravity of the character. To her son Ferdinand, Isabella is "too foul" for the name of mother; she is the "vilest of thy Sex [...] a thing I have miscall'd a Mother" (III.iii.137–8), who, because she has wallowed in her lust for the dark usurper, has enabled his insidious rise.

Whereas Laula's character, in *The Empress of Morocco*, is immutably evil, Isabella *develops* into an evil character. Behn adds psychological complexity to her characters by providing some details of their personal histories. We learn that at one time Isabella was considered an honourable woman and a loving mother. She tells her lover Abdelazer she "sacrific'd [her] Honour" (I.i.75) for their love and that her son Philip "prophan'd [her] purer flame" (III.i.149) for revenge. Philip says he remembers when she was "just [...] / And with a reverence such as we pay Heav'n / I paid my awfull duty" (I.ii.71–4). Like Shakespeare's Lady Macbeth and Abdelazer, Isabella must consciously remould herself to learn the arts of villainy: "Nature be gone, I chase thee from my soul" (II.i.230). At first she is apprenticed to Abdelazer: after her son Philip humiliates her, Isabella asks Abdelazer to "instruct [her] how t'undoe that Boy I hate" (II.i.214). Abdelazer tells the queen he will "instruct [her] in the way to [...] Revenge" (III.i.126). Eventually Isabella learns her skill and feels ready to act independently of her mentor: "I understand you, and more than I have time to be / Instructed in, I will perform" (IV.i.38–9). The queen mother's lust fuels her ambition and her wish for revenge, and in time her evil gains a life of its own. By the middle of the play, Isabella is "resolv'd upon the mighty pleasure" (III.i.148) of her carnage and, with sexual abandonment, she lets her need for gratification overtake the sin:

No rigid Virtue shall my soul possess,
Let Gown-men preach against the wickedness;
Pleasures were made by Gods! and meant for us,
And not t'enjoy 'em, were ridiculous. (II.i.233–6)

Like Laula, Isabella has broken free of any ethical constraint. She has renounced all moral responsibility and has gone past the point of no return. She even duplicates Laula's language: "My will's my King, my pleasures are my Gods" (*The Empress of Morocco* IV.iii). Isabella begins to be associated more and more with the devil. At the beginning of the play, Abdelazer is frequently referred to as a devil, but as the play progresses, the use of the epithet wanes for him and is picked up in references to Isabella. By the third act, she is associated with the devil several times. When the young king mourns Isabella's murder of Florella, he says of his mother, "'twas a Devils' hand who gave the wounds" (III.iii.135); Alonzo muses "[w]hat Devil reigns in Woman, when she doats!" (III.iii.245); and, as Abdelazer's henchman Roderigo is on the verge of killing Isabella, he tells her, "Thou mayst be Devil [...] for ought I know" (V.i.275). Isabella's sins are ultimately greater. Abdelazer has no emotional ties with his victims, whereas Isabella participates in destroying those she is supposed to cherish.

Outside the family, Isabella brings her malevolence to bear in her interactions with the Cardinal – another character greatly altered by Behn. In *Lust's Dominion* the Cardinal is a figure of ridicule, someone who willingly throws away his honour and beliefs in his lust for power. The Cardinal in Behn's play is vastly different. He is a man weakened by his obsession with Isabella and with ambition, but he fights these obsessions and retains his honour. Isabella attempts to declare her son Philip a bastard to exclude him from succeeding to the throne. In order to accomplish this, she tries to seduce the Cardinal into claiming paternity. In *Lust's Dominion* the Cardinal immediately gives in to her outrageous command. The Cardinal in *Abdelazer*, however, fights against it passionately:

Is't not enough I've given you up my power,
Nay and resign'd my life into your hands,
But you wou'd damn me too? – I will not yield –
Oh now I find a very Hell within me:
How am I misguided by my passion! (V.i.77–81)

But despite not conniving to cast doubt on Philip's legitimacy, the Cardinal ultimately ensures Philip's defeat against the forces of Abdelazer by holding back much-needed military support at the behest of Isabella. He subsequently gains expiation for his sins when he is led away to prison. As he reflects on his betrayal of Philip, his words echo the stoicism of Charles I, who, when on the scaffold, publicly repented for signing Strafford's death warrant:

The powers above are just, –
Thus I my Prince a Sacrifice first made,
And now my self am on the Altar laid. (V.i.148–50)[23]

Abdelazer's order to Isabella was to "undermine [the Cardinal's] Soul" (IV.i.29). Behn completes the association of Isabella with the devil as she fights to gain the Cardinal's (greatly enhanced) soul in this "very Hell within" him.

The threat to the royal family comes not from Abdelazer but from Isabella. Her passion for Abdelazer induces her to trespass beyond the boundaries of her assigned role as queen mother, thus putting the future of the dynasty at risk. Behn's characterisation of Isabella is that of an intelligent woman driven by carnal desire.[24] She is willing to abandon herself (and sacrifice her family) to the overpowering passion aroused by a sensual man and to subjugate all her other obligations and emotional ties to its powerful drive. For Behn, the theatrical device of the female villain allows her to exhibit overt sexuality in order to portray the use of power through sex. Behn needed a character that could step outside the normal confines of her society (and her place in it) and respond openly in an adulterous relationship with a highly sexual man.

In Abdelazer, Behn has created an overtly sexual man in contrast to his prototype in *Lust's Dominion*. Even though Abdelazer has tired of Isabella's passion before the play begins, the audience is able to see him in full sexual pursuit when he attempts to seduce Isabella's daughter, the princess Leonora. Abdelazer's language has a "rough harsh sound" (V.i.460): he says his love is "not to be resisted" (V.i.473). And in a sexually potent description, Abdelazer refers to his exotic heritage as inherently erotic.

> The lights put out! thou in my naked arms
> Wilt find me soft and smooth as polisht Ebony;
> And all my kisses on thy balmy lips as sweet,
> As are the Breezes, breath'd amidst the Groves,
> Of ripening Spices in the height of day:
> As vigorous too,
> As if each Night were the first happy moment
> I laid thy panting body to my bosom. (V.i.515–22)

Leonora does not succumb to Abdelazer's advances. This is in sharp contrast to her mother, whose carnal appetite is accentuated in a parallel scene, where she awaits Abdelazer, in expectation of sex:

> [...] his Power, like his Charms,
> His Wit, or Bravery! every hour renews [...]
> The thought comes o're me like a gentle Gale,
> Raising my bloud into a thousand Curls. (V.i.249–50, 253–4)

Both political power and sexual power are equated with sexual climax for Isabella.

In *The Empress of Morocco*, Elkanah Settle casts his queen mother, Laula, as the villain in the Protestant tradition of Catherine de'Medici. Laula's machinations and pitiless compulsion to control initiate the horror and death that envelops the court. Although her lover Crimalhaz is an outsider to the royal family, he is not a foreigner, and thus there is no connotation of alien evil. The source of evil in

The Empress of Morocco is clearly domestic: it emanates from inside the family, interpreting the family, as Derek Hughes argues, "as an archetype not of society but of the Hobbesian state of war."[25] It is also specifically female. Like Isabella, Laula is depicted as having stepped outside her socially approved familial roles as wife and mother. She has evolved into an androgynous figure most frequently described by male or 'kingly' attributes – her 'dread'ful aspects such as her fearlessness and bravery. Her son, Muly Labas, is in awe of her courage; he says she has a "dauntless spirit" which could "breath fire / To breasts as cold as Age" (IV.i). Laula speaks of her "Masculine heart" and curses "weak Nature" which her rage "unman'd" (V.i). She takes on a decisive and uncompromising leadership role, as her son confirms: "When she leads the way, / Though it were death to go, 'twere worse to stay" (IV.i).

The female appropriation of the male role is what drives the fear of female monstrosity in the horror plays. In Settle's *The Female Prelate* (King's 1680), not only is Joan/John boastful, proud and deceptive but also her overweening and, because she is a woman, *unnatural* desires for ambition and glory drive her to aspire to the popedom. She articulates, to her lover, her desire to reap the rewards of being both man and woman: "Glory, bewitching Glory; oh, for the Popedom! / [...] How 'twould please me / To reign the Christian World's dread Thunderer all / The day, and thy soft Venus all the night" (I.ii). Like Laula, who curses "weak Nature which my Rage unman'd, / A Masculine heart linkt with a Female Hand" (V.i), Joan has the body of a woman and the soul of a man:

> Could I but reach the Roman Diadem;
> I'd fit within my Romes Seven Hills as glorious
> As once the fam'd Semiramis within
> Her Babylonian Towers. Her Female Hand
> Did not the worlds Scepter guide, and why not mine?
> A Kingly Soul her borrowed manhood wore;
> Whilst like a God she sate within her Cloud,
> And moved her world beneath her. (I.ii)

Some earlier Restoration villainesses show developing signs of this manly aggression and ambitious drive for power. In John Dryden's *The Conquest of Granada* Part 1 (King's 1670), for example, the evil Lyndaraxa articulates her 'manly' features to the antithetical, 'womanly' Almahide, when she responds to the sounds of approaching battle: "Me thinks it is a noble, sprightly Sound. / The Trumpets clangor, and the clash of Arms! / This noyse may chill your Blood, but mine it warms [...]" (III.i.252–4).[26] In her campaign for power in *The Conquest of Granada* Part 2 (King's 1670/1), Lyndaraxa complains "how unequally in me were joynd / A creeping fortune, with a soaring mind!" (III.ii.27–8). Derek Hughes argues that Lyndaraxa is monstrous not only because her actions are nakedly ambitious and evil but also because, "unlike Almanzor, she is a woman."[27] Like Lyndaraxa, Laula's self-centred drive for illicit power leaves no room for fellow feeling or empathy. People whom she considers impediments to her plans are treated as mere obstacles rather than as the focus of spite or vindictiveness. She is able to murder without compunction, and, except for the murders of her husband and son, which are premeditated, Laula kills on impulse.

There are, however, important differences between Lyndaraxa as a prototype of the monstrous woman and the monstrous women of the horror plays. Lyndaraxa is not a fully formed sexual being. Two men are in love with her, and she uses their love in an attempt to achieve her ambition to become queen. She demands from Abdalla, for example, his brother's head before she says she will consent to marry him. But she remains sexually chaste – she exhibits no interest in or desire for sex for pleasure or as a tool to further her ambition. Lyndaraxa also aspires to queenship. She is an outsider trying to get in: having never known comprehensive political power she is driven to pursue it through whatever means (or men) are available: "I will be constant yet, if Fortune can; / I love the King: let her but name the Man." (*Conquest* Part 1, IV.ii.7–8). Laula and Isabella have been both queens and queen mothers. They have been in positions of supreme female power, but this is not enough: Laula in particular revels in the power game, creating uncertainty and fear and toying with other characters' hopes and expectations. She has already given up her position of queen once by disposing of her husband in order to place her malleable son on the throne. When this is no longer satisfactory, she removes the son to make way for her lover.

What distinguishes Laula the 'mother' from earlier evil mothers in literature and mythology is that her desire to orchestrate the destruction of her family appears chillingly motiveless. In classical literature there are many examples of women, such as Medea, Procne, Clytmnestra or Phaedra, who, as helpless victims of their inordinate lust, jealousy or vengeance, commit or condone the murder of husbands, fathers and children. Others, such as Leucippe and Agave, are driven 'insane' by the gods to commit similar crimes. On the Renaissance and Restoration stage, however, the majority of villainesses stop short of the murder of their own children (for example, Zempoalla in *The Indian Queen* or Tamora in *Titus Andronicus*). Lady MacBeth does not kill her children, although in order to shame her husband to murder she does give a disturbing description of how far she would go in order to see her plans to fruition:

> I have given suck, and know
> How tender 'tis to love the babe that milks me;
> I would, while it was smiling in my face,
> Have plucked my nipple from his boneless gums
> And dash'd the brains out, had I so sworn
> As you have done to this. (*Macbeth* 1.7.54–59)

This passage was retained in William Davenant's adaptation of *Macbeth* (Duke's 1673).

Other female villains in Restoration plays also have clear motivations for their evil deeds: for Zempoalla in *The Indian Queen* (King's 1664), Fulvia in *The Roman Empress* (King's 1670) and Deidamia in *Alcibiades* (Duke's 1675) it is lust; for Lyndaraxa in *The Conquest of Granada* it is ambition. In Settle's *Love and Revenge* (Duke's 1674), based on William Heming's *The Fatal Contract*, the evil queen, after poisoning her husband, tells her lover Clarmount that her sons must die. But, as with Isabella in *Abdelazer*, this is to enable her lover to access the throne. Jocasta in Nathaniel Lee and John Dryden's *Oedipus* (Duke's 1678) kills her children on the marital bed, but this is in a fit of despair after conclusive proof that she is Oedipus's mother. The female villain whose motiveless destruction most resembles Laula is Brunhalt from Beaumont, Fletcher and Massinger's *The Tragedy of Thierry and Theodoret*.

What Laula acknowledges as her motivation is unconvincing. She twice refers to the carnage she lets loose as stimulated by *love* for Crimalhaz, but Laula only uses the word ironically, either when she seeks to extenuate her nefarious actions and implicate Crimalhaz – "when Your Throne I on his Grave have built, / Remember Love was Author of my Guilt" (III.ii) – or when she wants to cast her actions in the noble light of sacrifice – "Is this your thanks for all her Love has done! / Who staked her Soul, to raise thee to a Throne" (V.i). Settle makes it clear, however, that Laula neither loves nor particularly lusts after Crimalhaz. There are no overt references to their desire for each other. When their adultery is discovered, Laula says they must meet their ruin simply because of "the slight excursions of a wanton flame" (III.i).

Laula's lover Crimalhaz appears only in a supporting role, as an instrument for her villainy. A strong man who is relatively undistinguished, he has the usurper's ambition to be king, but he has no motivation for engaging in the devastation that takes place. Crimalhaz could be any number of young, strong, ambitious courtiers, and he must learn his evil craft from Laula:

> I am a Convert, Madam [...]
> By your Examples I'll great Deeds pursue:
> My Thoughts shan't start at what my Hand dares do. (I.i)

Reinforcing the idea that he is merely an 'instrument' for Laula's evil, Crimalhaz also frequently shows signs of repentance and fear, as when he describes to Laula the king's death by poison:

> His Death so much of horror did present,
> I curst my Hand for being the *instrument*:
> A strange unusual trembling shook my Heart [...]
> Have you consider'd Madam what you've done [...].

In stark contrast to Crimalhaz, Laula never wavers. Her response to his fears is characteristic:

> Poisoned my Husband, Sir, and if there need
> Examples to instruct you in the deed,
> I'll make my Actions plainer understood,
> Copying in his Death and all the Royal Blood. (I.i)

There are allusions in this speech to the purported sentiments of Catherine de'Medici, who was also the power behind the throne in sixteenth-century France. In the *Discours*, the anonymous author "quotes" Catherine directly:

> We wish to exterminate all the heads of the nobility, those who are born or have become great by notable services [...] those who could legitimately oppose our evil machinations, those who because of their natural goodness could not assist in our evil machinations, those who because of their natural goodness could not assist in our deceits and treacheries.[28]

Catherine's alleged statement of purpose has no hint of moral questioning: no excuse or hesitation and no stimulus for action other than a desire to acquire more power at all costs. Similarly, Laula never once touches on the subject of guilt or culpability: "Let those, whom pious Conscience awes, forbear, / And stop at Crimes because they Vengeance fear" (IV.iii). She stabs herself rather than await state-sanctioned punishment and dies unrepentant and defiant:

> Hell! no, of that I scorn to be afraid
> I'll send such throngs to the infernal shade,
> Betray, and kill, and damn to that degree,
> I'll crowd up Hell till there's no room for me. (III.i)

In this she can once again be seen as taking on the male villain's role. Yet, because she is female her actions are adjudged to be more pernicious than had they been carried out by a man: "there's something / In Murder so beyond a Female Villain" (*The Female Prelate* V.i). A parallel can also be drawn between Laula and the evil Constable in John Crowne's *The Ambitious Statesman* (King's 1679). Like Laula, the Constable is consumed by ambition. He wants to kill off his son: "I'll kill him with more pleasure than I got him" (IV.i.p204); he does not care if it means he will go to Hell: he would rather create more destruction before he gets there. He has no interest in leaving a legacy on his death:

> what shou'd I do [with a Crown]?
> Palsies wou'd shortly shake it from my head.
> Nor wou'd I care to leave it to my son;
> 'Twill be all one to me when I am dead,
> [...] If he be crown'd, his glory will not shine
> Into my grave and warm my dust to see it:
> if he be victim'd there, I shall not feel it.
> 'Twill be no more than if they pluck'd
> Some pretty flower that grew out o'my dust. (II.i)

In fact, like Laula, he wishes for more sons to kill: "Had I more sons than would eclipse the sun, / I'd kill 'em all [...] Were all mankind my children, / I wou'd hang half, to rule the other half " (IV.i). But, once again, although the Constable and other fathers in Restoration drama, such as Solyman in Orrery's *Mustapha* (Duke's 1665), Mithridates in Lee's *Mithridates* (King's 1678) or King Philip of Spain in Otway's *Don Carlos* (Duke's 1676), are perceived of as villainous for wanting to kill their sons, their villainy (as will be shown in the following chapters) is conflated with their tyranny which has evolved through a loss of their minds: they are depicted as insane. Any moral indignation over their actions is inscribed onto their political life – their (in)ability to rule: they are rarely judged in their capacities as men or as fathers. Laula is still the ultimate aberration and much more monstrous, because she is both a woman and a mother.

The dangerous mix of female sexuality and illicit power in the queen mothers leads to emasculated sons. Neither Settle's nor Behn's play has a father figure to counter the powerful influence of the queen mothers. The kings, the heads of the patriarchy, never appear on stage; they are murdered soon after the plays begin.[29] In the other horror plays depicting monstrous women, Lee's *The Massacre of Paris* (written 1679) and Settle's *The Female Prelate*, the lack of father figures is equally striking. In *The Massacre of Paris*, the Queen Mother Catherine de'Medici's husband is long dead, leaving her effectively in control of the state. The plotline leading up to the massacre is built upon the Duke of Guise's desire for revenge for the murder of *his* father. He wrongly charges the Admiral with planning the murder when in fact it was Catherine who had orchestrated the older Guise's death. In *The Female Prelate*, the protagonist is also the son of a murdered ruler, the old Duke of Saxony, and it is the evil Joan who has dispatched him. With no men of equal strength or status to restrict her power, she becomes pope, controlling both church and state.

The evil influence of these monstrous women reverberates through their families and the state. The official shift of power from father to son excludes the mother/woman. J. Douglas Canfield argues that for a Restoration audience, "as the conduit for the succession of power and property and the state itself, woman is the aristocratic sign of societal stability."[30] The playwrights show the devastating results of women who act as destabilising agents by choosing to claim a place in the rigid patriarchal structure. And, those who are mothers insidiously retain and extend their power by exploiting the reflexogenic responses of obedience and filial devotion shown by their sons, the young kings. The subjection of the weak kings to their mothers is, in Susan J. Owen's words, "a paradigm of perverted authority relations."[31]

The relationship of Laula and her son in *The Empress of Morocco* has echoes of the reputed relationship between Catherine de'Medici and her children. Historically, three of Catherine's sons died young, after acceding to the throne: all were depicted in contemporary propaganda as weak and highly influenced by their Machiavellian mother. Catherine was also seen to be complicit in their early deaths. In his play based on the events leading up to the St. Bartholomew's Day slaughter, *The Massacre of Paris*, Lee plays heavily on the alleged relationship between Catherine and her sons, creating another monstrous, overbearing mother whose drive for power diminishes the sons' ability to rule effectively. What we hear of the eldest son sets the scene: early in the play the Duke of Guise refers to him as "the late puling King" (I.i.157). When Guise describes Catherine's second son, and the ruling monarch, King Charles, he uses similar imagery:

[…] his Mother's Poison
Boils in the Brains of the young drooping King […]
Mark how she tempers him betwixt her hands:
He has it in his Veins, the lingring draught that
moulders him away. (III.ii.194–5; 202–4)

As is the case in *The Empress of Morocco* and *Abdelazer*, Queen Mother Catherine is willing to kill her son to facilitate the rise of another; however, whereas Laula and Isabella both hope to place their lovers on the throne, Catherine says she will, if necessary, kill one son in order to put the favourite son, the Duke of Anjou, on the throne. Anjou's character is introduced as he sleeps in a chamber while his mother waits on him. The intimate surroundings are reminiscent of the langorous lovers' settings in the two earlier plays (cf. *Abdelazer* V.i.235: "A fine Chamber" where Isabella awaits Abdelazer and *The Empress of Morocco* III.i.1 where the scene opens to discover Crimalhaz and the queen mother sleeping on a couch). While Anjou sleeps, Catherine speaks to her son in the language of love: "O my Anjou […] the Darling of my doating Soul, / The Prince of my Eternal thought […]" (I.ii.1, 10–11). She complains that her plans for the massacre are not progressing as they should: "for want of one that knows to drive; / He sits too light upon the whirling Throne, / And totters […]" (I.ii.3–5). She says King Charles "must be ruled" or she will "melt [him] down" so that Anjou "may'st mount / Like Nero, tho' at Agrippina's Ruin" (I.ii.7–12). The sensuous setting and language, and the reference to Nero and his mother, underline the sexual/incestuous/aberrant nature of the relationship. As in the other plays, Catherine is the masculine force who dictates the young king's actions.

With Claws lock'd in, like Lions, couch to tear 'em,
Our Mother, thou so fierce upon the slaughter,
Direct thy Brood; we will not stir nor breath:
But when thou giv'st the Word, then start away,
Rush from the Shade, and make 'em all our prey. (I.ii.159–63)

When the young king has attacks of conscience or fears the repercussions of the slaughter, he is easily placated by his mother, who plays on his trust and love: "You fear ev'n Me; but I have liv'd too long. / Since my own Bowels, nay, my very Heart-Strings, / (For so I always lov'd and priz'd my Children) / Dare not confide in her that gave 'em Being" (II.ii.110–113). When the king becomes ill "bound in Conscience: He pukes at Drams […] spits Blood," Guise refers to the king's illness as "a fit […] o'th'Mother" (V.i.99–100). Like the other monstrous women in the horror plays, this mother provides no nurture or comfort to her offspring, only illness and death.

In *The Empress of Morocco*, the young king, Muly Labas, seeks his mother's counsel and never doubts her sincerity. When Laula tells him that Muly Hamet, the young king's loyal general, tried to rape her, he believes her story "since her blood does run within my Veins, / By instinct I know she all that's base disdains" (III.i). He is gullible and vacillating and proves a bad judge of character, ruled by emotion not reason. Even his fiancée Morena asks him to remove his "unmanly fears" and show "Courage" (I.i). Rather than use his power as king to protect himself when he is told that Crimalhaz intends to kill him, Muly Labas impotently asks if "there [is] no Policy nor Art that may / Prevent his Treason?" (IV.iii). It is his mother, ironically, who must remind him of his authority as king, and its potential power: "Can you Rebellion fear, or any thing / Who are my Son, and great Morocco's King?" (IV.i). Laula takes on the kingly attributes that should have been passed on to her son. She sees him as an "easie Fool," and she ridicules his naiveté: "'Tis pity Monarchs are so scarce – / Such gen'rous, easie, kind, good-natur'd things, / That one faign'd tear can rule the faith of Kings" (III.i). If she were a 'natural' mother and queen, Laula would see her son as a precious heir whose presence fulfils her obligation as queen. Instead she considers her son merely an encumbrance to her ambitious plans, so she disposes of him. In her study on gender and regency in early modern France, Katherine Crawford points out that widowed queen mothers were customarily named as their young sons' regent – allowing them governance of the nation. According to Pierre Dupuy, "[t]he principal reasons for this choice were founded [...] on the natural affection of mothers toward their children, and because they cannot fall under presumption or suspicion of presenting any danger to the Princes who are committed to their care." Crawford argues that Catherine de'Medici based her claim to power and authority on "accepted notions of female behavior as wife, mother and widow." She cultivated her image as a devoted wife who, after the death of her husband Henri II, was equally devoted to her children: controlling "the position of regent because she emphasized her maternal desire to keep the young king safe."[32]

In Behn's play, the young king, although a much more admirable character than his lascivious prototype in *Lust's Dominion*, is also weak, malleable and unable to see through his mother Isabella's lies and machinations. Like Isabella, he is afflicted and weakened by an uncontrollable passion. It is this weakness that is seen to be the greatest danger to the state. There are numerous allusions to Ferdinand's dream-like demeanour: his "Lethargy of Love" (II.ii.137). His brother Philip repeatedly tries to save him from being "drown'd in idle wanton Love" (II.i.48). Philip, whom Behn depicts as much more sane and more appealing than his prototype, becomes the foil for the young king. While his brother "will sleep away his anger," Philip tells his men "I'le be Active" (II.ii.131–3). As well as the contrast between Philip's active and Ferdinand's passive state, Philip also stands apart as he is not susceptible to Isabella's lies and machinations. He is the only person in court who sees through her deception and is not afraid to challenge her. Isabella's refusal to live up to the expectations of her 'natural' role as mother has repercussions on the whole family: it disturbs the interlinking set of social obligations and relationships that underpin the family hierarchy. In order for Philip to survive, he too must go against nature – to reinvent himself – and ruthlessly break his ties to his mother:

> [...] here upon my knees I vow,
> To shake all Duty from my soul,
> And all that reverence Children owe a Parent,
> Shall henceforth be converted into hate. (IV.i.56–9)

Philip's actions are justified by the trustworthy Alonzo, who confirms "A disobedience [...] to such a Parent, / Heaven must forgive the sin, if this be one" (IV.i.66–7). The 'sin' is the breaking of the Fifth Commandment – Honour thy father and thy mother – the foundation of the patriarchal structure. In the face of an unworthy mother, however, Philip's obligation can justifiably be abrogated for the good of the people.

For Behn the most dangerous result of the compulsive drive of illicit passion is the potential of illegitimate offspring to break the orderly succession of the patriarchal line. Behn intricately weaves themes of heredity and continuity through her play: hereditary succession is important for every one of her characters, especially Abdelazer, whose whole plan of destruction is motivated by his vision of himself as the rightful heir. Settle's characters, in contrast, place little importance on heredity or any kind of patrilineal dynasty. And, unlike Behn's characters, they bring no personal history to the play. Crimalhaz and Laula live very much in the here-and-now and are more concerned with satisfying their appetites than worrying about posterity. Laula has no interest in a legacy. Like Isabella, she seeks pleasure in the destructive swathe she cuts; but, unlike Isabella, she wants to kill sons for the sake of killing sons. Her main motivation seems to be to cut the heart out of her family; and the most effective way to do that is to kill off the bloodline:

> Let single murders, common hands suffice:
> I scorn to kill less than whole Families
> In all my Race, I nothing find that's ill;
> But that I've barren been: and wanted still
> More Monarchs to dethrone, more Sons to kill. (V.i)

When Crimalhaz accedes to the throne, he gives the hero Muly Hamet and his wife no offer of power while he lives, but the chance of a legacy on his death, as it is clearly of no interest to him: "though your hand and hers no Scepter bears, / You Lovers may get Kings to be my Heirs" (V.i). Crimalhaz is cynical about the idea that people gain greatness through heredity:

> Let cowards to their Fathers Thrones advance,
> Be great and Powerful by Inheritance [...]
>   I am to Courage born,
> Ambition is the rise of Souls, like mine
> Those Wreaths my Birth does want, my Brain shall win.
> They in advance to Greatness glorious prove,
> Who out of the dull track of Birth-right move.
> Birth-right, the Prop of an unpurchas'd Name,
> A weak alliance to an elder Fame,
> No glory by descent is never worn;
> Men are to Worth and Honour Rais'd, not Born. (II.i)

Both Crimalhaz and Laula also push the boundaries of nature in their attempt to satisfy their personal appetites. In a further defiance of any hierarchical order to the world, they justify their evil deeds by suggesting they can step outside of society's laws and revert to their primal state.

> LAULA. 'Tis not the blood of Sons nor Monarchs shakes
>   Those resolutions which my Courage takes.
>   O'er fear and vertue too, I have this odds:
>   My will's my King, my pleasures are my Gods. (IV.iii)

For Crimalhaz, in particular, to go back to the time when nature (not religion or society) dictated the rules, allows a freedom unattainable in his world. Nature is fierce and dangerous, but those who put themselves again into a state of nature are no longer subject to any external control.

In spite of his villainy and his position outside the royal family, Crimalhaz appears to be a better potential leader than either Laula's son Muly Labas or the 'hero' Muly Hamet, because of his ability to focus clearly on the business of governing. Not only is the true heir to the throne inept – unable to transcend his "Lethargy of Love" and deal with the issues of state – but also when he does take the throne on his father's death by his mother's hand, the weak and malleable Muly Labas also turns tyrannical. He wrongly charges his loyal friend and general, Muly Hamet, with the rape of Laula and unjustly sentences him to death, which is only commuted to banishment by Laula's intervention. The young king then estranges his only other ally, his sister Mariamne, for whom Morocco becomes a "barb'rous Town [...] Where Virtue mourns under a Tyrants frown" (III.ii). After Muly Labas's death and Crimalhaz's defeat, there is no guarantee with the crowning of Muly Hamet that tyranny will be crushed. His ability to govern effectively is questioned when, on his accession, he blithely states "[t]he charms of Crowns to Love but dull appears" (V.i). This statement (a clear allusion to Charles II) is contrasted to earlier perceptive comments made by Crimalhaz to the appropriate place for love:

> A silent Grotto, and a shady Grove
> Are far more proper scenes than Thrones for Love.
> Kings in so sublime a Region Move:
> They have Concerns that must take place of Love. (V.i)

The end of the play brings an uneasy resolution: a sense that the establishment of order and justice will be fleeting. Settle and Behn depict unrestrained ambition, fuelled by illegitimate love, leading only to tyranny. In both plays, the obsession of love/libido is portrayed as the will to power. Laula and Isabella take advantage of the sexual drive of their lovers to try to win dominion over them; to ensure the destruction of those who would thwart their plans; and ultimately to attempt to usurp kingly power. Thus the devious drive for unlawful political power, shrouded by sexual passion, is shown as an attempt to undermine legitimate rule.

The Empress of Morocco was probably first produced on the public stage in July 1673, although it was likely performed at court in 1671.[33] Certainly Settle had a place in court when he wrote the play, and he had the perspective of an 'insider.'

Laula, the female monster in Settle's play, represents the female principle: as a queen mother, she also represents the enemy within. It is an internal, feminine threat that is eating away at the stability of the state. In the early 1670s, Charles's much-hated mistresses, who had produced numerous illegitimate children, were blatantly using their influence at court over Charles in an attempt to wield power. Settle also revisits historical female characters and events. His evil queen mother reflects back on former times when other conniving women (in the main, queen mothers who purportedly used their position of power to influence their sons' policies) were seen to be threatening stability: in particular, the icon of anti-Catholic propaganda, Catherine de'Medici. Charles II's own mother, Henrietta Maria, was a member of the powerful Italian de'Medici family as well: daughter of the queen regent Marie de'Medici, who was also notorious for her abuse of power as queen regent during Louis XIII's minority. Henrietta tried desperately to control her son's political affairs. Her Catholic (thus nefarious) influence over her husband Charles I, and his policies, still resonated. In his diary Samuel Pepys notes her arrival back in England after the interregnum "doth please but very few."[34] In his *Account of the Growth of Popery and Arbitrary Government*, Andrew Marvell makes the memory of the past relevant to the present by comparing Charles I's marriage to Henrietta Maria to the Catholic James' recent marriage:

> [...] for his Royal Highnesse to marry the Princesse of Modena, or any other of that Religion, had very dangerous consequences: [...] [The King's subjects] have found by sad experience how such marriages have always increased Popery, and incorraged Priests and Jesuits to pervert his Majesties subjects.[35]

The fact that references to other malevolent female sources also happen to have been traditionally employed in Protestant propaganda is not a coincidence. Settle was, after all, to become a writer for the Whig Exclusionists and a member of the Green Ribbon Club. In *The Female Prelate*, Settle connects the feminine threat much more overtly with the Catholic Mother Church in his character of Pope Joan, "the Scarlet prostitute" (I.ii). This later play tunes into the fear of a loss of sovereignty through the spread of foreign hegemony by the Catholic church in Rome: a parallel and rival power structure drawing support away from the English crown through subversion by its English adherents. This does not mean, however, that Settle's anti-Catholic biases were not evident in a more subtle fashion in his earlier plays.

According to Settle's characterisation, female evil, while it is ostensibly innocuous, represents a decisive danger. Laura Lunger Knoppers argues that it is for precisely this reason that the Whore of Babylon is threatening: "[a]lthough monstrosity is usually defined by the grotesque, the ugly, the bestial, the horrifying [...] the most dangerous monster is the morally and sexually transgressive woman who allures rather than horrifies, seduces rather than disgusts."[36] As evidenced in *The Empress of Morocco* (and later in *The Female Prelate*), this form of monstrosity is menacing because its aberration is not (visibly) apparent: no one seems able to interpret the signs, to get beyond the physical evidence, least of all the ineffectual heir to the throne. Settle traces the crises of family and state authority to one destructive source. He uses the device of the monstrous woman as a triple threat. As a woman and a corrupt queen, Laula represents the malevolent aspect of women in power and the female capacity to infect the royal bloodline; in her comparison to icons used in anti-Catholic propaganda, she can be seen to manifest the Catholic menace. Above all, as an 'unnatural' mother who, rather than nurturing her family chooses relentlessly to destroy it; she represents the insidious danger of the enemy within: the familiar, the domestic.

Abdelazer was produced three years after the first public performance of the very popular *The Empress of Morocco*. Even though Behn's play was an adaptation of an earlier work, the plot and cast of both Behn's and Settle's productions were almost identical. Thomas Betterton played both Crimalhaz and Abdelazer; Henry Harris played the 'weak' sons Muly Labas and Ferdinand; William Smith played the characters who ultimately take over the reins of power: Muly Hamet and Philip; Mary Lee played Isabella after her recent success as the evil Deidamia in Thomas Otway's *Alcibiades*. Much of Behn's audience would have seen Settle's play (which was produced again in 1674), and comparisons would clearly be made. In both plays powerful women who wilfully reject the moral expectations and obligations implicit in their assigned roles are menacing. Behn's play, however, is much more nuanced: her characterisation is more complex and realistic; thus her depiction of evil is more chilling. Illicit passion drives a once-decent mother to make the deliberate choice of becoming a monster and destroying her family. Because she is also a queen, the damage she inflicts on her offspring and the implicit potential of producing illegitimate heirs also threatens the stability of the state.

Only a handful of years after *Abdelazer* was written, Behn became a propagandist for Charles II and the emerging Tory faction, at which time "she took many opportunities to attack the Duke of Monmouth, whom she saw as a danger to legitimacy and national stability."[37] *Abdelazer* is an early indicator of Behn's deepest political concerns. At a time when Shaftesbury and others were trying to exclude James from ruling, Behn emphasises the importance of continuity through legitimate hereditary succession. Behn comes close to making the play a revenge tragedy. She is sympathetic to Abdelazer's state: his hatred of the Spanish royal family is justified. But, incensed by retributive violence, he does not ultimately have providence on his side. He fails in his attempts to infiltrate the royal family insidiously. In the play, power is hereditary, and it is the royal family who ultimately has the right to rule. For Behn, patriarchal stability and security are reliant on both men *and women* in positions of power fulfilling their obligations; and the legitimacy of the royal line depends as much on the probity of the queen as it does on the morality of the king. An eroticised queen, such as Isabella, threatens to nullify the legitimate succession to the throne and imperils the country's political and social security.[38] Because of her position of providentially secured power, it is a weakness in Isabella, rather than in Abdelazer, that brings the country to an internal chaos such as that experienced in England's recent past.

In each play, the wanton queen mothers are contrasted with young virginal women. There is an implication that if women progress from virgin to 'pious' mother, they pose very little danger. Yet these women are overtly libidinous beings who, even when they become mothers, seek sexual relationships – with men other than their husbands. Worse is that they remain sexual creatures even as queen mothers, a revered but symbolic role considered to be beyond sexuality and beyond power.[39] Behn and Settle portray female libido as a destructive force; a force that is benign only when its expression is severely restricted to approved societal channels. In the context of the two plays, a sexually aggressive woman is an evil aberration of normal womankind and becomes infinitely more dangerous the more privileged her position. Without the protection her assigned roles afford her, a woman is quite unable to sublimate her desires. Thus, whether she is a helpless prey to her sexuality, as in Isabella's case, or uses it as a weapon, as in Laula's case, under its spell she becomes capable of initiating and encouraging the most despicable crimes.

In the horror plays, the monstrous woman is a disruption of the natural order of things – an evil symbol of a world turned upside down. For many of those attending the performances, she is an embodiment of anxieties and fears returning from the past to haunt. These monstrous women are also, most importantly, mothers: mothers willing to destroy their own families. Despite the differing political views of Settle and Behn, each playwright identifies the potential source of danger as coming not from outsiders but, rather, from those at the very centre of power, close to home.

Endnotes

[1]   Sandra Clark's research on early modern English responses to female crime confirms this: "although in incidents of spouse-murder husbands were far more often the perpetrators, there was a far higher proportion of accounts of murders by wives, [...] the literature of child-killing is almost entirely a literature of women's crimes [...]. [A]nd of course the extensive literature of witchcraft is in multiple ways a literature of women [...] (*Women and Crime in the Street Literature of Early Modern England* [Basingstoke: Palgrave Macmillan, 2003] 53). Susan C. Straub comments on the fascination of the seventeenth-century's popular press with "murdering mothers" and its "almost obsessive concern with female violence" (*Nature's Cruel Stepdames* [Pittsburgh: Duquesne UP, 2005] 7, 60). This fascination and repulsion with evil women has not diminished in our time. Murderesses such as Myra Hindley and Rose West continue to stir up prurient interest beyond that of their male partners in crime. In 1998, the first woman executed from Texas's death row generated more media interest than any of the men executed in the past ten years. Commenting on the (child) murderess Mary Bell, Emma Forest states: "In reporting on murder, there is an unspoken tabloid rule: when men kill, it's bad. When women kill it's evil" ("Iconography: The Mary Bell tolls for you" *Guardian*, 4 May 1998: 8).

[2]   Laura Lungers Knoppers, Introduction, *Monstrous Bodies*, ed. L. Knoppers and Joan B. Landes (Ithaca and London: Cornell UP, 2004) 6.

[3]   David Cressy, "Lamentable, Strange, and Wonderful: Headless Monsters in the English Revolution," *Monstrous Bodies* 48.

4   Kittye Delle Robbins, "Tiamat and Her Children," *Face to Face: Fathers, Mothers, Masters, Monsters – Essays for a Nonsexist Future*, ed. Meg McGavran Murray (Westport and London: Greenwood, 1983) 52.

5   Straub 39, 59. Although Straub's study provides sound evidence of the period's interrogation of maternal authority through the press's fascination with female criminality, I find the arguments somewhat contradictory at times. Dealing with female murderers of both husbands and children, Straub argues in one instance that, "husband murder – far more than infanticide or child murder – posed the greatest threat to the social order" overturning "the domestic hierarchy" (19); however, in another instance she argues that, "even more than the murdering wife […] the murdering mother reveals the instability inherent in the family-state analogy" (42).

6   *The Female Prelate: being the History of the Life and Death of Pope Joan* (London 1680). All references to Settle's *The Female Prelate* are from the 1680 edition and are hereafter cited parenthetically in the text.

7   John Knox, *The First Blast of the Trumpet against the monstrous regiment of Women* (Geneva, 1558) 13.

8   South, 571–2.

9   South 572–3.

10   Knoppers, in Knoppers and Landes, *Monstrous Bodies* 13.

11   David Cressy, *Travesties and Transgressions in Tudor and Stuart England* (Oxford: OUP, 2000) 41, 37.

12   Knox 9, 12.

13   Bruce Thomas Boehrer, *Monarchy and Incest in Renaissance England* (Philadelphia: U of Pennsylvania P, 1992) 73–4.

14   *Discours* held a continued interest: it appeared as an important part of Simon Goulart's *Memoires de l'estat de France sous Charles neufiesme*. As propaganda against female rulers, the *Discours'* impact was long-lasting: "it was used against Marie de'Medici in the seventeenth century and against Marie-Antoinette in the eighteenth" (R.J. Knecht, *Catherine de' Medici* [London and New York: Longman, 1998] 164–5).

15   *Discours merveilleux de la vie, actions et deportemens de Catherine de Medicis, Royne-mere*, ed. Nicole Cazauran (Geneva: Librarie Droz., 1995) 127–9; Robert M. Kingdon, *Myths about the St. Bartholomew's Day Massacres 1572–1576* (Cambridge, Mass., and London: Harvard UP, 1988) 203, 208–10.

16   N.I. Matar, "The Renegade in English Seventeenth Century Imagination" *SEL* 33 (1993): 491–3.

17   Lord Henry Howard had been sent on a trade mission to Taffaletta, 'Emperor' of Morocco. The port of Tangier was part of the dowry of Catherine of Braganza, and Charles II had spent what was considered by many to be an inordinate amount of money in improving the harbour and fortifications. Taffaletta snubbed Charles's ambassadorial party; they finally returned to England nearly a year later, empty-handed. See John Martin Robinson, *The Dukes of Norfolk* (Oxford: OUP, 1982) 125–6. Settle does not appear to have used any of the details of Howard's travels in his play, except for the name of a character called Taffalet, who is a fierce but honourable leader. Although he shows the Moroccan court as immoral and brutal, the fact that Settle would set his play in Morocco after such a foreign-affairs embarrassment could be seen as a slight against Charles and his wife.

18   L.S., *A letter from a gentleman of the Lord Ambassador Howard's retinue, to his friend in London* (London, 1670) 2, 23.

¹⁹ John Burbury, *A Relation of a Journey of ... my Lord Henry Howard from London ... to Contantinople* (London, 1671) 212.

²⁰ Thomas Dekker, *The Dramatic Works of Thomas Dekker*, ed. Fredson Bowers, 4 vols. (Cambridge: CUP, 1953–61). All references to *Lust's Dominion* are from Bowers's edition, vol. 4, and are hereafter cited parenthetically in the text.

²¹ Aphra Behn, *The Works of Aphra Behn*, ed. Janet Todd, 7 vols. (London: Pickering & Chatto, 1992–96). All references to *Abdelazer* are from Todd's edition, vol. 5, and are hereafter cited parenthetically in the text.

²² Jacqueline Pearson similarly argues that, "Behn significantly expands on Abdelazer's vengeful resentments against the Spaniards, who dethroned and murdered the king his father, and who now rule the land of which he believes himself rightful king. He acts as he does not because Blacks are naturally evil, but because of his dispossession within Spanish society" ("Slave princes and lady monsters: gender and ethnic difference in the work of Aphra Behn," *Aphra Behn Studies*, ed. Janet Todd [Cambridge: CUP, 1995] 227–8).

²³ "God forbid that I should be so ill a Christian as not to say God's judgements are just upon me […] an unjust sentence that I suffered for to take effect, is punished now by an unjust sentence on me." Quoted in Pauline Gregg, *King Charles I* (London: J.M. Dent & Sons Ltd., 1981) 444; and Kerrigan, "Revenge Tragedy Revisited" 207.

²⁴ I disagree with Jacqueline Pearson's view that "Behn is prepared to allow a sexually autonomous woman the dignity of being a tragic hero, while her predecessors are not" (Pearson, in Todd, *Aphra Behn Studies* 234). Isabella is certainly distinguished by exceptional fortitude, but there is very little else to commend her to tragic hero status. Although I would agree she is a slave to her lust (much in the same way that Abdelazer is a slave to his misfortune), I do not feel that her lust is a tragic flaw. She stepped over the line when she consciously remoulded herself: "Nature be gone, I chase thee from my soul" (II.i.230). I also disagree with Susie Thomas, who argues, in reference to Pearson's statement, "There remains the question: why should a white woman seem more dignified by being made full-bloodedly evil, when the reverse is true of a black man?" (Susie Thomas, "This Thing of Darkness I Acknowledge Mine: Aphra Behn's *Abdelazer, or The Moor's Revenge*" *Restoration* 22:1 [1998]: 38). I do not believe that the queen is accorded any more dignity than Abdelazer. Both are certainly given more dignity than their prototypes, but the queen mother dies a victim – under layers of deception – whereas Abdelazer is given the opportunity to face his murderers in full strength (one man alone cannot kill him) intimidating his adversaries to the end.

²⁵ Hughes, *English Drama* 93.

²⁶ *The Works of John Dryden.,*. All references to *The Conquest of Granada Parts 1 & 2*, are from the California edition, vol. 11, ed. John Loftis et al., (1978) and are hereafter cited parenthetically in the text.

²⁷ Hughes, *English Drama* 81–2.

²⁸ *Discours*, quoted in Kingdon 208.

²⁹ Behn omits the scene in *Lust's Dominion* (I.iii) where the old king appears on his deathbed.

³⁰ Canfield, *Heroes and States* 60.

³¹ Owen, *Restoration Theatre and Crisis* 246.

³² Katherine Crawford, *Perilous Performances* (Harvard UP, 2004) 24, 4. Pierre Dupuy, *Traite sur la Majorite de nos Rois*, 1:43, quoted in Crawford 3; Dupuy first published his treatise in 1655.

³³ Frank C. Brown argues *The Empress of Morocco* was first acted at court in 1669/70 and at Dorset Gardens in 1671. His dates originate from Settle's claim, in *Ibrahim*'s "Preface to the Reader," that *The Empress of Morocco* was "Acted in less than three years after *Cambyses*." Brown dates the production of *Cambyses* after John Downes's assertion that it was "the first new play that was acted" by Davenant's company, after the fire. Brown also quotes Anthony A. Wood, from *Athenae Oxonienses*, who says the play was acted in 1671 (*Elkanah Settle: His Life and Works* [Chicago, 1910] 12). I believe it is most likely that the 1671 production referred to by Wood was the amateur production. I agree with Eleanor Boswell that the winter of 1671/72 is the earliest the play could have been produced: "previous commentators seem to have overlooked Settle's definite statement in his dedication to Henry Howard, Earl of Norwich, that he owed the story to the Earl's embassy to Africa. Reference to the Calendar of State Papers reveals the fact that Howard [...] went to Morocco in June, 1669, and returned in October, 1670. Settle could scarcely have had the play ready that season – unless indeed, he wrote it in a few weeks, in which case, he would certainly have boasted of it – and moreover, since the Court must at that time have been occupied with preparations for the Grand Ballet or Masque danced in February, 1670/71, it would not have been ready for another undertaking of so elaborate a nature" (*The Restoration Court Stage 1660–1672* [London, 1932] 132).

³⁴ Pepys 1:282.

³⁵ Marvell, *Growth of Popery* 48. C. Condren and A. Cousins point out the use of "the past tense tars Mary with the same brush as Henrietta Maria and the damage her religious coterie had done to Charles I" (*The Political Identity of Andrew Marvell* [Aldershot: Scolar, 1990] 296). John Milton also refers to Henrietta Maria's malevolent influence over Charles I in *Eikonoklastes*. "[I]t is op'nly known that her Religion wrought more upon him, then his Religion upon her, and his op'n favouring of Papists, and his hatred of them call'd Puritants [...] made most men suspect she had quite perverted him" (Chapter VII: 422) (Milton, *Complete Prose Works of John Milton*, ed. Don M. Wolfe, 8 vols. [New Haven: Yale UP, 1953–82]). All references to *Eikonoklastes* are from Wolfe's edition, vol. 3, and are hereafter cited parenthetically in the text.

³⁶ Laura Lunger Knoppers, "'The Antichrist, the Babilon, the great dragon': Oliver Cromwell, Andrew Marvell, and the Apocalyptic Monstrous," *Monstrous Bodies*, ed. Knoppers and Landes 122–3.

³⁷ Todd, "Aphra Behn," *DNB*.

³⁸ ·This is not to suggest that Behn thought queens should never be erotic, simply that they should restrict their eroticism to their own marriage. Behn does eroticise monarchy in her later poetry. In *A Pindarick Poem on the Happy Coronation of His most Sacred Majesty James II*, for example, James and Mary of Modena are depicted as Jove and Juno. The poet Behn tries to coax James out of bed, to prepare for his coronation: "Shake off the downy pleasures from thy eyes; / And from the softest Charms of *Love*, Arise!" (*Works of Aphra Behn* 1:96–7). Mary of Modena, who is also aligned with Venus and with Petrarch's beloved Laura in the poem, is the "*inchanting Ravisher*" who uses the "Musick of Her Tongue; / Her Angel Eyes, and Voice, so conqu'ring" (102–4) to keep James with her in bed.

³⁹ R.J. Knecht notes that, although Catherine de'Medici tried to influence her husband's policy her political influence was minimal during his lifetime. In other words, her (abuse of) power occurred during the time that she was regent/queen mother (Knecht 46).

Chapter 4
Degenerate Rulers:
Nathaniel Lee's *The Tragedy of Nero* and
The Rival Queens

The queen mothers in the horror plays are evil because each abuses her position in an effort to subvert the legitimate right of succession to the throne. The power of the queen mothers to orchestrate destructive events is related to both role and gender. As the relicts and mothers of kings, they are accorded obligatory deference from the court and respect and obedience from their sons. Adding leverage to these social and psychological sources of influence is erotic power: each of the queen mothers uses her sexual allure to align herself with an ambitious man eager to abet her in increasing her power and his. Yet the queens in both *The Empress of Morocco* and *Abelazer* fail. In these plays the power of the state is held by men in direct line of succession. In contrast to the power wielded by the queens, the power of the kings is a legally and religiously sanctioned power deriving from their roles as sovereigns in a hereditary system strongly favouring male heirs. But despite being endowed with all the social and political power in the state, the male rulers (legitimate or otherwise) are depicted in the horror plays as being no less morally abhorrent than the monstrous queens.[1] As with the depiction of monstrous women, the degenerate rulers also represent a domestic threat to stability. There is, however, an important distinction between the two: attempts to stretch the limits of their monstrous power prompt the queen mothers knowingly to commit evil; whereas the opportunities to exercise virtually limitless power drive the kings into madness, diminishing their culpability for their crimes.

Nathaniel Lee's *The Tragedy of Nero* (King's 1674) and *The Rival Queens* (King's 1677) were popular and influential. *Nero* was acted several times during its opening season; it spawned a reproduction of an earlier anonymous play, *Piso's Conspiracy*, at Drury Lane and went on to influence Otway's early plays as well as Settle's *Ibrahim* and Shadwell's *The Libertine* at Drury Lane the following season. *The Rival Queens* was also in demand: on the second recorded performance of the play, the house was twice as full as it had been for the performance of Dryden's *All For Love* earlier the same month: a total attendance of 513 compared to 279.[2] Hart's performance of Alexander was particularly sought after. According to John Downes, whenever Hart acted Alexander, "the house was fill'd as at a New Play [...] he Acting that with such Grandeur and Agreeable Majesty" (41). The play's popularity continued: it was performed for the king and queen several times between 1681 and 1685 and "revived in one form or another almost every season on the London stage until well past the middle of the nineteenth century."[3] In a discussion on players, apparently written by a contemporary of Lee's and attributed to Thomas Killigrew, the writer looks back to the Restoration theatre and the importance of *action* in retaining the audience's attention: "the more constant and violent the Action is, the more it will be attended by them; wherever there is Passion, there must necessarily be Action; those Tragedies therefore, that have a perpetual Succession of Passion, can never miscarry." With specific reference to Lee's *The Rival Queens*, the writer says it is

> this Quality that has preserv'd and still keeps up the Tragedy of *Alexander the Great*, which Mr. Crown found fault with, in a Discourse with me one Day, because, it was continually on the fret, as he call'd it, from the Beginning to the End; that is, the Passions were lively and strong through the whole Piece, which so took up the Audience, that they had no Leisure or Interval of Quiet to grow weary and be disgusted.[4]

The cast for *Nero* and *The Rival Queens* was similar in important ways: Charles Hart played Nero and Alexander; Rebecca Marshall played the evil women, Poppea and Roxana. Even though these two plays were produced three years apart, the casting supported important links between the absolute rulers in both plays (diminishing Alexander's role as a hero by associating him with the tyrannical and depraved Nero) as well as the evil, lustful females whose overtly sexual relationships with the rulers aided in the overall breakdown of familial and patriarchal roles. The two plays frame an important period of development in the horror play as dramatists from both companies responded to key themes in Lee's work, questioning the nature of power as well as the existence of providential justice.

The plays trace, in some detail, the rapid moral decline of two rulers who had, at an earlier time, deserved the loyalty and admiration of their subjects. By the end of the plays, both realms have suffered a progressive and dangerous deterioration of orderly rule in concert with the psychological degeneration of the rulers. According to one contemporary source, the aetiology of madness in the seventeenth century was attributed to "divine retribution, diabolical possession, witchcraft, astrological influences, humoral imbalances, or to any combination of these forces."[5] Nathaniel Lee posits another cause: one which was articulated 100 years later, in January 1770, by William Pitt, Earl of Chatham, in a speech to parliament: "Unlimited power is apt to corrupt the minds of those who possess it [...]."[6] The examination of the nature of power and its relationship to justice is a recurring theme in Lee's work. *Lucius Junius Brutus* (Duke's 1680) and *The Massacre of Paris* (written 1679), considered Lee's more overtly political plays, were banned for their anti-Catholicism and republican sentiments only a handful of years after *The Rival Queens* was written and produced. It is clear that at this earlier stage in his career, Lee was already focusing on the pathology of kingship.

Nathaniel Lee was born into a scholarly family. As a child and young man, he had had access to his father's extensive library, which comprised a diverse range of historical, philosophical and religious works. It is unlikely that Lee was unfamiliar with the ongoing theological debate on God's justice and reason versus His will.

The supporters of the doctrine of the Divine Right of Kings argued that God is justice: He acts in a certain way because it is a just and reasonable way. Because a king derives his power directly from God, he is inherently 'just' and deserves absolute obedience; because he is divinely appointed, he rules for life. In contrast, Hobbes and others argued that elevating justice above God would limit His power. God's actions were seen to derive not from His justice, but from His will – in Hobbes's words, His "Irresistible Power [...] [and] it is from that Power, that the Kingdome over men, and the Right of Afflicting men at his pleasure, belongeth Naturally to God Almighty; not as Creator, and Gracious; but as Omnipotent" (*Leviathan* 31:246–7). Ideas of Divine Right lost some currency during the 1670s. A subject of regular discussion in the forties, fifties and early sixties and then again during the Exclusion Crisis, there was little written on the subject in the decade of the horror plays.[7] However, the question of whether resistance to lawful authority could ever be justified was an important theoretical problem at the time. In 1675, a bill was brought forward to require all members of both houses of parliament to declare the unlawfulness of resistance and an oath not to endeavour any alteration of the government or state.[8] The subject of Divine Right kingship was debated in the 1670s, and the most vocal proponents remained the clergy. Early in 1674, the bishops met to discuss the proposal to exclude the Catholic James from succession to the crown. According to K.H.D. Haley,

> [t]he Archbishop of York, supported by the Bishop of Winchester and 'cheered by the rest of the bishops,' put forward the pure divine right theory that obedience was due, not only to a Popish King, but to a tyrant and even a pagan, and described the proposal as 'diabolical.'[9]

For Lee, the threat to the stability of the state stems from corrupt power at the top of the hierarchy. He suggests sovereign power is not inherently just, and he rejects absolutism outright. In fact, in his depiction absolute power – over time – will *always* lead to injustice. Lee's focus in the plays discussed here is the destructive sequelae of despotic kingship. His two protagonists are, in a sense, victims of their rise to that pinnacle of power. Lee traces the pathology of the 'disease' of tyranny, exploring how a tyrant is created through the exercise of absolute power. Given no moral boundaries or consequences to their actions, Lee's intemperate kings engage in impulsive and often cruel behaviour which causes intense discord and fear among their subjects. In both studies, the kings undergo the process of mental and moral degeneration while still on the throne. Lee demonstrates that the kings' madness is not caused, like King Lear's, by personal tragedy; rather, it is the corrupting effects of the office of autocratic kingship that drives their psychological and moral collapse: their descent into madness. As a counterpoint to the madness of the kings, Lee introduces characters in both plays who, as a result of summary actions of the kings, have been driven 'mad.' Unlike the all-powerful kings, however, they are constrained from rash reactions by the counsel of their friends or by their helplessness in the face of tyranny.

Madness was still little understood by the medical profession or the general public in the late seventeenth century, and mad people were often objects of derision and fear. Madness did hold a fascination though, as evidenced by Robert Burton's still influential *The Anatomy of Melancholy*, written in the years before the civil wars; as well as the numerous treatises which appeared after 1660 on 'diseases of the head.' For those writing on the subject in the years between 1663 and 1689, the general consensus was that madness clearly indicated a loss of reason. The writers of treatises generally agreed that there were four types of madness: Delirium, Phrensie, Melancholia and Mania. A Delirium was a "dotage [...] not long induring;"[10] A Phrensie was a "perpetual [...] deliry [...] with a continued Fever";[11] Melancholia was "a raving without a Feavour or fury, joined with fear and sadness."[12] The most extreme of all was Mania, which was "a loss of the wits, with raging and fury, but without a Feaver."[13] It is a descent into Mania, or acute insanity, that Lee depicts in his rulers. To the general public, this was considered the most frightening form of madness. The notes of the astrological physician, Richard Napier, characteristically describe the victims of acute insanity as "terrifyingly wild and incomprehensible [...] likely to be hostile, angry, or violent, to laugh strangely, babble or scream incoherently."[14] In *Two Discourses concerning The Soul of Brutes*, Thomas Willis further delineates the three main characteristics of people with Mania:

> First, That their Phantasies or Imaginations are perpetually busied with a storm of impetuous thoughts, so that night and day they are muttering to themselves various things, or declare them by crying out, or by bauling out aloud. Secondly, That their notions or conceptions are either incongruous, or represented to them under a false or erroneous image. Thirdly, To their Delirium is most often joyned Audaciousness and Fury, contrary to Melancholicks, who are always infected with fear and Sadness.[15]

Laws pertaining to those considered insane are relevant to this study. Michael Dalton's *The Countrey Justice* (republished in 1665) indicates that under law 'lunatics' who committed a felony could enjoy immunity from certain severe penalties – as, like children, they were considered *non compos mentis*. Dalton explains that "there are three sorts of persons who can be accounted non compos mentis to this purpose and the like. 1. A fool natural ... 2. He who was once of good and sound memory and after [...] loseth his memory. 3. A lunatic [...] [and] if one that is non compos mentis [...] kill a man, this is no felony."[16] People who were considered mad were, by and large, taken care of by their families or through their parishes. The only public asylum in England was Bethlem (Bedlam) Hospital in London, but it retained only a small number of inmates. John Strype wrote a description of Bedlam, stating that "from the Year 1684 to 1703 [...] there had been in this Hospital 1294 Patients; of which Number had been cured and discharged 890, which is above two Patients in Three."[17] Although the hospital was making attempts to 'cure' its patients, Bedlam was in no way a retreat. It was, in fact, open for public 'entertainment' – observers regularly streamed through to observe the unfortunate occupants. After its shift to larger quarters in 1676, Bedlam's connotation with spectacle and entertainment grew. Even a respected physician like Thomas Willis could describe Bedlam as a foreign country whose wild inhabitants could be gawked at as if they were on theatrical display:

> There is no need to illustrate the nature of this Disease with Histories and Examples, or to describe the manifold Types of it; but rather let them go to the Hospitals of mad people where they may behold, not without a wonderful spectacle, as it were a new and monstrous nation of men, contrary to rational people.[18]

Nathaniel Lee himself was confined in Bedlam between 1684 and 1688. His friend, William Wycherley, wrote a poem to Lee in Bedlam in which he refers to the abuse of the inmates through starvation, whipping and exhibition:

> You, best because you starv'd, fell mad before,
> Now Starving, does your Wits to you restore; [...]
> You did, before that you were mad, engage
> With Numbers, and in your Poetic Rage,
> Lash'd (as your Keeper you) the madder Age; [...]
> And now, the Rabble to thee does resort,
> That thy Want of Wits may be their Sport.[19]

Not surprisingly, Bedlam and Bedlamites were the models used for madness by the Jacobean playwrights from Shakespeare's *King Lear*, where Edgar feigns madness as the ex-Bedlam beggar Tom O'Bedlam, to Thomas Middleton's depiction of a madhouse in *The Changeling*. Although, like the Jacobean ideas on madness, notions of madness in the Restoration would have been influenced by Bedlam and Bedlamites, it is worth noting that there are no Bedlamites in the horror plays. Lee and other horror writers of the Restoration did not situate their madmen in madhouses; rather, the mad characters hold pivotal roles in society. In the context of the time, the madness of an ordinary citizen, although potentially frightening if the person was violent, was controllable. A mad person, or lunatic, was a limited danger. In *The Tragedy of Nero* and *The Rival Queens*, Lee creates disturbing scenarios of the disastrous consequences of having a mad, hostile head of state, an absolute ruler accountable to no one: a ruler whose habitual ethical and moral restraints have been overcome by the conviction of his omnipotence.

In Lee's satirical explication of Divine Right, the mad kings, Nero and Alexander, add to their imagined God-given right to rule the equally strong delusion that they are gods. A commonly held belief was that madmen often saw themselves as someone else: "some think themselves to be Kings, Princes, Prophets."[20] In his handbill (c.1674) advertising his madhouse on Clarken-well Green, James Newton describes a man who "commanded the standers by to take off my head, for he would be K Charles II."[21] In Lee's depiction the irrationality inherent in his characters' assumptions that they are gods can potentially destabilise an entire kingdom and undermine the imparting of justice.[22]

The Rival Queens opens with early signs of discord and evidence of Alexander's capriciousness. Two of Alexander's courtiers, Lysimachus and Hephestion, are fighting each other, and the opening line of the play equates their dissent with ideas of madness. Alexander's loyal general Clytus, attempting to intervene in the sword fight, asks: "What, are you Mad-Men!" (I.i.1).[23] Four lines later Clytus once again calls Lysimachus "mad" for wanting to kill his rival over the love of a woman. Lysimachus loves a captured princess and is beloved by her. But they have had their love denied because Alexander has decided to give the princess in marriage to his favourite, Hephestion. The discord between the men is the result of this arbitrary decision. In this case, no harm results because they are made to see reason by Clytus.

As Lysimachus and Hephestion leave the stage, the idea of a madness or discord enveloping the state is further developed by the immediate introduction of a plot against Alexander's life. Cassander, the leader of the plot, enters and speaks of dark portents for Alexander's destruction. He has had foreboding visions and has been visited by "A mad Chaldean in the dead of Night" (I.i.146). As the plotters meet, they express profound grievances against "bloody Alexander" (I.i.242) who "[w]ou'd be a God" and "is cruel as a Devil" (I.i.222). The audience learns of Alexander's violent and unjustified actions against former companions and faithful generals whom Alexander had tortured and killed after (apparently groundless) fears that they were plotting against him. These men are described by the plotters as innocent; and their martyrdom is given credence later in the play when more trustworthy and impartial characters, such as Clytus and Eumenes, describe them as "our great Friends" (III.i.2–3), "great Parmenio, and his slaughter'd Sons: / [...] who did many brave exploits / Without the King, – the King without him nothing" (IV. i.479–81).

The first act ends with yet another example of Alexander's fall from virtue: his sexual betrayal of his wife Statira. On his way back from his most recent battle, he once again had sexual relations with his former wife Roxana. Alexander's sexual betrayal causes derangement and despair in Statira, and she joins the other victims of his heedless actions. She speaks of the "burning torture," and even though she pleads for 'justice,' it is not to be found: "I will have remedy, I will, I will, / Or go distracted; Madness may throw off / The mighty Load, and drown the flaming Passion" (I.i.400–403). Before we are even introduced to Alexander, then, Lee has drawn a tyrant; and he has illustrated the repercussions of Alexander's actions on his people and on the state by repeatedly characterising images of disorder with the adjective "mad."

We finally meet Alexander in Act 2, but because Lee has already questioned the traditional historical depiction of Alexander as a conquering hero, his ostensibly heroic entrance from yet another successful war is ironic.[24] Some hint of Alexander's state of mind is soon evidenced by his inability to recognize his own kin and his determination to ignore divine omens. Both Plutarch and Curtius mention several incidents where it is believed that Alexander ignored potent omens. Lee, however, accentuates Alexander's disdain for the sources of the portentous signs. He also includes an omen – not in Plutarch or Curtius – just before Alexander drinks the poison that kills him:

A pale Crown'd head flew lately glaring by me,
With two dead hands, which threw a Chrystal Globe
From high, that shatter'd in a thousand pieces. (IV.i.80–82)

Alexander's dismissal of portents is further evidence of his gradual detachment and stems from an overweening pride in his absolute power, fuelled by continual flattery from his courtiers. His demeanour foreshadows the biblical rebuke that "Pride goeth before destruction, and haughty spirit before a fall" (Proverbs 16:18). Lee's contemporaries linked pride with madness. Thomas Willis claims ambition and pride have "made some mad" and that "mad men are not as Melancholicks, sad and fearful, but audacious and very confident, so that they shun almost no dangers, and attempt all the most difficult things that are."[25] Thomas Tryon says pride is "the chief Procatarick, or remote original cause of Madness":

[…] for an abusive Self flattering Perswasion […] or Esteem of falsehood, do at first Seduce a person into Presumption, and a despising of others, or into an Indignation of Self-Love, Anger, Hatred, or Wrathfulness, towards his Neighbour.[26]

Halfway through the play, Alexander rejects his ancestry. He luxuriates in Persian riches, disdaining Macedonian traditions by insisting that he and his courtiers dress in opulent Persian fashions. He also denies he is the son of a mere king (Philip) and claims divine origin: "By all my Kindred in the Skies Jove made my Mother pregnant" (IV.i.358). Previously, both Alexander and his flatterers had referred to him as "young Ammon," but this is the first direct repudiation of his parentage. Alexander's closest comrade (and 'step'-father) Clytus reproaches him for disowning his heritage. While his flatterers repeatedly insist on Alexander's divinity, Clytus is driven to speak the truth: he tells of Alexander's "blasphemies […] [and] the riots of a most debauch'd, and blotted life" (IV.ii.472). Lysimachus tries to protect Clytus from Alexander's growing anger by suggesting "the old man rav'd" (IV.i.444), but Alexander impulsively kills Clytus. It is after Clytus's death that Alexander begins the final stages of his own disintegration into madness: "[t]hy Friends will shun thee now, and stand at distance, / Nor dare to speak their minds, nor eat with thee, / Nor drink, lest by thy madness they dye too" (IV.i.518–20).

In the final act Roxana, driven 'mad' by Alexander's sexual rejection of her: "O you have ruin'd me, I shall be mad […] My brain is burst" (III.i.37,52), and spurred on by the "madness" of personified Envy (III.i.72), kills her rival Statira. After Statira's death – and after he himself is poisoned – Alexander falls into the deep theatrical madness of raving and "strange wild look[s]" (V.i.297). It is at this final moment that Lee brings unexpected pathos to Alexander's situation, much like Shakespeare does to Antony, by allowing us a glimpse of his former, 'heroic' self. As he raves, Alexander recalls his friendships with Parmenio and Clytus, men he subsequently killed. He once again speaks of acts of heroism on the battlefield and talks disparagingly of the "gaudy Persians" (V.i.337). Lee implies that Alexander's earlier virtue was unsustainable: unrestrained state power in the hands of an individual has an inalterable destructive effect not only on those who live under it but on the ruler as well.

Alexander's delusive omnipotence is a censure of absolutism, but it is also censure of its adherents – in particular, monarchs such as Louis XIV. Historian John Spurr argues that the perceived malevolent influence of Louis and France on England was exacerbated by the eagerness of the English to "import hither the air and carriage, and assurance of the French":

> With foreign manners came 'foreign softnesses,' and this was the slippery slope to luxury, the sybaritic and heedless consumption of unearned delights, which sapped the native vigour of the people and drained the nation of money to pay for imported wines and silks.[27]

The English satirists of the mid-1670s regularly aligned Louis and Charles II and condemned the relationship between the two monarchs. In John Ayloffe's *Brittania and Raleigh* (1674/5), Louis's regime is personified in a dame "bedeck'd with spotted pride" who demands of Charles to "shake off those baby-bonds [and] Taste the delicious sweets of sov'reign power / 'Tis royal game whole kingdoms to deflower" (*POAS* 1:96, 98–9). And there is a satirical suggestion that Charles II is a doppelganger:

> A colony of French possess the court;
> Pimps, priests, buffoons i'th' privy-chamber sport.
> Such slimy monsters ne'er approach'd a throne
> Since Pharaoh's reign, nor so defil'd a crown,
> I'th'sacred ear tyrannic arts they croak,
> Pervert his mind, his good intentions choke,
> Tell him of golden Indies, fairy lands,
> Leviathans, and absolute commands.
> Thus fairy-like the King they steal away,
> And in his place a Louis changeling lay. (25–34) [28]

Louis XIV and Lee's other autocratic ruler, Nero, are also linked through their despotism. Bishop Burnet, among others, made the direct connection, calling Louis as vainglorious as "the worst of the Roman Emperours."[29] As already argued, Lee is particularly fond of using analogies from Roman history to reinforce his study of degenerate rulers. Between 1674 and 1679, five of Lee's six plays centre on tyrannical, arguably 'mad' monarchs: two of these are Roman (Nero and Augustus Caesar in *Gloriana*) and one, Caesar Borgia, is groomed by Machiavel to aspire to the glories and the tyranny of ancient Rome. Lee was not alone in using Roman analogies to identify contemporary tyranny and decadence. Shakespeare's *Julius Caesar* was reproduced several times in the 1670s and 1680s. Many poems from the early to mid-1670s, such as Andrew Marvell's *Further Advice to a Painter* (1671), the anonymous *A Dialogue between the Two Horses* (1676), John Lacy's *Satire* (1677) and John Ayloffe's *Marvell's Ghost* (1678) clearly criticise the absolutist tendencies of Charles II and his court through a comparison with such tyrannical characters from history as Commodus, the corrupt Assyrian king Sardanapalus, Nero, the Antonine emperor Heliogabalus and the Roman autocrat Tarquinius Superbus. In *Eikonoklastes*, Milton had, of course, made similar analogies between Charles I and despotic Roman emperors Nero and Caligula.[30]

As in *The Rival Queens*, there are early indications in Lee's *The Tragedy of Nero* that things in the state are not as they should be. Fear and paranoia have engulfed Nero's court: people are "hang'd for looking suspitiously" (I.i.157). We are told that Nero despises reason: he is "[i]mpatient of wise councel, and reproof " (I.i.49), and he "can't endure a man / that's given to meditation; hates a Philosopher, as much as he / loves a Fidler" (I.i.163–4). One courtier advises another not to be thoughtful, as that morning a friend "by the Emperor's Order, had his throat cut, for being thoughtful" (I.i.168–9). Nero has even brutally assaulted his own family: we are introduced to him as he is taking his mother, Agrippina, to execution. Even when one of Nero's courtiers sheds tears of pity for Agrippina's fate, they are construed as "a sort of liquid Treason" (I.ii.178).

At the same time, however, Lee sets up a history of the character of Nero and his court, which was once renowned as "a full Orb / Of matchless glory" (I.i.40–41). According to the courtier Otho,

> Nothing appears, alas, as heretofore;
> The darkness of his horrid vices, have
> Eclips'd the glimmering rays of his frail virtue
> His cruelties, like birds of prey, have pick'd
> All seeds of Nobleness from his false heart
> And now it lyes a sad dull lump of earth. (I.i.43–8)

At one time Nero had some virtue, but his potential for nobility was never realised. The process of degeneration implies a fall away from previous virtue or excellence. Portraying Nero as simply *mad* from the start to the finish of his life would be meaningless. It would imply that the defect was in the individual – one bad seed – which when destroyed could be replaced with someone or something better. But Lee's kings *become* mad because of the inability of any absolute ruler to be proof against the pathology of supreme power.

One of the sources for Lee's play is the anonymous *The Tragedie of Nero* (1624). This was reproduced as *Piso's Conspiracy*, with minor alterations by the King's Company in 1675, after the success of Lee's play. A comparison between the two protagonists can help to illuminate Lee's characterisation of Nero as a man whose moral degeneration leads to madness. In the earlier play, Nero is depicted as ruthless and unforgiving, but there are no references to madness. Although he is universally despised for his tyranny, and his desire to see himself as a great actor and writer causes embarrassment and disdain, the character is consistently insightful about his position. When Nero hears of Piso's conspiracy against his life, he reflects in soliloquy on the responsibilities of greatness that have been thrust upon him:

> O sweet dispised joyes of pouerty,
> A happiness vnknowne vnto the Gods ...
> Mother, thou didst deseruedly in this,
> That from a priuate, and sure state, didst raise
> My fortunes, to this slippery hill of greatnesse;
> Where I can niether stand, nor fall with life. (IV.i)

Whereas Lee's Nero is depicted as very much the exclusive source of evil in the play, throughout the earlier tragedy the emperor is associated with his corrupt flatterers and is not seen as the sole source of evil. Abetted by his flatterers, he does see himself as a god; however, at the end of the play when his followers desert him in his time of need, his clarity of thought belies 'madness' as an excuse for his tyranny:

> The people may forsake me without blame,
> I did them wrong to make you rich, and great,
> I tooke their houses to bestow on you:
> Treason in them hath name of libertie
> Your fault hath no excuse, you are my fault,
> And the excuse of others treachery. (V.i.)

In the anonymous play, the emperor Nero chooses to play the game because he can, but he never loses sight of reality. Conversely, Lee's Nero is compelled to execute his tyrannical actions: the increasing severity of his madness gives him no insight and no choice.

Another important distinction between the two plays is that the earlier tragedy is based on the events surrounding Piso's conspiracy and occur after Nero's violent murder of his family. Lee's play, however, focuses very much on the loss of moral responsibility inherent in a degree of madness that enables Nero to blithely destroy his family in his reckless drive for omnipotence. The play begins with Nero's destruction of his mother and moves through the murder of his wife, his stepbrother and his father-figure Seneca. This focus on family slaughter is central to other horror plays, including many of Lee's plays, such as *Caesar Borgia* (Duke's 1679), where Borgia commits atrocity after atrocity, eventually murdering his brother, father-in-law and his wife. Like Borgia, Nero in Lee's play moves inexorably towards literal madness, in front of his audience's eyes.

Having broken the taboo of incest, by daring to rape his mother, Nero exults in his feelings of omnipotence after he commands her execution. Hearing of Agrippina's death, he gleefully acknowledges that his "soul now free does walk, / And shall no more be clogg'd with moral talk" (I.ii.21–2). Nero feels empowered by his ability to perform the most unnatural acts with apparent impunity. Not only does he rape and kill his mother, he also gelds his lover Sporus in another attempt to subvert nature: "Who, but a GOD, like me, could Sexes change? / Sporus be witness of my Mighty art; / Sporus, now Lady, once Lord of my heart" (I.ii.34–6). This incident is reduced to one passing comment in the anonymous version of *Nero*, but in his version of the play, Lee accentuates the perversity of the event as yet another indicator of Nero's deluded and growing belief in his own divinity:

I am God; my self I Canonize [...]
I ransack Nature; all its treasures view;
Beings annihilate, and make a new:
All this can I, your God-like Nero do. (I.ii.28, 40–42)

Before Nero orders his death, Seneca tries to bring Nero back to his senses. He attributes Nero's actions to "murd'ring pride [...] [that] dost all reason kill" (I.ii.70). Rather than listen to the elder Seneca's wise counsel, however, Seneca's words inflame Nero's boasting. Nero brags that when he sits at the right hand of Jove, he will settle for nothing less than human sacrifice.

No blood of Bulls, nor Goats, shall there be spilt; [...]
The best of humane gore shall wash my Shrine;
Heroes shall bleed, and they are half Divine [...]
Each common God shall, in his turn, be Priest,
And for your lower world make his request:
Then offer up a grateful Sacrifice,
Kings heads, Queens hearts, and charming Virgins eyes. (I.ii.73, 76–7, 80–83)

Like Alexander, as Nero's tyranny grows, the effect on his subjects is devastating. Once again, Lee uses the term 'mad' to describe the irrationality that can be associated with extreme emotional states when rulers lose all normal moral restraints and there is a sense of powerlessness in the population. Feelings of injustice and despair are endemic. After Seneca is killed by Nero's order, even the normally loyal Drusillus refers to Nero as "the raging Fiend" and asks "[w]hen will his black impieties have end?" (II.i.1–2). When Octavia refuses Nero's demand that she kill her brother Britannicus, Octavia looks in vain for justice: "Oh Gods, can you your vengeance keep? / Where is your Thunder? [...]'tis you that sleep" (II. iii.125–6). When Britannicus finds her, stabbed by Nero, he makes a futile plea to a higher power for redress: "Gods! Gods! but they are deaf, or will not hear" (II.iii.153). Britannicus's grief over Nero's impulsive and unpunishable murder of Octavia – combined with his belief that his lover has died – drives him to profound despair, producing, in his own words, a "madman" (IV.i.31).

Nero's ruination of Poppea incites a desperate rage in her brother and her husband. Otho says he is "lost [...] my heart's sick [...] / Down, down, my swelling heart; O, I am sad: / Hold, my weak eyes; this sight has made me mad" (IV.ii.21, 25, 39–40). Piso calls himself "mad. / This night he whore's my Sister" (III.iii.91–2). Rather than seek vengeance in heaven, however, Piso looks to Hell to hear his "pray'r." Despite the guilt and shame brought about by Nero's debasement of her, Poppea is impelled by the intoxicating madness of unbridled lust to seek new sexual adventures.

I've gone too far to think of a return;
I must enjoy him: O my heart does burn!
My blood boils high, and beats with strange desires:
'Tis just that madness mingle with such fires. (IV.i.109–12)

It is Nero's unlicensed exercise of power that leads to the 'madness' of his subjects. When a leader is irrational, capricious and arbitrary and there are no standards of virtue or honour, the moral confusion spreads out into the state. As with Alexander, the effects of arbitrary power do eventually destroy Nero as well. The final disintegration of his mind takes place after Caligula's ghost appears to the sleeping Nero, challenging him to even greater wickedness under the veil of his madness:

> By Traytors hands I fell: O that I could,
> For every drop they shed, Spill Seas of blood.
> Oh Heav'n, I'de do what cannot be exprest!
> With raging Plagues I'de fill each Roman brest:
> Burn Palaces: like Thunder, I would rove,
> Tear the tall woods, and rend each Sacred Grove.
> But Oh! by pow'rful Fate I am confin'd
> And must not reak the madness of my mind [...]
> With my pale hand I stroak thy troubled sense;
> All poison Hell contains I do dispense [...]
> Go on, be mad. (IV.iv.11–18, 21–2, 29)

This 'meeting' of tyrants aligns the two and Caligula's anger and madness inspire Nero's:

> The forked tongues of Furyes can't express
> The rage that burns within me: Sulphur's less [...]
> Famine, Plagues combine;
> Your madness trebled cannot equal mine;
> All you faint emblems of my fury are;
> No tender Sex, nor age my wrath shall spare. (IV.iv.33–4, 41–4)

It is apparent that Nero has now succumbed to Mania, the most extreme of the four types of madness, with its attendant raging and fury.[31] From this point on, Nero takes on the characteristics of the more acutely or theatrically 'mad' character and begins to truly rave. When reports have reached the court that the French are ready to bring the war to the gates of Rome, Plautus says the emperour "laughs; slights them, and swears he'll hang 'em all" (V.ii.7).

Lee's fictionalised kings are transformed into tyrants when their feelings of omnipotence loosen the bonds of the moral and ethical restraints that define their virtue. As argued, the resulting 'madness' brings destruction to the state and, finally, to the tyrant himself. It is of note that at the end of both plays, the tyrants find themselves in the same state of helplessness which characterised their subjects. In the confusion and anxiety of his final hour, Nero turns to Petronius in vain for help: "Speak, my true friend; I'le be advis'd by you; / What more remains, in these extreams, to do?" (V.iii.210–11). After killing Clytus, Alexander also expresses, to his courtiers, a sense of helplessness: "O, you have undone me! / Excuse it not, you that cou'd stop a Lion, / Could not turn me; you shou'd have drawn your Swords, / And barr'd my rage with their advancing points; / Made Reason glitter in my dazl'd eyes [...]" (IV.i.526–31).

In *The Rival Queens* and *The Tragedy of Nero*, as madness is a metaphor for absolute power, Lee also likens the moral degeneracy stemming from perceived omnipotence to the slowly spreading contagion of syphilis – its causes, its symptoms and its treatment – in tropes of depravity, poison and burning. As venereal disease causes devastating debilitation of mind and body, unrestrained political power undermines the integrity not only of the present body politic but also, in a hereditary monarchy, its future. The term most commonly used for syphilis in the seventeenth century was 'Lues Venerea': 'lues' meaning 'pestilence' or 'corruption.' Contemporary medical treatises most frequently refer to the deceptive and polymorphic character of the disease:

> though there appear no Sign nor Symptom of a Disease for the present, yet it may be latent and lurking within the Body, many years, before it make any discovery of it self either in its own nature, or in the discuise of other Diseases.[32]

In a political analogy which Nathaniel Lee might have relished, Gideon Harvey declares that "the Pox is a Monarch, all other Diseases are its subjects."[33] It is, he says, "an universal Disease" which skips "like a Grashopper" from one part of the body to another: "From the part first attackt to the Liver, thence to the Brain [...] till it hath made an entry [...] upon the intire Manor of the Body [...] it's here there and every where."[34]

Syphilis continued to infect the population in epidemic proportions in seventeenth-century England, and popular treatises on syphilis proliferated after 1660. It had a tangible presence at Charles II's court. The disease afflicted (or was believed to have afflicted) several major figures. William Davenant was disfigured by it.[35] There were rumours about Prince Rupert; in January 1667 Pepys recounted that

> Prince Rupert is very bad still; and so bad, that he doth now yield to be trepan'd. It seems [...] it is a clap of the pox which he got about twelve year ago – and hath eaten to his head and come through his Scull; so his Scull must be opened and there is great fear of him.[36]

There were also rumours that James's mistress, the Countess of Southesk, had deliberately infected him with the pox.[37] Venereal disease was associated with profligate, illicit sex. Those who became infected were seen as having brought it upon themselves:

> By God's just judgment [the pox] hath assailed Mankind, not only in France, but in most parts of the World, as a scourge or punishment, to restrain the too wanton and lascivious lusts of impure Persons [...] The searing droplets of this cruel sickness fall on those who are hot with love and dirtied with lust; it is a punishment for their misdeeds and their shameful desires.[38]

Alexander's sexual promiscuity in *The Rival Queens* is linked to his degeneration and the spread of disease. In one of Lee's sources, *Plutarch's Lives*, Alexander is remembered as a man who controlled his sexual passions. According to Plutarch, Alexander's response to having Darius's women as captives in his camp was judicious: "Alexander, so it seems, thought it more worthy of a king to subdue his own passions than to conquer his enemies, and so he never came near these women."[39] Lee's Alexander, however, has little control over his sexual desires. Alexander has promised fidelity to his new wife, Statira, but on his way back to Babylon he allows himself to be seduced by his first wife, Roxana. The sexual betrayal will produce a bastard, and it is also the catalyst that eventually leads to the destruction of Statira and Alexander himself.

Alexander's inability to control his rapacious sexual appetite is invoked as a deadly weakness throughout the play by dependable characters, such as the loyal and honest Clytus: "O that a Face should thus bewitch a Soul / And ruine all that's right and reasonable" (I.i.56–7); "This comes of Love, and Women, 'tis all madness (II.i.405). For Clytus, Alexander's sexual compulsion "unmans" him and deprives him of distinction in combat, and in matters of state:

> Two Wives he takes, two Rival Queens disturb
> The Court; and while each hand do's beauty hold,
> Where is there room for glory? (I.i.67–9)

Lee's lines echo contemporary English satirical verse on both Charles II and Louis XIV. Two years before *The Rival Queens* was performed, Rochester's *Timon* refers to Louis XIV's two mistresses:

> We chanced to speak of the French king's success;
> My lady wondered much how heaven could bless
> A man that loved two women at one time,
> But more how he to them excused his crime. (57–60)[40]

Lee's lines also resonate with contemporary satire on Charles II, such as Rochester's lampoon:

> [...] he loves f---ing much.
> Nor are his high desires above his strength:
> His sceptre and his p---k are of a length,
> And she may sway the one who plays with t'other. (9–12)

And John Lacy's *Satire* from 1677: "Was ever prince's soul so meanly poor, / To be enslav'd to ev'ry little whore? (7–8). Gilbert Burnet confirms contemporary anxieties that Charles's immoderate sexual desires were, among other things, taking him away from important matters of state. Referring to rumours of the king's response to the Dutch fleet being in the river Medway in 1667, Burnet writes: "[...] it was given out, that he was very cheerful that night at supper with his mistresses, which drew many libels upon him, that were writ with as much wit as malice, and brought him under a general contempt. He was compared to Nero, who sung while Rome was burning."[41]

Like Charles II, Lee's Nero is seen to distance himself from the matters of state in favour of his sexual exploits: "Let phlegmatick Dull Kings, call Crowns their care: / Mine is my wanton [...] My Scepter, like a charming rod, shall raise Such sports" (I.ii.35). When Galba and other European powers are advancing toward Rome, Petronius makes a desperate plea for action from Nero. Nero responds as if to an insolent interruption: "Do you consult, while I my pleasures mind" (V. ii.46). Other degenerate rulers in the horror plays suffer from the same unruly passions which jeopardize the state. In William Joyner's *The Roman Empress* (King's 1670), as the emperor Valentius nears death and his crimes become clear, the loyal Statilius tells him, "'tis thought you were uxoriously / Subject to the ill government of women / Whose practises should ever be suspected" (Act V, p59). And in Lee's *Caesar Borgia* (Duke's 1679), Machiavel, frustrated with Borgia's obsession with Bellamira complains he must "rouze" his protégé:

> He is my Champion prince, Italian Tyrant,
> Not form'd to languish in a Womans arms.
> Oh --- 'tis a fault, were I so fram'd for greatness,
> E're I would amble in a Female Court [...]
> I would be Gibbetted i'th'Common-way. (I.i.206–9, 211)

Also like Charles II, Nero's frenzied sexual exploits bear no fruit; he has no children – no legitimate heirs. Alexander is similarly unable to spread his seed to produce legitimate offspring. His 'illicit' sexual relations with Roxana have impregnated her; but he has abandoned her as his wife, leaving his child illegitimate. Lee implies that the progeny of Alexander and Roxana's liaison is something debased when Alexander tells her:

> O that thou wert a man, that I might drive
> Thee round the world, and scatter thy Contagion,
> As Gods hurl mortal Plagues when they are angry. (V.i.195–7)

In *The Tragedy of Nero*, the protagonist's sexual depravity and the court's moral degeneracy are the source of the moral disease that spreads in ever-increasing circles. There are numerous references to Nero's diseased and debauched life, his corruption of innocence and his unnatural desires. His sexual assaults begin at home with the horrifying revelation of his mother's rape: "Monster of men, who alter'd nature's course, the stream ran backwards, and found out the Source" (I.i.147–8). In the larger arena of the court, vice and debauchery have become the norm. Men and women are terrified; Nero rapes and murders on a whim. By the second act, the court can no longer contain Nero's vices. Nero's pimp, Petronius, has had to go further afield – into the realm of the country – in order to find new flesh for Nero. There he finds the beautiful Poppea, Otho's wife. In Acts 2 and 3, Lee rapidly alternates the scenes between court and country to accentuate the emperor's sexual deviancy spreading from the court like a crippling venereal disease, threatening to destroy the moral fibre of the whole country. The 'golden Circle' of the court becomes 'a fatal Circle [...] it carries poison [...] [and] a thousand Devils [...] tempting innocence" (II.ii.20–22). The action climaxes in the middle of the play – Act 3, scene 3 – when the emperor himself enters the realm of the country and consummates the relationship with Poppea. Once she has been seduced, Poppea herself becomes diseased. Her words are "pesilent, the blasting issue / Of a corrupted heart, diseas'd and deadly" (III.ii.55–6). Like an uncontrollable epidemic, the contagion continues to spread as Poppea, in her turn, lusts after Britannicus:

> [...] Just Heav'n has sent
> On my inconstancy this punishment [...]
> My blood boils high, and beats with strange desires:
> 'Tis just that madness mingle with such fires. (IV.i.107–8, 111–12)

Poppea then goes further and tries to seduce her own brother, Piso, when he approaches her in disguise:

> Oh pow'r of Love! his words my Soul invade!
> Sure 'tis some GOD, delighting in a shade:
> The Glories of his eyes [...]
> charm my wounded sight [...]
> Since I am made the Empress of the World,
> Since all's my choice, why do I doubtful stand,
> And wish a pleasure which I may command? (V.iii.18–20, 21, 23–5)

Lee's idea of moral degeneracy – a corrupting disease opening itself up into wider and wider circles, infecting innocent parties or generations – fits in with contemporary understanding of syphilitic infection. William Clowes refers to a girl "who was greatly infected with this sicknesse in many parts of hir body [and who] received the infection, either from the parents [...] or else [...] by sucking the corrupt milke of some infected nurse"; and Marchamont Nedham discusses "Hereditary Propagation" of the disease.[42] Interestingly, the imagery inherent in the sixteenth- and seventeenth-century tracts on the contagion changes very little into the nineteenth century. According to the *Annales d'hygiene publique* (1841), hereditary syphilis was

> slowly and surreptitiously sapping the strength of succeeding generations [...] It attacks the very essence of life, poisoning it at the source and grinding down the spirits. The more it infects individuals, the more it poisons families, the more it insinuates itself into the masses, the more it brings about the degradation and degeneration of the human race.[43]

This vivid description of hereditary syphilis echoes the tropes of madness, venereal disease and poison which Lee employs to give expression to his vision of the repercussive effects of despotism. Poison unites the sexual and degenerate elements of physical and mental breakdown in these plays. Once in the body, poison spreads rapidly and prodigiously: a prelude to death by arsenic poisoning is madness. Arsenic was also commonly used to treat syphilis. Associations between poison, blood and madness were well established by the time of the Restoration. Thomas Willis reports "the taking of some poisons, are wont to stir up Madness."[44] Robert Bayfield and other writers promote the use of bleedings and leeches (to extract the 'poison' in the blood) as part of a cure for madness.[45]

In medical treatises and in literary works, poison was conflated with the venom of a snake, which in turn was a common metonym for venereal disease.[46] Lee's contemporaries Marchamont Nedham, Gideon Harvey and Richard Wiseman, who wrote treatises on syphilis, all refer frequently to its "venom."[47] In their work the disease is characteristically seen as corruptive and cunning. Nedham writes, "this Infection many times steals into the Body, and [...] silently it may lodg there, without any manifestation of its Venom in the person." He refers to "this Serpentine Evil," which "hath twined it self with our corrupted Nature" stinging "many to death invisibly, and poysons the rest of the world with new Ferments."[48]

The association of poison and syphilis was echoed in literature by images of syphilitic poison and corruption. Edmund Spenser calls it a 'foule euill [...] [t]hat rotts the marrow and consumes the braine." Erasmus argues "the condition of the body [infected with syphilis] has its effect on mental power. Undeniably, this disease usually depletes whatever brains a man has. So it comes about that rulers of states may be men who are healthy neither in body nor mind."[49] Shakespeare uses the metaphor of the serpent for syphilis and its poisonous effects.[50] And he, along with many Jacobean playwrights, uses images of syphilitic decay, disease and degeneration to mask hidden corruption. *Hamlet*, *2 Henry IV* and *The Revenger's Tragedy* all contain images of "rank diseases" poisoning and corrupting the body from the inside out; while others, like Thomas Dekker, deal more specifically with "[t]he Harlots poyson" (*The Honest Whore* III.ii.41–2).[51] In *Sylva Sylvarum*, Francis Bacon refers to "the venom of the French pox,"[52] and John Donne writes of the "serpentine crawling and insinuation" of the pox.[53] In the later seventeenth century, John Milton uses syphilitic metaphors for corruption. In *Defensio Secunda* he sees his adversary Alexander More as a "most wanton creature, whose very breath, befouled by venereal corruption, every pure man would shun" (647–8). In *The Ready and Easy Way to Establish a Free Commonwealth*, he refers to supporters of the established church as "new fanatics of not the preaching but the sweating-tub, inspir'd with nothing holier then the Venereal pox" (453).[54] The Earl of Rochester often makes political use of the metaphor, as in *On the Women about Town*, when diseased (in this case, Irish) women "invade" Charles's court: "They carry a fate which no man can oppose: / The loss of his heart and the fall of his nose" (9–10).[55] Although the political messages of these writers differ, Nathaniel Lee chose his metaphors of degeneration specifically to take part in this long-term and ongoing discourse on syphilis and corruption.[56]

In both *The Rival Queens* and *The Tragedy of Nero*, characters are killed by poison. But poison in this case can be understood to mean not only 'venom' but also moral corruption. Exploiting their tyrannical power, the kings become sexual predators; and the poison causing their deaths can be read as a metaphor for the syphilitic contagion associated with licentiousness, which ultimately leads to madness and death. Thus the temptations of supreme power lure the kings into depravity and, ultimately, to destruction. Some evidence for this interpretation can be gathered from the addition of "burning" to the poison-syphilis-madness paradigm. Burning was slang for syphilitic infection in the Elizabethan and Restoration periods, but as early as the mid-sixteenth century, the disease was already being compared to "an occult flame."[57] Burning evokes images of the punishments of Hell and a (guilty) soul in torment as well as describing the hideous pain of death by poison. In *The Rival Queens*, Alexander is assassinated with poison. The conspirator Cassander describes its effect in detail:

> O we shall have him tear [...]
> The world to Atoms; for it scatters pains
> All sorts, and through all nerves, veins, arteries,
> Even with extremity of frost it burns;
> Drives the distracted Soul about her house. (IV.i.256, 258–61)

When Alexander begins to feel the effects, there is a frenzy of burning:

> O I am shot, a forked burning Arrow
> Sticks cross my shoulders, the sad Venom flies
> Like Lightning through my flesh, my blood, my marrow [...]
> I am all Hell, I burn, I burn again [...]
> My vital Spirits are quite parch'd, burnt up,
> All my smoaky Entrails turn'd to ashes. (V.i.315–17, 325, 356–7)

In *The Tragedy of Nero*, the most fascinating example of the paradigm occurs between Acts 4 and 5. At the end of Act 4, when the ghost of Caligula visits Nero "[f]rom the Infernal cave" (IV.i.1), he says he will dispense "[a]ll poison Hell contains" (IV.i.22) to aid Nero in the destruction of Rome. Nero responds to the imagery:

> Nothing but flames can quench my kindled Ire:
> Blood's not enough; Fire I'le revenge with fire.
> Fierce as young Phaeton I will return:
> Great ROME, the World's Metropolis, shall burn. (IV.iv.55–8)

Lee collocates all the images in these parallel scenes: the next act opens with Britannicus, the true prince of the blood, in his death throes. Already a victim of Nero's moral corruption, he is finally poisoned on Nero's orders.

> Fire, fire, I'm all one flame, fly, my friends fly,
> Or I shall blast you; O my breath is Brimstone
> My Lungs are Sulphur, my hot brains boil over [...]
> I burn, I burn. (V.i.1–3, 7)

As a group, Lee's kings are boastful, egocentric, self-serving, ineffectual and corrupt. In both *The Tragedy of Nero* and *The Rival Queens*, it is the equation of royalty with the sublime that sparks off the fatal stage of the kings' corruption. It is only when the kings – in a frenzy of madness – covet and reach for God's (absolute) power, that they lose all control. Yet, once again, the point that Lee (and others writing in the genre) emphasise is that the greatest danger to the state comes not from the failings of individual rulers but from sovereignty itself, when the crown is a metonym for omnipotence. By 1674, when *The Tragedy of Nero* was produced, sweeping powers were ceded to the king:

> Charles was restored without conditions; he was protected against seditious talk by a special treason act; he was given absolute control over all the armed forces; his judges often considered themselves merely the mouthpieces of the royal will; he was empowered by statute to remodel corporations[...] Still more, the Test Act of 1673 and the Act of 1678 imposed a state religion, for a political purpose and by secular penalties; with this cement Charles established an impregnable power.[58]

Although Charles's power was limited by parliament, during the 1670s he was still able to silence opposition and rule on his own, much as his father had:[59]

> Until 1679 Charles did not suspend parliaments themselves, but new parliaments. In their place he created the second 'Long Parliament' of the century, and managed it by adjournments and (particularly) prorogations. By these means, from 1673 to 1678, parliament was kept in being but largely out of session.[60]

Under the patriarchal system, obedience by subjects is implicit. Subjects must obey all royal commands, whether or not they countermand divine laws such as 'thou shalt not kill.' According to proponents of Divine Right, such as Robert Filmer, subjects have no recourse to any other authority:

> The prince, whom you may justly call the Father of the country, ought to be to every man dearer and more reverend than any Father, as one ordained and sent unto us by God. The subject is never to be suffered to attempt anything against the prince, how naughty and cruel soever he be.[61]

The king's motives cannot be questioned; the absolute ruler is answerable only to God, and only God can judge him. When Nero plans to kill Agrippina – and threatens the life of his wife Octavia as she tries to intervene – Britannicus protests vehemently: "Tyrant, this must not be, while I draw breath" (I.i.100). But Britannicus backs down almost immediately from challenging Nero's paramountcy: "When e're I rise against that Sacred head / In thought, may loads of Thunder strike me dead / You are my Master, and Rome's Emperour" (I.i.107–9). Nero commands his courtiers Drusillus and Otho, against their will, to kill Agrippina. When Otho returns with the body he imputes blame for the murder to Nero: "She is, as you would have her" (I.ii.1).

Lee shows how such a system, under a degenerate ruler who *is* the law, can be tantamount to slavery for the subjects. It does not matter how the subjects –

be they opponents or supporters – respond to their circumstances; their fates are determined solely by the will of the king. Punishment and reward alike are arbitrary. The most honest and trustworthy followers, such as Clytus and Britannicus, die simply because they are victims of moments of sudden anger. As he stabs Clytus, Alexander declares "let bold Subjects learn by thy sad Fate, / To tempt the patience of a man above 'em" (IV.i.500–501). Obedience is unquestioned, most often passive and the result of fear of reprisal. In their attempts to protest against egregious commands, the subjects resort to flattering the kings, appealing to their better natures or extolling their reputations for justice, but all pleas are futile. Similarly, any covert threats to rebellion are empty. Nero's guard Drusillus responds with horror to Nero's exploits and declares "some noble Roman should dare to be glorious, dangerously good / And kill this Tyrant" (II.i.17–8). Yet Drusillus remains loyal to Nero. When Galba's army approaches he pleads with Nero: "fly Sacred Sir, you'r lost" (V. iii.198).

The doctrine of Divine Right presupposes the king to be the moral and political bedrock of the family and the state: he is expected to be just: to guide, direct and protect. But, if we look at the microcosm of the family that Lee creates, Nero and Alexander represent the antithesis of model patriarchs. Nero uses his position in the hierarchy not to protect and guide his family but to abuse and destroy it. He begins with the sexual abuse and murder of his own mother and continues with the destruction of his wife and his obsessive sexual desires for new mistresses. Although less pathologically sexual, Alexander is no more a model family head. His 'family' consists of two wives: the one he despises is carrying his child. He denies his real father's existence, and he murders his 'stepfather' Clytus. Because both Nero and Alexander's fathers are dead before the plays begin, Clytus and Seneca appear as the only 'father-figures' in the plays. But the important balance their wisdom and guidance as patriarchs should provide is completely disregarded – if not disdained – by Alexander and Nero.

Both the rulers' incapacity to deal effectively and judiciously in personal matters extends to their failure to dispense justice in the state. When Alexander dies, he bequeaths his empire "to him that is most worthy" (V.i.371). But a quick sweep of the remaining candidates gives no reason to believe that the next king will be any more just or competent. Lysimachus is the frontrunner to the throne. But, like Alexander, although he is brave he has also shown himself to be distracted by love, irrational and foolhardy. Even at the end of the play he remains blind to Alexander's degeneration, insisting on referring to Alexander as "the [...] best of Kings" (V.i.387). He has been so inculcated into the doctrine of Divine Right of Kings that there is little question that he will repeat the pattern when he himself assumes the office.

As other horror dramatists do, Lee poses the question: if a head of state is mad, corrupt, or unjust, from where can the people search out and find justice? The absence of justice is remarked upon several times in *The Tragedy of Nero*: "Justice is robb'd, her sword and scales you move; / Sweet Mercy starts, and, shrinking, flyes above" (I.i.77–8); "where is Astrea fled? / Foul vice Triumphs, trampling on Virtues head" (II.iii.90–91); "Honour is stabb'd, and all the Virtues bleed" (IV.i.16). Britannicus calls out in vain for justice: "Gods! Gods! but they are deaf, or will not hear" (II.iii.153). And, although Nero does eventually die, the pattern of man-god-tyrant is clearly set up to repeat itself when his conqueror is hoisted on the shoulders of the people, as the new ruler, and "made a God." In *The Rival Queens*, the conspirators and regicides see their aim realised, and, in an ironic subversion of justice, they escape punishment. Roxana also gains her freedom and goes unpunished after murdering the innocent Statira.

In an absolute monarchy, the administration of justice is reliant on the virtue of the monarch bolstered by the sanctity of his vows to protect and care for his people. Subjects are expected to give allegiance to the king, and in his 'God-given' role, the king in return is expected to dispense 'perfect' justice as if it is coming straight from God. But rulers are human and, when handed supreme power, even the 'best' of them can over time be drawn into a delusional certainty of their own omnipotence to the extent that they, like madmen, lose rational control of their emotions and moral standards and become derelict in their duties to their subjects. Thus, in the horror plays, the chaos in the state is depicted as not only emanating from within the hierarchy in power but also from the very top of that hierarchy: the absolutist kings have no accountability to their subjects, and justice is lost.

When the viability of justice is contingent on both parties keeping their vows then the sanctity of oaths is paramount. In these plays, oaths are not kept; there is a proliferation of meaningless vows; threats and promises are as profuse as they are empty. Neither Alexander nor Nero keeps to their marriage vows, nor do they keep their oaths as patriarchs to protect their families and subjects. Statira's oath never to see Alexander again (II.i.346–9) holds no more meaning than Alexander's vow, to his physicians, that he will make them "Kings" if they save Statira's life (V.i.137). Word meanings are arbitrary. To Nero "[v]irtue is a name; Religion is a thing" (I.ii.31) and "[v]irtue is the greatest crime" (IV.i.80). Critics routinely pinpoint rant and bombast in the horror plays as evidence of the poor quality of the writing. As argued in Chapter 1, there is a case that can be made that the use of rant and bombast was appropriate and deliberate – an extension of the fatuity of solemn words. Nero, after Poppea's death, rants "[i]f she were dead, I would restore her breath, / And she should live, / Spight of her self, spight of the Gods, and Death" (V.iii.186–8). When Roxana kills Statira, Alexander declares:

> [...] thank Statira that thou art alive;
> Else thou hadst perish'd; yes, I wou'd ha' rent
> With my just hands that Rock, that Marble heart;
> I wou'd have div'd through Seas of bloud to find it, To tear the
> cruel Quarry from its Center. (V.i.182–6)

These phrases are as absurd as they are empty; and the self-deluding statements of the mad rulers match the laudatory but hypocritical words of the subjects. The courtiers, for example, use bombastic language when addressing the rulers – "dread

Sir," "Sacred head," "son of Jupiter" – even though they despise them and secretly hope for a rebellion.

One insight into Lee's use of false praise can be found in the drama of Seneca. Gordon Braden contends that Seneca's aphorisms on *imperium* provide a central message that "power is the unanswerable fact in human dealings, more fundamental even than truth." Braden goes on to argue that

> [t]he tyrant knows that the adulation he receives does not mean what it says, but the very discrepancy confirms the real and satisfactory content of such praise: his ability to command it. Absolute power inserts itself between words and their significations and rewrites them as their opposites.[62]

It is an expression of the ruler's might that he can force his subjects to utter false and empty words. He can compel a coded language in which what is said is not what is meant, knowing that there is hypocrisy on both sides of what is essentially a duologue. This perverse expression of power, which produces a level of pleasure or satisfaction in the autocratic ruler, is equally evident in Lee's depiction of his mad kings. In Lee's plays the covenant between the absolute king and his subjects has been broken, and the result is disorder and dislocation. For Lee,at a time when the parliament was "kept in being but largely out of session," the vacuity of the words can also be seen as a symptom of that breakdown.

Hyperbole is integral to the language of the horror plays: its extravagance matching the violent overstatement of the theatrical spectacle. Further, to historians of post-traumatic writing such as Dominick LaCapra, hyperbole is a stylistic tool that enacts the fact that one is affected by excess and trauma. LaCapra speaks of the "thought-provoking and fruitful role of hyperbole in emphasizing what one believes is given insufficient weight [...] in the ongoing attempt to articulate possibilities in a discipline or in the broader culture" after traumatic events.[63] The combination of empty but grandiose rhetoric and extreme physical spectacle in these plays generates an overwhelmingly violent theatricality that plays out as an inexorable repetition of corruption and defeat.

The kings of the horror plays commit criminal acts. Like 'lunatics' under law, they appear as a special class of criminal. Their positions of limitless power, like their madness, allow them to destroy rather than protect, to arouse fear rather than provide safety, to murder rather than nurture. Unlike the lustful tyrants of the heroic plays, the deaths of these criminals do not provide a new beginning for the remaining characters in the play. The criminal rulers do not represent 'one bad seed' in a society that will restore itself after the tyrant's death. The disease and madness of the criminal rulers comprehensively destroy the healthy state; but, more disturbingly, they leave behind the legacy of the same diseased system which endorsed them.

Endnotes

[1]   Other examples of degenerate rulers in the horror plays include the kings in Thomas Otway's *Don Carlos*, William Joyner's *The Roman Empress*, Rochester's *Vallentinian* and Lee's *Mithridates* as well as Borgia in Lee's *Caesar Borgia* and Augustus Caesar in Lee's *Gloriana*. Chapters 5 and 6 will further analyse these kings and their degeneracy.

[2]   *The London Stage* 205–6.

[3]   *The Works of Nathaniel Lee*, ed. Stroup and Cooke 213. Also see note 55 in Chapter 1 of this book.

[4]   *Miscellanea aurea: or, The golden medley* (London, 1720) 37–8. Quoted in Ham 74. The epistolary essays were written by several people, but "chiefly by T. Killigrew."

[5]   Richard Napier in Michael MacDonald, *Mystical Bedlam* (Cambridge: CUP, 1981) 7.

[6]   W. Cobbett, *The Parliamentary History of England*, vol. 16 (London, 1813) 665.

[7]   The handful of tracts that comment on Divine Right, printed in the mid-1670s, have as their main focus popish and Episcopal concerns. They include Robert Sanderson's *Episcopacy as established by law in England not prejudicial to regal power* (London, 1673); Peter Walsh's *The third and fourth of The controversial letters or, Grand controversie, concerning the pretended temporal authority of popes over the whole earth* (London, 1673) and *The eleventh and twelfth of The controversial letters ...* (London, 1674).

[8]   K.H.D. Haley, *Politics in the Reign of Charles II* (Oxford: Blackwell, 1985) 4.

[9]   K.H.D. Haley, *The First Earl of Shaftesbury* (Oxford: Clarendon, 1968) 360.

[10]   Robert Bayfield, *A Treatise de Morborum Capitis Essentiis & Prognosticis* (London, 1663) 32–3.

[11]   Bayfield 36; William Drage, *A Physical Nosomony* (London, 1665) 64.

[12]   Drage 64; Bayfield, 39; Thomas Willis, *Two Discourses concerning the soul of brutes* (London, 1683) 188. A Latin edition of Willis's work appeared in 1672.

[13]   Thomas Tryon, *A Discourse of the Causes, Natures and Cure of Phrensie, Madness or Distraction* (London, 1689) 250.

[14]   MacDonald 123.

[15]   Willis 201.

[16]   Michael Dalton, *The Countrey Justice* (London, 1666) 243.

[17]   John Strype *A survey of the cities of London and Westminster ... Written at first by John Stow ... Corrected, improved, and very much enlarged ... to the present time; by John Strype*, 2 vols. (London, 1720). Quoted in Richard Hunter and Ida Macalpine, eds., *Three Hundred Years of Psychiatry* (London: OUP, 1963) 308.

[18]   Willis 208.

[19]   William Wycherley, *The Complete Works of William Wycherley*, ed. Montague Summers, vol. 3 (New York: Russell & Russell, Inc., 1964) 233–7.

[20]   Bayfield 41.

[21]   Hunter and Mcalpine 200.

[22]   Michel Foucault argues that in the nineteenth century, "the initial model of madness would be to believe oneself to be God, while for the preceding centuries it had been to deny God" (*Madness and Civilization*, trans. Richard Howard [New York: Pantheon, 1965] 264).

[23]   *The Works of Nathaniel Lee*, ed. Stroup and Cooke. All references to *The Rival Queens* are from Stroup and Cooke's edition, vol. 1, and are hereafter cited parenthetically in the text.

[24]   Plutarch, *The Age of Alexander*, ed. Ian Scott-Kilvert (Hamondsworth: Penguin, 1973).

[25]   Willis 203–5.

[26]   Tryon 256.

[27]   Spurr 8.

[28]   Propaganda by the French Crown regularly linked "Louis le Grand" with the historical, heroic "Alexander the Great." The epistle to the King in Racine's play *Alexandre le Grand* makes flattering references to the similarities between the two men. Charles le Brun's series of paintings on Alexander were similarly created to glorify Louis: "the Crown had the paintings engraved for inclusion in the state-financed Cabinet du Roi volumes, and sent them throughout the world to advertise the greatness and rightness of the reign of Louis le Grand" (Donald Posner, "Charles Lebrun's Triumphs of Alexander" *The Art Bulletin* 41 [1959]: 244–5). This propaganda was not unknown in England. John Locke's journal of 1677, for example, refers to the king as "Lewis le Grand."

[29]   Burnet, *Bishop Burnet's history of his own time* 1:609.

[30]   Henry Foulis is another writer who utilises the analogy, primarily as anti-Catholic propaganda:

> Many of the ancient Heathens, as Caligula, Commodus, Heliogabalus, nay the Physitian Menecrates, prided themselves not a little, in being held and accounted to be Gods by the people, and so to be sacrificed to: Hence the Emperour Domitian used to Stile himself (a) Lord and God: […] This Caligula used to threaten the Air if it rained upon his sports, as Xerxes would have the Seas whipt, because not presently calm at his command; as if they were related to the King of Catona, who swears at his Coronation, that during his Reign, it shall not rain unseasonably, neither shall there be Pestilence or Famine […]'Tis pretty to observe with what Thundring and Impertinent Titles some of the petit Kings in Asia and other places do attribute to themselves, as if they were Lords of the Sun and Moon, terrible to those who never heard of them; and though their Dominions be but of small extent, yet would grudge not to be thought Gods, and Conquerours of the whole world […] At these and such like extravagances we are apt to smile, and to censure not onely as foolish but profane, and pitty the ignorance and credulity of such Pagan Fondlings; and yet in the mean time, those who account themselves the onely Christians are too guilty of the same folly." (Henry Foulis *The History of Romish Treasons and Usurpations ...* [London, 1671]: 1–2)

[31]   It was proverbial in the sixteenth and seventeenth centuries that anger itself was a form of madness: "Wrath and Madnesse they say be all one" [Morris Palmer Tilley, *A Dictionary of the Proverbs in England* (Ann Arbor: U of Michigan, 1950) 14]. Robert Burton writes, "there is no difference betwixt a mad man, and an angry man, in the time of his fit" (*The Anatomy of Melancholy*, ed. Thomas C. Faulkner, Nicolas K. Kiessling, Rhonda L. Blair, vol. 1 [Oxford: Clarendon, 1989] 2.3.9).

[32]   Marchamont Nedham, *Medela Medicinae* (London, 1665) 63.

[33]   Gideon Harvey, *Little Venus Unmask'd* (London, 1670) 27.

[34]   Harvey, *Little Venus* 25–6; Gideon Harvey *Great Venus Unmasked*, 2nd ed. (London, 1672) 33–4.

[35]   John Aubrey, *Aubrey's Brief Lives*, ed. Oliver Lawson Dick (London: Secker and Warburg, 1949) 86.

[36]   Pepys 8:34–5. See also Pepys 8:40–41 and 6:12.

[37] See *POAS* IV:203, 236–7; Pepys 9:154–5.

[38] John Harris, *The Divine Physician* (London, 1676) 34; Jean- Baptiste Lalli, "La Franceide ou le Mal francais, poeme burlesque" (translated into French from the Italian, original edition, 1629).

[39] Plutarch, *The Age of Alexander* 256–7 (section 21).

[40] The reference to Rochester's *Timon* (1674) is taken from *The Complete Poems of John Wilmot*, ed. Vieth 67.

[41] Burnet, *Bishop Burnet's history of his own time* 1:458. See also Pepys 8:282 and 8:286.

[42] William Clowes, *A brief and Necessary Treatise ...* . (London, 1596) 151; Nedham, *Medela Medicinae* 62, 168.

[43] *Annales d'hygiene publique* (Paris, 1841) xv. Quoted in Claude Quetel, *History of Syphilis*, trans. Judith Braddock and Brian Pike (Cambridge: Polity, 1990) 166–7.

[44] Willis 204.

[45] Madness itself is also referred to as 'poison' in Bayfield 49.

[46] The first published account of syphilis in 1497 by Ruy Diaz de Isla is entitled *Tractado contra el Mal Serpentina (Treatise Against the Evil Snake)*. Early writers such as Girolamo Fracastoro discuss how the infection "passes through all the veins, and poisons the juices of the body" (Girolamo Fracastoro, *Fracastor*, trans. Heneage Wynne-Finch [London: William Heinemann, 1935] 1:81). (This poem was translated by Nahum Tate in 1686.) In 1548 Jean Fernel compared the disease to "the poison of a scorpion or a rabid dog [that] spreads imperceptibly throughout the whole body from the first part to be infected" (*Joannis Fernelu ... de Abditis rerum causis* [Paris, 1548]).

[47] Nedham, *Medela Medicinae*; Harvey, *Little Venus*; Richard Wiseman, *Several Chirurgicall Treatises* (London, 1676).

[48] Nedham, *Medela Medicinae* 74, 84, 171–2.

[49] Edmund Spenser *The Faerie Queene*, ed. A.C. Hamilton (London: Longman, 2001) I: iv: 26:7–8; "A Marriage in Name Only" *The Colloquies of Erasmus*, trans. Craig R. Thompson (Chicago: U of Chicago P, 1965) 147.

[50] See G.W. Bentley, *Shakespeare and the New Disease: The Dramatic Function of Syphilis in Troilus and Cressida, Measure for Measure and Timon of Athens*, diss., U of California, Davis, 1985.

[51] *The Dramatic Works of Thomas Dekker*, ed. Bowers vol. 2.

[52] Francis Bacon, *The Works of Francis Bacon*, ed. J. Spedding, R.L. Ellis, and D.D. Heath, vol. 2 (Edinburgh 1857–74) 439.

[53] John Donne, *Paradoxes and Problems* "Why Doth the Poxe so Much Affect to Undermine the Nose?" *Complete Poetry and Selected Prose*, ed. John Hayward (London: Nonesuch, 1962) 352.

[54] *Complete Prose Works of John Milton*, ed. Wolfe. All references to *The Readie and Easie Way to Establish a Free Commonwealth* are from Wolfe's edition, vol. 7, and are hereafter cited parenthetically in the text; all references to *Defensio Secunda* are from Wolfe's edition, vol. 5, and are hereafter cited parenthetically in the text. According to translator Donald A. Roberts, More, a clergyman of the Reformed Church, was the editor/ publisher of the anonymous libel to which Milton refers, although it was most likely written by Anglican priest Pierre du Moulin. See Raymond A. Anselment, "Seventeenth-Century Pox" *The Seventeenth Century* 4 (1989): 197.

The Horror Plays of the English Restoration

55 *The Complete Poems of John Wilmot*, ed. Vieth 47.

56 Again, although the periods and their politics (and the politics of medicine) differ, Jonathan Swift and William Hogarth are only two examples of writers who carry the discourse into the eighteenth century. In Hogarth's *A Harlot's Progress*, disturbing images of venereal infection are used satirically as a symbol of wider social corruption. In poems such as *A Beautiful Young Nymph Going to Bed* and *The Lady's Dressing Room*, Swift's 'heroines' Corinna and Celia paint over their physical corruption ("begumm'd, bematter'd, and beslim'd"), which is itself a mark of their moral corruption. For Swift the prostitute embodies moral corruption, but she is only a symptom of what is wrong with society. In France, 'political pornography' produced in tracts against Marie Antoinette and others overtly suggests "sexual degeneration went hand in hand with political corruption" (see Lynn Hunt, ed., "The Many Bodies of Marie Antoinette," *Eroticism and the Body Politic* [Baltimore: Johns Hopkins UP, 1991] 119).

57 Leonardus Botallus, *Luis Venereae Curandi Ratio*, in Luigi Luigini *De Morbo Gallico ...*, 2 vols. (Venice, 1566–67).

58 David Ogg, *England in the Reign of Charles II*, 2nd ed., vol. 2 (Oxford: Clarendon, 1955) 745–6.

59 Contemporaries used the terms 'limited' and 'mixed' monarchy in describing the constitution that supported Charles. (K.H.D. Haley quotes Andrew Marvell: "unlike other countries, England had only a limited monarchy" [Haley, *Shaftesbury* 438]).

60 Scott, *England's Troubles* 177. Scott offers more examples of contemporary concern over the prorogations – pamphlets, he says, that "both echoed the parliamentary arguments of the first crisis of parliaments, and anticipated those of the next" – i.e., *Letter from a Parliamentman to his Friend* (1675), *The Long Parliament Dissolved* (1676) and *The Debates of Arguments for Dissolving this Present Parliament* (1676). See also "On the Prorogation," *POAS* 179–84.

61 *The Necessity of The Absolute Power of all KINGS: And in particular of the King of England by John Bodin* (London, 1648), Sir Robert Filmer, *Patriarcha and Other Political Works of Sir Robert Filmer*, ed. Peter Laslett (Oxford: Basil Blackwell, 1949) 325. Filmer's essay consists entirely of extracts from Jean Bodin's *Republique*. The *Republique* had been a textbook at English universities since 1606 (Louis Teeter, "The Dramatic Use of Hobbes's Political Ideas" *English Literary History* 3 [1936] 154).

62 Braden, *Renaissance Tragedy and the Senecan Tradition* 30–31.

63 LaCapra 35.

Chapter 5
Patrilineal Discord:
Nathaniel Lee and John Dryden's *Oedipus* and Thomas Otway's *Don Carlos*

The bond of kinship was the cornerstone of societal unity in seventeenth-century England; it was the basis from which people established their status in the community. If a person was so disaffected that he could not name his mother or father, he could be proven to be a lunatic. "To indicate that a lunatic was insensible, one might note that he did not know his family or 'friends.'"[1] People who sought to menace the harmony of their family or cause harm to kin were seen to be undermining their own best interests and were thus considered irrational.

> English laymen thought that the stark Bedlam madman was dangerous, inclined to murder and assault, arson and vandalism. Unlike a criminal, however, he could reap no conceivable benefit from his violence, because he threatened or attacked people and property that were essential aspects of his own social identity.[2]

The higher up in the social hierarchy, the more far-reaching were the consequences of family discord: in royal kinship groups, intra-family strife might well have political consequences for the whole nation, especially if it involved the issues of religious affiliation or succession. At the very least, loyalty to the crown might falter in the face of a house divided against itself.[3]

In the horror plays, violent family discord is a key recurring motif. As is the case in the two previous chapters, family unity is under siege because of the moral turpitude of the parents, who are also, importantly, the rulers of the state. This breakdown from the 'top' affects every family member. The normal development of sons and daughters is perverted, because the father's traditional role as paternal guardian is defiled by incestuous lust and jealousy. The heads of the families are shown as morally weak; they act against their own children: those who trust them the most, and who are least able to defend themselves. Incest is portrayed as an act of supreme selfishness, admixed with cupidity and a remorseless drive for possession, which overcomes all normal barriers of moral and social inhibition. The results are estrangement and displacement within the family and a profound sense of loss. Although the deleterious consequences of their actions ultimately affect the safety and the social structure of the state, the corruption of their paternal prerogative into incestuous control is played out in the microcosm of the family.

In *Incest, Drama and Nature's Laws*, Richard McCabe contends that incest in Renaissance and Restoration drama functions "as a political and social metaphor rather than as an imagined potential sphere of human relations [...] Regarded as the ultimate breach of natural law, incest becomes a powerful metaphor for other forms of social or political corruption."[4] A notorious example of the incest taboo being used not as a metaphor but as a political ploy was Henry VIII's redefinition in 1534 of statutes prohibiting incest. Citing biblical validation, Henry succeeded in his efforts to annul his marriage to Anne Boleyn. The new statutes were based on the biblical verses in Leviticus 18:6–18 and, styled in the same rhetoric, interdicted against relationships not only between those tied by blood but also by marriage:

> [...] that is to say, the Son to marry the Mother, or the Stepmother, the Brother the Sister, the Father his Son's Daughter or Daughter's Daughter, or the Son to marry the Daughter of his Father procreate and born by his Stepmother, or the Son to marry his Aunt, [...] or to marry his Uncle's Wife, or the Father to marry his Son's Wife, or the Brother to marry his Brother's Wife, or any Man to marry his Wife's Daughter, or his Wife's Son's Daughter, or his Wife's Daughter's Daughter, or his Wife's Sister.[5]

Catherine had been married to Henry's older brother, Arthur. Under the new statutes, Henry's marriage to "his Brother's Wife" was incestuous, thus illegal. These statutes eventually led to incest being considered a crime in England, but it was not until the Commonwealth that parliament first designated incest as a criminal offence punishable by the secular magistrate.

In *Monarchy and Incest in Renaissance England*, Bruce Thomas Boehrer cites these laws and argues that Henry's assertion of patriarchal prerogative focuses on sexual control of the royal family. Henry alters the social significance of his wives by "wrapping them in a thick gauze of incestuous narrative; he told stories about them that authorized particular kinds of action – demoting one wife [...] promoting another [and that] Henry's heirs, and their heirs in turn, wrote family fictions to countervail and absorb the ones that Henry had written before them." Thus, he says, the monarchy since that time was never free from its own desperate attempts to prove itself legitimate: "the subject [of incest] surfaces repeatedly in royal strategies of self-promotion and self-legitimation [...] because the incest prohibition serves as a highly flexible, extremely powerful political tool – authorizing particular alliances, prohibiting others [...]."[6] Incest subsequently emerges as a noteworthy structural motif in many literary texts. Associated with the vices and aspirations of the upper classes, these works, from Henry's time forward, concern themselves with and parallel "the social arrangements and anxieties of English royal absolutism in the early modern periods."[7]

The motif of incest as an expression of paternal absolutism and corruption is established in a great deal of sixteenth- and seventeenth-century literature. In *Shakespeare's Darker Purpose*, Mark Taylor argues that "Shakespearean fathers dread no circumstance more than the loss, to other men and to maturity, of the daughters whom they desire for themselves." The desire "expresses itself in very strange behaviour – in acts that are arbitrary, selfish [...] cruel." Of course these incestuous feelings are not always overt but "manifest themselves through sublimations, compensations, and displacements."[8] John Milton employs the incest motif to express his fears of arbitrary government. *Eikonoklastes* is Milton's attempt to break down the icon of Charles I as martyr, created in *Eikon Basilike*, and replace it with the image of Charles as tyrant. Milton compares Charles to Roman autocrats such as Nero, Domitian and Caligula in order to set up an historical pattern of tyranny to which Charles falls heir. In Milton's central image of incest, Charles is depicted as having sex with his mother, the parliament. It is an expression of the anxieties of absolute rule and political ambition:

> And if it hath bin anciently interpreted the presaging signe of a future Tyrant, but to dream of copulation with his Mother, what can it be less then actual Tyranny to affirme waking, that the Parlament, which is his Mother, can neither conceive or bring forth *any autoritative Act* without his Masculine coition: [...] What other notions but these, or such like, could swell up *Caligula* to think himself a God? (XI: 467)

As with Nathaniel Lee's plays, self-love and the overrating of oneself – inevitable results of absolute monarchy – lead to degenerate, in this case incestuous, acts. For Milton, this is an inevitable consequence when a king expresses "contempt and disdain for the subjects who originally empowered him." Incest then develops as "a figural equivalent for the set of political attitudes that includes divine-right proprietarism, royal paternalism, and patriarchal absolutism."[9]

Satirists of the 1670s take up Milton's mantle and use images of criminal incest as representations of kingship gone awry: as kings responding with disdain and injustice to their subjects and to power. The anonymous author of *Nostradamus' Prophecy* (1672) exposes the disarray and tyranny that assails a state whose rulers indulge in unnatural acts against it:

> When *Sodomy* shall be prime Min'sters Sport,
> And *Whoring* shall be the least Crime at Court:
> When Boys shall take their *Sisters* for their Mate,
> And practise *Incests* between Seven and Eight: [...]
> Then th' *English* shall a greater *Tyrant* know
> Than either *Greek* or *Latin* Story show.[10]

In the anonymous *Hodge* (1679), Charles II's aspirations to God-like absolutism are directly identified with incest. The gods give the 'humble' Hodge far-reaching sight so he is able to spy "the goatish god [Charles] [...] in his Alcove, / The secret scene of damn'd incestuous love." The newly enlightened Hodge pleads: "Cease, cease, O Charles, thus to pollute our Isle; / Return, return to thy long-wish'd exile."[11]

The joyous mood gripping the nation at the Restoration had been replaced by bitter disappointment. The prevalence of incest themes in the horror plays could be interpreted as a symptom of the miasmata of betrayal pervading English society at this time: in particular, concern over the behaviour of Charles II in his paternal role as father of the country. As has already been argued, by the mid-1670s Charles was estranged from parliament and the English people. Satirists were suggesting that he was not living up to his side of the bargain – to his duty, as monarch, to provide peace and security for the people. Rochester's quip, "God bless our good and gracious King, / Whose promise none relies on" gives air to the belief that the king was untrustworthy; but on a more sinister level, parliament (and the people) were depicted as "being [...] betrayed."[12] Charles's attempts to constrain parliament and to restrict supreme power within a small, easily controlled circle could be seen as a flagrant mark of self-absorption and paternal absolutism. Incest is a perfect metaphor for the vanity of this self-seeking pattern of recycling and reproduction.

Familial strife and incest are, of course, not exclusive to the horror plays. There is father-son rivalry in Dryden's *The Assignation* and *Aureng-Zebe*, which also features the evil Nourmahal, who loves her stepson. In Thomas Otway's *The Orphan*, brothers betray each other, and when one incestuously takes his brother's place on his wedding night, it leads to tragedy and the death of the lovers. In Behn's *Oroonoko*, a grandfather lusts after and abducts his grandson's wife into his seraglio. In her Oedipal short story *The Dumb Virgin*, a brother unknowingly has sex with his sister and kills his father. And there is incestuous desire between father and daughter in Dryden's *Fables*. In the absence of violence and guile, however, family stability is not affected by incestuous feelings, especially between mutually attracted brothers and sisters. This is the case in Behn's *The Young King* and *The Dutch Lover*. The comic plot of Dryden's *The Spanish Fryar* is similar in its depiction of narrowly averted sibling incest, as is the apparent brother-sister incest theme in *Love Triumphant*. In another of Dryden's plays involving sibling incest, *Don Sebastian*, the young lovers are mutually attracted to each other and are ignorant of their blood relationship until after they have consummated their love. A clear distinction is made between breaking the taboo with full knowledge and breaking it in ignorance. When the shocking truth is revealed by the family's friend Alvarez, he is at pains to tell the young lovers, "[t]hough Incest is indeed a deadly Crime, / You are not guilty, since, unknown 'twas done, / And, known, had been abhorr'd" (V.i.445–7).[13] For the sake of poetic justice, however, the lovers must be punished for breaking the taboo. They make the painful decision never to see each again. Their suffering adds pathos to their situation; the audience remains sympathetic to the lovers' plight, and their decision to part in some way makes reparation for their 'sin.'

Incest in the horror plays, in contrast, invariably reflects dangerous rifts within the family. For the most part, it is depicted between father and child. The 'love' is most often forced, violent and one-sided – a disturbing exercise of patriarchal privilege and domination. It is also depicted not as an exclusory personal tragedy but as an integral part of an overall breakdown of family and state structure. And, with perhaps one exception, the perpetrator(s) commit the crime with full knowledge of their kinship to their victim. It can be argued that the one play where the crime is committed in ignorance is John Dryden and Nathaniel Lee's *Oedipus* (Duke's 1678). As we will see, however, the refashioning of the ancient play in 1670s London provides a concerted focus on the incest theme, and, unique to Dryden and Lee's version, the protagonists – Jocasta and Oedipus – continue to exhibit overt sexual interest in each other even after the revelation of their mother-son relationship.

A brief look at only a handful of the horror plays, then, conjures up grave doubts about the possibility of maintaining the integrity of the family (and state) when it is being assaulted from within, by those whose job it is to nurture and sustain it. In Nathaniel Lee's *The Tragedy of Nero* (King's 1674), the emperor rapes his mother and then has her put to death. In Thomas Otway's *Alcibiades* (Duke's 1675), the king orders the death of his chosen 'son' Alcibiades and lusts after Alcibiades's betrothed; the queen lusts after Alcibiades. In a violent extension of the father-son rivalry, Lee's *Mithridates* (King's 1678) depicts the father/king raping and marrying his son's fiancée; he also orders the death of one son and unwittingly poisons another. In John Crowne's *Thyestes* (King's 1680), one brother rapes the other's wife, and a father is made to eat his own son. The Thyestean banquet is, of course, also present in Edward Ravenscroft's reworking of *Titus Andronicus* (King's 1678) – another play which focuses on the dissolution of father-child relationships. In William Joyner's *The Roman Empress* (King's 1670), the heir to the Roman throne is unrecognised: he is lusted after by his stepmother and executed by his father. In Thomas Otway's *Don Carlos* (Duke's 1676), the father, King Philip of Spain, forcibly marries his son's betrothed and then orders the death of them both. The archetypal theme is revisited in Lee and Dryden's reworking of the familiar story of *Oedipus* (Duke's 1678), where the son kills the father and marries the mother.

The bodies of the mothers and daughters in the horror plays are inscribed with incest. Most of the mothers are stepmothers, the kings having remarried much younger spouses, and are not consanguineously related to the sons. In all of the plays, however, these stepmothers relate *sexually* to the sons. In *Oedipus*, *The Roman Empress* and *Alcibiades*, the Phaedra-like mother-figures lust after their sons, eventually leading to the son's destruction. In *Mithridates* and *Don Carlos*, stepmother and son are mutually attracted, having originally been betrothed to each other until the king/father figure lusts after the woman and forces her into marriage with him. In *Don Carlos*, the princess who comes to marry Carlos, but stirs the king's lust, is first daughter then wife to the king (and thus sister and mother to the son):

> When I arriv'd to be the Princes bride
> You then a Kind Indulgent Father were [...]
> Not your own Daughter could have lov'd you more. (V.i.148–9, 154)[14]

In *Mithridates*, the daughter-figure Semandra also arrives in court as the prince Ziphares's betrothed. When she is brought before her stepfather Mithridates, he is captivated by her beauty. Mithridates loses all self-control; demanding that Semandra marry him, he declares war on his son:

> [...] till I saw your Eyes, I lov'd
> The virtue of my Son; I lodg'd him near
> My Heart, and set him down my Successor:
> But now [...]
> I hate him more than I did ever love him. (II. 202–5, 209) [15]

The competition between father and son for the body of the daughter/mother leads to the destruction of natural familial bonds. The more Semandra pleads to be returned to Ziphares, the more aroused Mithridates becomes until his jealousy overtakes his reason and his judgement and he suggests attainment of the sexual object is more vital than his kingship.

> Had he conspir'd my Death, usurp'd my Throne,
> Perhaps I might have doom'd him to be slain,
> Yet sure I shou'd have wept to see him die;
> But now, since he must Ravish that lov'd Gem,
>   [...] shou'd I my Empire give
> To buy his Fate, I'de think it vastly sold. (II.211–14, 217–18)

The central metaphor for incest and the female body in these plays is the womb. It is rarely, however, described as a life-sustaining entity, which is comfort-giving, all-encompassing and protective. It is, rather, "[t]he fatal source, the occasion, and cause / Of all miseries, and servitude" (*The Roman Empress* IV p52). It is a locus of discord: a place where two rivals – father and son – meet. It is most frequently pictured either as being ravaged or as rejecting its incestuous burden through images of abortion. As *Oedipus* begins, the city of Thebes is gorged with the diseased and dying: the gods' punishment for the murder of the old king Laius. The opening scene is graphic: "Dead Bodies appear at a distance in the Streets; Some faintly go over the Stage, others drop" (I.i). The Thebans crowd to the palace to implore help from the new king Oedipus. As the prodigies light up the night sky, Oedipus and his wife/mother Jocasta come forward to view the spectacle:

> OEDIPUS. Why from the bleeding Womb of monstrous Night,[16]
>   Burst forth such Miriads of abortive Stars?
>   Ha!. My Jocasta, look! the Silver Moon!
>   A setling Crimson stains her beauteous Face!
>   She's all o're Blood! [...]
>   A vast Eclipse darkens the labouring Planet:
>   [...] sound all our Instruments of War; [...]
>   And beat a thousand Drums to help her Labour. (II.i.33–7, 39–40, 42)

The bleeding womb, abortive stars and the bloodstained labouring planet are, of course, analogous with Oedipus's incest. The images foretell the results of such an assault on the mother's body by the son. A bleeding womb either aborts its offspring or produces something aberrant, as Jocasta suggests when she asks Oedipus why he remains gazing at the sky "as if the Gods / Had some new Monsters made" (II.i.71–2). When the womb is depicted as a place of comfort in *Oedipus*, it is a false comfort. When his life and sanity are threatened by the unfolding of the prophecy, Oedipus seeks comfort in womb-like images of Jocasta's arms:

> Tho' round my Bed the Furies plant their Charms;
> I'll break 'em, with Jocasta in my arms:

Clasp'd in the fold of love, I'll wait my doom;
And act my joys, tho' Thunder shake the room. (II.423–6)

[sleepwalking]: O, my Jocasta! 'tis for this the wet
Starv'd Soldier lies all night on the cold ground [...]
To be thus circled, to be thus embrac'd
That I could hold thee ever! (II.337–8, 341–2)

Oedipus yearns to return to the womb/mother for comfort, to reject the external world, but, as he soon discovers, he has already made the journey to the womb which bred him and has violated it. Nature has been "forc'd back again upon her self " and, like a whirlpool, made to "swallow her own streams" (I.i.551–3). Any safety or comfort he seeks is impossible. For Oedipus, "the sacred Veils that wrapt thee yet unborn" (IV.606–7) deceive him: they are the cause of, not the protection from, his tortures. When Jocasta realises Oedipus is her son, images of the womb are integral to her language. They are, however, images of ravishment and destruction: a plundering of Mother Earth. As Jocasta searches frantically for somewhere to hide from the horror of her reality, she demands that the "Earth open, or I'll tear thy bowels up" (V.249). She equates the act of incest to "a monstrous Gap [hew'n] in Nature / A flaw made through the Center" of the earth (IV.i.425–6). In the end, however, Jocasta's final call to Oedipus is to return to her womb, in death: "I'll wrap thy shivering Spirit in Lambent Flames! / And so we'll sail." (V.i.430–31).

Lee and Dryden use three main sources for their adaptation of the Oedipus myth: Seneca, Sophocles and Corneille. One of the distinguishing features of Lee and Dryden's play is the unique portrayal of the sexual relationship between Oedipus and Jocasta.[17] Early on in the play, they make ironic use of the customary filial affection expected of a son and the piety of son-mother relationship by parodying that bond before it is destroyed.

OEDIPUS. So well I love, words cannot speak how well.
        No pious Son er'e lov'd his Mother more
        Than I my dear Jocasta.

JOCASTA. I love you too
        The self same way [...]
        For I love Lajus still as wives shou'd love:
        But you more tenderly; as part of me:
        And when I have you in my arms, methinks
        I lull my child asleep. (I.i.524–8, 531–4)

In Seneca, Sophocles and Corneille, Jocasta's realisation of her incest immediately drives her to commit suicide; she and Oedipus have very little left to do with each other. Lee and Dryden's Jocasta regularly makes physical comparisons between her two husbands, and the playwrights create in the two lead characters a deep sexual longing that endures even after the revelation of their kinship:

> JOCASTA. In spight of all those Crimes the cruel Gods
>   Can charge me with, I know my Innocence;
>   Know yours: 'tis fate alone that makes us wretched,
>   For you are still my Husband.
>
> OEDIPUS. Swear I am,
>   And I'll believe thee; steal into thy Arms,
>   Renew endearments, think 'em no pollutions,
>   But chaste as Spirits joys: gently I'll come,
>   Thus weeping blind, like dewy Night, upon thee,
>   And fold thee softly in my Arms to slumber. (V.218–26)

Lee and Dryden also emphasise the offspring of this incestuous union more than their sources do. Their Oedipus can only fully understand the true horror of his actions when he considers the legacy he leaves his children. He verbalises the derangement of identity between parents and children when caught in a cycle of incest:

> What shall I call this Medley of Creation? [...]
> Here one, with all th'obedience of a Son,
> Borrowing Jocasta's look, kneels at my Feet,
> And calls me Father; there a sturdy Boy,
> Resembling Lajus just as when I kill'd him,
> Bears up, and with his cold hand grasping mine,
> Cries out, How fares my Brother Oedipus?
> What, Sons and Brothers! Sisters and Daughters too! (V.i.156–63)

Milton's imagery in *Paradise Lost* is comparable. In his epic poem, Sin and Death are the incestuous offspring of Satan. There is distinctly similar familial confusion as Satan addresses his children as "Fair Daughter" – "[t]hy daughter and thy darling [...] and thou son and grandchild both" (II 870, X 384). Sin sprang out of Satan's head. Sin tells the story of how her father then became attracted to her: "[t]hy self in me thy perfect image viewing / Becamest enamoured." Satan responded to her with lust:

> [...] such joy thou took'st
> With me in secret, that my womb conceived
> A growing burden.
>
>   [...] my womb
> Pregnant by thee, and now excessive grown
> Prodigious motion felt and rueful throes.
> At last this odious offspring [...]
> breaking violent way
> Tore through my entrails, that with fear and pain
> Distorted, all my nether shape thus grew
> Transformed [...]. (II 765–7, 778–85)

The incestuous lust does not end here. Satan's incestuous spawn, the Oedipal Death, then turns on his own mother, and the cyclical pattern of rape and incest on the body of the mother continues.

> I fled, but he pursued (though more, it seems,
> Inflamed with lust then rage) and swifter far,
> Me overtook his mother all dismayed,
> And in embraces forcible and foul
> Ingendering with me, of that rape begot
> These yelling monsters that with ceaseless cry
> Surround me [...] hourly conceived
> And hourly born, with sorrow infinite
> To me, for when they list into the womb
> That bred them they return, and howl and gnaw
> My bowels, their repast [...]. (II 790–800)

The pattern repeats endlessly and opens out into wider and wider circles with even more destructive, disfigured progeny. The unnatural horror of Satan/tyrant/Charles I's incest/paternal absolutism in Milton's poem follows an historical pattern of tyranny and spawns cyclical and unending pain and devastation. At the same time, Milton subverts Stuart royalist panegyric, in which the divine nature of the king is seamless – Christ-like Charles I is reborn in Charles II. Rather, he depicts familial (Stuart) betrayal in which the offspring is inevitably doomed to become heir to the degeneracy of the father.[18]

Dryden in particular shows Milton's influence throughout *Oedipus*, and he and Lee arguably focus on the progeny of incest for political reasons similar to Milton's.[19] Familial betrayal spawns a relentless cycle of evil. In what could be interpreted as an attempt to stop the perpetuation of parental depravity, Jocasta kills her "preposterous" children. As the scene draws on Jocasta's suicide, the audience sees the innocent victims of her incest "slain upon the Bed" – "her Daughters hang[ing] / On the Bed Royal; and her little Sons / Stabb'd through the breasts upon the bloody Pillows" (V.ii.406–8). Maximillian Novak argues that, "the children are much less important in Dryden's version than they are in Sophocles's or Corneille's even."[20] The children, however, do not exist in any tangible form in the other plays. Although it is true that Sophocles and Corneille allow Oedipus's children to live in order to "anticipate the children's troubled future," Dryden and Lee do not look forward to a sequel: instead, they treat the ghastly deaths of the progeny of Oedipus and Jocasta as a focal point of their play.

The incest motif is of paramount importance to Lee and Dryden's tragedy; it is constantly highlighted, in contrast particularly to the tragedies of Corneille and Sophocles, where references are limited. As in Seneca's play, the ghost of Laius rises from the dead to emphasise Oedipus's incestuous acts: "who murder'd me? / 'twas Oedipus: / Who stains my Bed with Incest? Oedipus [...] From Thebes, my Throne, my Bed, let him be driv'n" (III.i.368–9, 376). The subplot of Eurydice and Adrastus, taken from Corneille, is also given an aberrant sexual focus: in a parallel to the destructive sexual triangle of Laius/Oedipus/Jocasta, Creon lusts after (and plans to rape) his niece Eurydice, who despises him and loves Adrastus. Creon's sister Jocasta had promised Eurydice to Creon, but Oedipus will not let the marriage take place, as he considers the relationship incestuous. To Oedipus, incest is the most evil of all evil acts:

> I'd rather
> Embrue my arms up to my very shoulders
> In the dear entrails of the best of Fathers,
> Than offer at the execrable act
> Of damned Incest. (IV.i.288–92)

Questions of free will versus fate are central to Sophocles's depiction of the tragedy. The taboos have already been broken before the play begins, and Sophocles makes it clear that it is ultimately Oedipus's *choice* to discover the truth or not. Sophocles's arrogant but heroic king desires the truth, and he is the driving force, doggedly pushing for answers and even a public inquiry into the crime – against the advice of Tiresias, Jocasta and Creon. Where the earlier play depicts a supportive, trustworthy Creon who is distrusted by a sceptical Oedipus, Lee and Dryden invert these characteristics: their Creon is a feisty, rebellious would-be usurper modelled on Richard III (or, more topically, the Earl of Shaftesbury). Their Oedipus, however, is a subdued and relatively naïve version of Sophocles's king. And it is Creon – not Oedipus – who is the primary precipitator of the events. It is his stirring up of the people against Oedipus that keeps the relentless ball rolling and unfolds the truth. There are other striking moments in Sophocles which question whether human life is trapped in a pattern of its own or others' making; or, as Jocasta suggests, if all is random:

> Fear?
> What should a man fear? It's all chance,
> chance rules our lives. Not a man on earth
> can see a day ahead, groping through the dark.
> Better to live at random, best we can.
> And as for this marriage with your mother –
> have no fear. Many a man before you,
> in his dreams, has shared his mother's bed.
> Take such things for shadows, nothing at all –
> Live, Oedipus,
> as if there's no tomorrow! (1068–78)[21]

But this line of questioning is omitted in Jocasta's speeches in the Dryden/Lee version. Every time Jocasta joins Oedipus on stage, her function (aside from the imparting of information towards the end of the play) is to anticipate the revelation by adding dramatic irony to the sexual attraction between two lovers who are unknowingly mother and son. One of her last lines, "'tis Fate alone that makes us wretched" (V.i.220), indicates that more than any other horror play, this is a personal tragedy involving incest; but more than any previous version of the Oedipus story, her revised role produces a tragedy with an emphasis on the act of incest.

A comparison of the plays' endings is also significant. Lee and Dryden's drama ends bleakly with Oedipus's suicide after the destruction of his entire family. In other adaptations, Oedipus's tragedy is mitigated by some form of redemption. In Corneille's drama, for example, *Oedipe* is an oppressor, who blinds himself in the end. But in doing so, he undergoes a form of apotheosis: the letting of his blood exonerates him and ends the Theban plague. In Sophocles's play Oedipus also blinds himself and becomes an exile; but he is a man who, through his self-mutilation, acknowledges his moral blindness – ignorance is replaced with knowledge. Both endings give evidence of a level of human dignity and significance in the face of indifferent gods and overwhelming horror. At the end of Seneca's *Oedipus*, however, there is no redemption of human dignity. With Oedipus's exile, the plague leaves Thebes, but Oedipus, alone and unenlightened, demands that "[d]estructive Fates and sickness' trembling fear, / wasting, black plague, dementia – come here, / be my companions!" (1116–18). Although Lee and Dryden acknowledge Sophocles's influence, it is Seneca's bleak play that sets the tone of their drama. G.K. Hunter argues that Renaissance imitations of Seneca diverge from the original in their attitude to fate: "While allowing the cruelty of tragic destiny, [Elizabethan drama] is also strongly assertive of the redeeming features of a tragic existence [...] the renewed faith." The Senecan world, however, because its gods are unjust, depicts "a world of total injustice."[22] At the close of Lee and Dryden's *Oedipus*, all the main characters die unenlightened: there is no sense of redemption, no alleviation of the misery, no lesson learned.

In the horror plays, when natural law at such a fundamental level has been corrupted, the external replicates the internal: the personal, familial wars that the characters take part in parallel growing external civil strife. The warring father and son represent "brothers fighting brothers." In *Oedipus*, when the prophecy is made real and Jocasta and Oedipus understand that they are mother and son, the family begins destroying itself: Oedipus, Jocasta and their children, Eurydice (Oedipus's sister/daughter) and her betrothed Adrastus all die violently. As Jocasta loses her sanity and prepares to kill her children in the royal palace, her brother Creon is making a bloody attempt to take over the city. One of Oedipus's men tells the prophet Tiresias to "Charm [...] [t]hese feuds within: while I without extinguish / The furious Creon; / That Brand which sets our City in a Flame" (V.310–13). In Otway's *Alcibiades* (Duke's 1675), the eponymous hero makes similar analogies between 'disjoynted' nature and civil strife when he discovers that he has stirred the lust of his stepmother:

Sure at my birth the Heavens themselves did mourn.
Disjoynted nature did her course forbear,
And held within her Womb a civil War. (V.i.2–4)

The internal, normally safe and nurturing haven of the womb is overrun by unnatural disruptive forces such as rivalry and lust and is turned inside out: the internal and the external are synonymous and, as Oedipus expresses, the collapsing family is civil anarchy.[23]

Fall darkness then, and everlasting night
Shadow the Globe [...]
Through all the inmost Chambers of the Sky,
May there not be a glimpse, one Stary spark,
But Gods meet Gods, and justle in the dark. (IV.622–3, 626–8)

The rivalry between father and son over the body of the mother/daughter incapacitates all of these characters, but most particularly the paternal heads of family and state. Distracted by reckless passion, they are unable to distinguish truth from fantasy and fail to perform their roles as fathers and, more tellingly, as rulers with any effect. Thus they become a danger not only to their families but also to the state. After falling in love with his son's betrothed, King Philip of Spain in Otway's *Don Carlos*, influenced by "Veracious Varlets, Sordid Hangers on" (V.95), can see his son only in terms of an aggressive rival: "Thinking my Youth and Vigour to decrease, / You'd ease me of my crown to give me peace" (IV.495–6). In Joyner's *The Roman Empress* (King's 1670), Emperor Valentius has his son Florus put to death after accusing him of trying to seduce his stepmother Fulvia. After the innocent Florus is executed, Valentius is the only one who, still blinded by his rage and jealousy, cannot discern the truth – the deceptive and monstrous nature of his beloved.

In dynastic ideology, a son is the desired result of marriage. Only a son can produce immortality for the father by carrying on the patrilineal line. In all of the plays dealt with here, the rulers have a male heir, but – without exception – the existence of the son/prince is a reminder of the constant threat of replacement to the father/king. The archetypal father-son relationship in monarchical history is "repeatedly mythologized as a potentially patricidal struggle for authority."[24] The fathers in these plays distrust, despise and fear their sons with an intensity that is unprecedented. They produce the desired offspring only to be overwhelmed with fear of the threat to their own mortality, which threat they seek to counter by positioning themselves as hostile rivals to their sons. This destructive cycle is taken to an extreme in Otway's *Don Carlos*. The first scene of the play opens with the king having just married his son's betrothed. As the older man proudly displays his young bride, he suggests to Don Carlos that he is now in a position to create possible alternatives for Carlos's throne:

From this Fair Charmer, and our Royal Bride,
Shall such a Noble Race of Heroe's spring,
As may adorn the Court when thou art King. (I.i.20–22)

Through marriage with a new, much younger bride, the king not only seeks to renew or re-establish his youth but also wants to usurp his son's position – taking his bride, his youth and his virility. His desire to suppress his son's sexuality effectively takes away his son's ability to become a father or a future ruler. The king's posturing also contains overt threats. The "Noble Race of Heroe's" will maliciously be created to compete with Don Carlos's position of heir to the throne. They will also challenge his dominance, growing to find their strength as young heroes at the same time that Don Carlos approaches his father's current age (i.e., begins his decline). It is Don John, the king's brother, who summarises the king's foolishness in positioning himself as rival to his son and sole heir.

> Why would you cut a sure Succession off,
> At which your Friends must grieve, and Foes will laugh
> As if since Age has from you took away
> Increase, you'd grow malicious and destroy? (V.73–6)

The king is not adhering to the natural laws of kinship or kingship and is thus depicted as a figure of ridicule, not of power. His bid to retain his potency and youth in rivalry with his son demands that his son lose not only his natural right as heir but also his life. The loss of the son's life, by extension, also affects the hope and security of the state. As Semandra says of Mithridates: "he blushes / To think he cou'd so monstrously Decree / To murder the sweet hopes of all his Kingdoms" (II.244–6).

The fears of the fathers in these plays, however, are never correspondent to the actions of the sons: it is not the son's ambition for political or social power that leads to the conflict but, rather, the father's refusal to give it up. The fathers are attempting to pre-empt an event that seems unlikely to have occurred in any case. With the exception of Oedipus, who does so unwittingly, the sons ironically never come close to fulfilling the role of rebel so anticipated by their fathers. In *The Roman Empress*, *Mithridates*, *Alcibiades* and *Don Carlos*, the sons attempt verbally to placate their fathers and defend their rights – to the body of the daughter and to the throne – but their arguments and entreaties are never recognised by their fathers. Don Carlos is the only son who looks to action: he considers joining rebels in another country to fight his father politically:

> Rob'd of my Love, and as unjustly thrown
> From all those hopes that promis'd me a Crown,
> My heart, with the Dishonour's to me done,
> Is poison'd, swells too mighty for my breast;
> [...] *Father!* and *King!* both names bear mighty sence:
> Yet sure there's something too in *Son*, and *Prince*.
> I was born high, and will not fall less great,
> Since Triumph Crown'd my Birth, I'le have my Fate,
> As Glorious and Magestick too, as that [...]
> Let th'Common Rout like Beasts Love to be Dull.
> Whilst sordidly they live at ease and full,
> I am a Prince have had a Crown in view,
> And cannot brook to loose the prospect now. (IV.i.7–10, 16–19, 27–8, 31–2)

His grand, brave plans are short-lived, however, and his desire for his stepmother demands that he stay and once more "asswage [his] angry Father's rage" (IV.i.379) through submission.

The idea that the men who are bred to take over power have no voice is admirably dealt with by Nathaniel Lee in *Mithridates* (King's 1678). Mithridates meets his son's fiancée, Semandra, in the first act of the play. Captivated by her beauty, he sings the praises of the woman whom he will soon rape and force into marriage:

> Had I as many Tongues as I have Languages,
> Skill'd in all Speeches of the babling World,
> And cou'd at once speak to as many Nations,
> With such a grace as might make Athens blush.
> By Mercury, and by the Father of
> The Muses, I shou'd never speak Semandra. (I.i.433–8)

The king's lust for Semandra immediately prompts his campaign to bring about the emasculation of his son. Five lines later, under Mithridates's questioning, Ziphares simply responds to his father: "Let me be dumb for ever from this moment" (I.i.443). As Mithridates imbues Semandra with a complex language, he takes his son's voice away. From this early stage in the play, Ziphares's words, needs and desires (like those of other sons in these plays) are consistently ignored by a father who finally destroys him because of the threat he poses.

Even though the sons are never able or willing to rebel against the fathers, epithets for the son focus on images of rebellion. In *Don Carlos*, the king compares his son to Satan (IV.593–4): he uses terms such as "th'Usurper" (IV.261), "Rebel" (IV.487), "bold encroacher" (III.i.390) and "monster" (III.i.312). Oedipus more than once refers to himself as "monster," and his stepbrother Creon (the only other male family member alive) describes him as "[t]his barbarous stranger, this Usurper, Monster" (IV.i.26). References are also regularly made in *Oedipus* to the fear of the son, even though when the play begins Oedipus's father Laius is already dead. The oracles prophesying that Laius's son would murder are retold several times; and there are numerous references to the boy Oedipus's legs being pinned when Laius, out of fear for his own life, orders that his son be abandoned on a mountainside. Oedipus fulfils the role of rebel son; but none of his actions is consciously that of a son actively securing his birthright. On the contrary, when he is told of his fate by the oracles, Oedipus runs away from the home of those he believes are his parents so he cannot commit crimes against them, even though it means he must lose his birthright. He commits the ultimate rivalrous act towards his father – having sex with his mother – unknowingly. It is interesting to note that in Lee and Dryden's adaptation of the play, Oedipus sees his sins as an attack on his father:

> [...]'twas my Fate
> To kill my Father, and pollute his Bed,
> By marrying her who bore me. (III.564–6)

This is yet another case of rival father-son factions fighting over the same female body; but the ravishment of that body is specifically seen as a defiant act towards the father, not the mother. It is depicted in relation to its outcome on the father-son relationship, just as the fathers' rapes of the daughter-figures in *Don Carlos* or *Mithridates*, for example, are seen as an act of violence towards the rival son.

The inability of the son or the father to fulfil his role and the subsequent breakdown of the patrilineal/familial structure produces images of displacement in the family. In these plays, there are recurring references to exile and alienation – to the family as a group of strangers, antagonistic to each other. The king in *Don Carlos* tells his son that his blood is "a stranger like thy soul to me" (IV.i.463). Trying to rally the citizens against Oedipus, the rebel Diocles tells them that "Oedipus pollutes the Throne of Lajus, / A stranger to his Blood" (I.i.294–5). This language typifies the father-son relationship in all of these plays: even though they are of the same blood, fathers and sons are strangers – they know nothing of each other, they are blind and deaf to each other's needs and, in their ignorance, they invariably destroy each other. Images of banishment are also common and act to distance the son further from what should be his source of nurture. Don Carlos speaks of his "exile" after his father banishes him: "I am left / Alone, a naked wanderer" (III.i.441–2). John Crowne picks up on this theme of loss, exile and the movement towards "nothingness" in *The Destruction of Jerusalem by Titus Vespasian* (King's 1677), produced six months later.[25] Oedipus is a "fugitive" who must be "cast out to Banishment" (IV.i.142). He refers to himself as "out-cast Oedipus" (IV.i.621). Mithridates says he will "cast [his son Ziphares] out, / That Bosom-Wolf, who laps my dearest blood" (III. ii.135–6). In the final scene of *Thyestes*, Atreus declares, "Man is a vagabond" (V p55). *Alcibiades* opens with Alcibiades fleeing from Athens to Sparta, the enemy camp, for refuge. The first concrete information we have about Alcibiades, then, is that he is willing to "change sides." Otway never clarifies who Alcibiades is, nor does he give any details about his background or family history. We meet only his sister Draxilla, but she gives no information about her family either. When she discovers Alcibiades has run away, she refers to herself as "an Orphan destitute and bare" (II.i.17). Alcibiades's vague and uncertain roots produce an uneasy silence and work to alienate him from the audience early on in the play.

There are two father-son relationships in this play, and both are disastrous. Alcibiades's 'stepfather' is the king of Sparta, but he misunderstands Alcibiades and wrongly accuses him of treason and of seducing the queen. This relationship eventually destroys both Alcibiades and the king. The other father-son duo is Alcibiades's friend Patroclus and the old general Tissaphernes. But these two characters have no commonality, and the earnest and loyal Patroclus is abused by and becomes alienated from his evil father who, through murder and deceit, aspires to the throne. There are two similar relationships in *The Roman Empress*. The hero, Florus, despises the man he believes to be his real father – the rebel General Arsenius. Florus becomes the 'step'-son to the Roman emperor Valentius, who refers to himself as Florus's "[f]ather by adoption / Which merits more then if I were by nature" (IV, p39). It eventually emerges that Valentius is Florus's true father, but not before Florus is wrongly accused by Valentius of treason and of seducing the queen, and both father and son are destroyed.

In the perverted, restrictive and unnatural environment that the family units provide, the offspring grow into dysfunctional, weak sons/princes who are averse to their assigned places in the hierarchy. They prove not only incapable of protecting their interests but also, indeed, of surviving. These princes may be physically heroic and courageous – most are powerful warriors who lead troops to victory against foreign enemies – but this is where their roles as 'heroes' end. David R. Hauser suggests that, along with the ability to feel passions strongly, "great self-control [is] a necessary premise to heroic action."[26] The sons in these plays display little or no self-control. As already indicated, even though Don Carlos has been banished and forbidden to see the queen again, he rejects the opportunity to escape and lead the rebels against his father because of his desire to see his beloved: to "lay […] down at [the Queen's] feet and dy" (IV.i.348). The sons are so incapacitated by passion for their mistresses and fear of their fathers that they lose their ability to reason and to gain any personal position of power. In his dedication to *The Conquest of Granada*, John Dryden delineates the attributes of an heroic character when describing Almanzor:

> I have form'd a Heroe, I confess, not absolutely perfect, but of an excessive and overboyling courage: but *Homer* and *Tasso* are my precedents. Both the *Greek* and the *Italian* Poet had well consider'd that a tame Heroe who never transgresses the bounds of moral vertue, would shine but dimly in an Epick poem […]. [27]

Dryden continues the argument in his essay *Of Heroique Playes*.

> [G]reat authors […] made their Hero's men of honour; but so, as not to divest them quite of humane passions, and frailties. They contented themselves to shew you, what men of great spirits would certainly do, when they were provok'd, not what they were oblig'd to do by the strict rules of moral vertue.[28]

The 'heroes' in the horror plays, however, are moral cowards, and they are incapable of addressing any wrongs done to themselves or to others. Jessica Munns calls Otway's Alcibiades "a bungler, neither entirely virtuous nor heroically overreaching but instead an unobservant and confused participant in struggles over power and pleasure to which he is central but which he fails to understand." She compares him to Plutarch's "ambitious and sexually promiscuous Alcibiades [who] exemplifies the energy of power invested in a single man" and finds him lacking. "In contrast, Otway's 'squeamish Gentleman' never initiates action but picks his way ineptly through political and sexual minefields and demonstrates the ways in which power is felt rather than enacted."[29] In *Mithridates*, when he finds out Semandra has been forcibly married and raped, Ziphares's response is dishearteningly feeble: "Oh, at thy feet, let me for ever lye, / Thus hang upon thy knees with dying grasps, / Thou most wrong'd Innocence, abus'd Semandra" (IV.i.563–5). These emasculated sons will not exact revenge. Yet any act of vengeance against such extreme paternalism could be acceptable: if they did act, they would be seen as tragic but effective. In *The Art of Rhetoric*, Aristotle states that "[t]o take vengeance on one's enemies is nobler than to come to terms with them; for to retaliate is just, and that which is just is noble; and further, a courageous man ought not to allow himself to be beaten."[30] Not one of these characters tries to overthrow the icon of despotism which is threatening his life, and all are depicted as ridiculous and weak for not doing so.

The sons are also portrayed as inactive and impotent in the political and social sphere. They are shown as unable to produce strong and trustworthy leadership, let alone provide any political stability or security for the country or their people. The prince Ziphares, like many of the other sons, resolves to die when forbidden to possess his love. The general Archelaus asks him to live and protect his country:

> [...] which must fall without you,
> Your bleeding Country must obtain at least
> That you wou'd live to free her from her Foes [...]
> That you would save your Country from the Romans. (V.ii.83–5, 87)

But the prince has abandoned any condition of leadership that his birth demands: "Were I to live, I wou'd not fight again: / The World shou'd neither better be, nor worse / For me" (V.ii.92–4). The sons are not discerning: they are incapable of reading critical danger signs and are consistently misreading people and situations. Neither Alcibiades nor *The Roman Empress*'s Florus is able to anticipate or defend himself from the virulent attacks of his lustful stepmother. Lee and Dryden's Oedipus blindly trusts his evil stepbrother and misreads his motivations. He calls Creon "honest" (III.i.53) and "worthy" (IV.i.111). Creon's comment, "[m]y body opens inward to my soul, / And lets in day to make my Vices seen / By all discerning eyes, but the blind vulgar" (I.i.179–81), further accentuates Oedipus's inability to discern the true character of even those closest to him. And, like the other sons who make it to the throne in these plays, Oedipus's inability to read people puts his crown and his people in jeopardy. Oedipus says Creon has earned his protection: that the palace "is a Sanctuary, / The King himself's thy Guard" (IV.i.98–9), all the while Creon works actively to convince Thebans that Oedipus is an enemy who must be overthrown.

The effect of the profound schisms in these dysfunctional families is inescapable to the offspring who inherit the reins of power. The offspring's weaknesses invariably lead them to self-destruct, and what they leave behind is a rudderless society. Robert Ornstein suggests that, "the myth and ritual critics tell us that the tragic hero is sacrificed for the good of the community or the state and that the sacrificial pattern purges pity and fear."[31] In all of these plays (with the exception of *Don Carlos*, where the king "Runs off raving"), both the fathers and their sons are dead by the conclusion. The sons are sacrificed, but there is no purgation of pity and fear in the plays. The deaths figure no end to the corruption or any improvement in the condition of the state: there is certainly no sense of renewed hope or faith – no restoration of decency in the Elizabethan or Jacobean mould. Any potential or apparent restoration of peace does not hold up as such under close scrutiny, as the new rulers indicate a repetition of old patterns. The contamination of the incestuous family has already spread outward and those who are left to reign are impaired by it even if they are not tied to the family by blood. In *Alcibiades* Patroclus takes over the crown, but, as Jessica Munns suggests, he is a "king of grief [...] his father is a traitor, his friends are dead, and his mistress is lost."[32] The downfall of Alcibiades – the passion for his mistress which overrides his desire for self-control or self-preservation – is mirrored in Patroclus. In the short space of time between finding his best friend dying and being crowned king, Patroclus concerns himself with a desperate search for his absent mistress. His urgent language parallels Alcibiades's and indicates the same weaknesses: "Quickly let after her be made pursuit: / I'll ransack all the World to find her out" (V.i.520–21).

In *Don Carlos*, the king's brother Don John is the only character left to rule, and, although he can discern others' defects, his words and actions have already begun to parallel those of his brother, the king of Spain, signalling an unsettling and potentially enfeebling infatuation with love:

> How vainly would dull Moralists Impose
> Limits on Love, whose Nature brooks no Laws:
> Love is a God, and like a God should be
> Inconstant: with unbounded liberty
> Rove as he list. (III.i.15)

The king of Spain was himself a strong and honourable ruler before his infatuation overcame him, so there is little doubt that Don John will be susceptible to reproducing the pattern which preceded him. In *Oedipus*, Lee and Dryden kill off Oedipus as well as his children. The 'hero' Adrastus, who would take over the crown if this were an heroic drama, is also killed off. The courtier Haemon is the only character left to rule, but, as is the case with Alcibiades, we know nothing of him: he has no history and is an unsettlingly vague character. *Mithridates* ends perhaps most bleakly, with all the main characters dead and the country under siege from Roman forces.[33]

Like the cyclical and inward-looking pattern associated with incest, society, in these plays, is depicted as being caught up in a tragic reinforcing cycle of corruption and defeat. No character emerges unscathed; and certainly those characters who would normally be expected to provide some leadership and stability are not to be found. The recurring images of desolation and loss suggest a society bereft of its traditional verities. But the chaotic state is arrived at not only because there is no one of any worth at the helm; there is also a sense that some of the responsibility for it lies with the people. It is the citizens themselves who perpetuate the unjust and tyrannical rule under which they suffer. As we saw in the previous chapter, after Nero is destroyed in Lee's *The Tragedy of Nero*, the courtier Piso tells us there is celebration as the people eagerly await their new hero, the conqueror Galba.

> With all the Pomp 'O th'Court his Camp wee'll meet,
> And his approach with Joyful shoutings greet:
> Proclaim him Emperour with Trumpet Sound
> While he, now made a God, shall scorn the ground,
> And, on our shoulders ride, with Lawrels Crown'd. (V.iii.244–8)

Within minutes of disposing of one tyrant, then, the court is busily creating another royal 'God.' Lee depicts the king's subjects as blindly abetting the king in the continuation of their own servitude. Similarly, in the plays discussed in this chapter, the people share the sons' fear of rebellion: all submit to repression by the king without protest, and the people arguably end up with the government they deserve. The princes can lead their country to fight external enemies, but no one – neither the princes nor the people – will fight for freedom from tyranny at home.

The idea that history is cyclical, and that people appear to be compelled to repeat the same patterns and thus the same mistakes, is common to writers and thinkers of the Restoration period. Just as Dryden depicts the Theban mob in *Oedipus* as fickle followers of whoever woos them effectively, in his satire on the Exclusion Crisis, *Absalom and Achitophel* (1681), Dryden speaks of the "fickle rout," (785) the "giddy Jews" (the English) who, "govern'd by the Moon," (216)

> Tread the same track when she the Prime renews:
> And once in twenty Years, their Scribes Record,
> By natural Instinct they change their Lord. (217–19)[34]

The capricious – even 'lunatic' – nature of the people is also prevalent in the work of writers of a completely different political persuasion, such as John Milton. Milton's work also focuses on the cyclical nature of the drama of history; and the English people are most often depicted as the worst perpetrators of their own bondage. From fear or apathy, they do nothing to save themselves; and even after so much blood is shed to gain their freedom, they learn nothing from their experiences and return to slavery under leaders who ultimately betray them. In *Eikonoklastes*, Milton argues that the restitution of Charles I or

> these precepts giv'n to his son [...] unavoidably would have set us in the same state of miserie, wherein we were before; and have either compell'd us to submitt like bond slaves, or put us back to a second wandring over that horrid Wilderness of distraction and civil slaughter. (XXVII: 579–80).

In *The Readie and Easie Way to establish a free Commonwealth*, Milton sees his fears of backsliding realised:

> [F]or this extolld and magnifi'd nation [...] to fall back or rather to creep back so poorly as it seems the multitude would to thir once abjur'd and detested thraldom of Kingship [...] to throw away and forsake, or rather to betray a just and noble cause for the mixture of bad men who have ill manag'd and abus'd it [...] and by thus relapsing, to verifie all the bitter predictions of our triumphing enemies [...] not only argues a strange degenerate contagion suddenly spread among us fitted and prepar'd for new slaverie, but will render us a scorn and derision to all our neighbours.

Milton argues that if the country "after ten or twelve years prosperous warr and contestation with tyrannie" decides once again "to run their necks [...] into the yoke which they have broken," they are only worthy "to be for ever slaves [...]" (422, 428). Milton reiterates the point elsewhere, for example in *Samson Agonistes*, where he argues that people have a choice and Englishmen, like the men of Judah, actively choose to love "Bondage with ease [more than] strenuous liberty" (356).[35]

Milton's *History of Britain*, published in 1671, continues to explore the English compulsion to enslave itself under a tyrannical power. As David Loewenstein argues, the *History*'s "story of failed historical promise reinforces a sense of historical repetition."[36] Although the *History* is a record of struggle, Jonathan Sawday suggests that "it is not so much a record of past triumphs, but rather an ironic catalogue of the English refusal to grasp liberty when it was offered: the history of England is revealed as one of 'sad continuities.'"[37] In the *History*, Milton again implies that time and again the English people actively choose slavery over freedom. Like the horror plays, however, the wrong patterns are being repeated, and the cycle is impossible to break because nobody learns from the mistakes that are made: no one is willing or able to enforce change. As in the horror plays, in Milton's *History* conquering armies and their leaders are interchangeable – all who fall under the sway of absolute power ultimately become corrupt: "The *Saxons* were now full as wicked as the *Britans* were at their arrival, brok'n with luxurie and sloth, either secular or superstitious" (v. 259).[38] Because of their incapacity to act against the aggressors, however, it is above all the "unteachable" (451) English who are responsible for perpetuating their enslavement.

As trauma theory contends, after traumatic events, such as the English civil wars and the social and political dislocation that followed, the severely split psyche is compelled to remember the event by perpetually troping it. The English psyche was not allowed to come to terms with its trauma. In fact, through the Act of Oblivion, there was a conscious and, it would appear, universally approved agreement to pretend the events never happened. But the fear of return "to a second wandring over that horrid Wilderness of distraction and civil slaughter" was foremost in people's minds. The horror playwrights suggest that, in spite of these overwhelming fears, in spite of any determination not to repeat mistakes of the past, the English people were caught up in recurrent patterns over which they felt they had no control. England had found itself right back where it was on the eve of the first civil war. The English people were staring at the potential of their own worst fears realised, but, once again, they were inert: they were proving incapable of saving themselves from yet more tyranny and civil chaos.

Endnotes

[1]   MacDonald 126.

[2]   MacDonald 142.

[3]   St. Mark 3:25: "And if a house be divided against itself, that house cannot stand."

[4]   Richard McCabe, *Incest, Drama and Nature's Laws* (Cambridge: CUP, 1993) 5, 21.

[5]   *Statutes at Large from the First Year of King Edward the Fourth To the End of the Reign of Queen Elizabeth.* 67 vols. (London, 1786–1866) 25 Henry VIII c22. Quoted in Boehrer 1.

[6]   Boehrer 3.

[7]   Boehrer 12.

[8]   Mark Taylor, *Shakespeare's Darker Purpose* (New York: AMS, 1982) x.

9 Boehrer 113.

10 *A Collection of Poems on Affairs of State by A.M. and other eminent wits....* (London, 1689) 15–16.

11 I am quoting the edition of the poem by Elias F. Mengel, Jr., from vol. 2 (1965) of Lord, ed., *Poems on Affairs of State*. The poem was originally and erroneously attributed to Andrew Marvell and is known by several different titles. See *A Collection of Poems on Affairs of State by A.M. and other eminent wits....* 5–7.

12 John Wilmot, Earl of Rochester, *Impromptu on Charles II* in *The Complete Poems of John Wilmot*, ed. Vieth 134; Anon, *On the Prorogation* in *POAS* 1:184.

13 *The Works of John Dryden*, ed. Swedenberg, et al. All references to *Don Sebastian*, ed. Earl Miner, are from the California edition, vol. 15, and are hereafter cited parenthetically in the text.

14 *The Works of Thomas Otway*, ed. Ghosh. All references to *Don Carlos* are from Ghosh's edition, vol. 1, and are hereafter cited parenthetically in the text.

15 *The Works of Nathaniel Lee*, ed. Stroup and Cooke. All references to *Mithridates* are from Stroup and Cooke's edition, vol. 1, and are hereafter cited parenthetically in the text.

16 This line is reminiscent of *Paradise Lost*: "the wide womb of uncreated night" (II.150). *The Poems of John Milton*, ed. John Carey and Alastair Fowler (Harlow: Longmans, 1968). All references to *Paradise Lost* are from Carey and Fowler's edition and are hereafter cited parenthetically in the text. It is also evocative of E.F. Watling's translation of Seneca's *Oedipus*: "the dark womb / Of everlasting night" (III 593–4) (*Seneca: Four Tragedies and Octavia* [Harmondsworth: Penguin, repr. 1972]).

17 I am aware of Candy Schille's argument that it is commonplace for modern critics of *Oedipus* to suggest that Lee and Dryden "emphasize the erotic nature of the incestuous relationship between Oedipus and Jocasta." At the risk of redundancy, however, I believe it is an important point to make. In emphasising the sexual relationship, I seek to argue that, even when the facts of the incest are discovered, feelings of repugnance and guilt in these plays are overcome by the irresistible compulsion of degenerate desire (Schille, "At the Crossroads" *PLL* 40:3 [2004]: 305). See also Maximillian E. Novak, "Commentary to *Oedipus*" in *The Works of John Dryden*, ed Swedenberg, et al. 13:464.

18 For a helpful argument on Milton's political use of Satan and its links with Charles I, see Joan S. Bennett, "God, Satan, and King Charles" *PMLA* 92 (1977): 441–57.

19 For example, *Oedipus* I.i.192–202 closely parallels the opening lines to *Samson Agonistes*; *Oedipus* III.i.65 is similar to *Paradise Lost* II 600–604; *Oedipus* I.i.5–8 is similar to *Paradise Lost* III 588–90.

20 Novak, "Commentary to *Oedipus*" in *The Works of John Dryden*, ed. Swedenberg, et al. 13:452.

21 Sophocles, *The Three Theban Plays*, trans. Robert Fagles (New York: Penguin, 1982).

22 G.K. Hunter "Seneca and English Tragedy," *Seneca*, ed. Costa 170, 173.

23 The womb as a locus of discord or civil war appears as well in Milton's *Paradise Lost* where Hell is described with its "gates wide open [...] like a Furnace mouth" (II 884, 888). Beyond Hell lies "The Womb of Nature:"

> The secrets of the hoary deep, a dark
> Illimitable Ocean without bound [...]
> where eldest Night
> And Chaos [...] hold
> Eternal anarchy (II 891–6).

[24]　Lynda E. Boose and Betty S. Flowers, eds., *Daughters and Fathers* (Baltimore and London: Johns Hopkins UP, 1989) 32.

[25]　See Vanita Neelakanta, "Exile and Restoration in John Crowne's *The Destruction of Jerusalem by Titus Vespasian*" *Philological Quarterly* 89:2–3 (2010): 185–207.

[26]　David R. Hauser, "Otway Preserved: Theme and Form in Venice Preserv'd" *Studies in Philology* 55 (1958): 482. Quoted in Munns 29.

[27]　*The Works of John Dryden*, ed. John Loftis et al., vol. 11 (Berkeley and Los Angeles: U of California P, 1978) 6.

[28]　*The Works of John Dryden* 11:16.

[29]　Munns 27.

[30]　*Rhetoric* 1367a in *The Art of Rhetoric*, ed. and trans. John Henry Freese (London: William Heinemann Ltd., 1926) 97.

[31]　Ornstein 275.

[32]　Munns 36.

[33]　The trustworthy General Archelaus remains alive, but he is too old to produce further worthy heirs. More importantly he has pledged to die if the prince Ziphares dies, and because he keeps to his word, there is little chance of his surviving much past the play's end.

[34]　*The Works of John Dryden*, ed. Swedenberg et al., vol. 12. Swedenberg comments, "[i]n reference to recent English history, Dryden apparently was thinking of 1640, 1660, and 1680" (252).

[35]　*The Poems of John Milton*, ed Carey and Fowler. All references to *Samson Agonistes* are from Carey and Fowler's edition and are hereafter cited parenthetically in the text.

[36]　David Loewenstein, *Milton and the Drama of History* (Cambridge: CUP, 1990) 87.

[37]　Sawday 194.

[38]　*Complete Prose Works of John Milton*, ed. Wolfe. All references to *The History of England* are from Wolfe's edition, vol. 5, and are hereafter cited parenthetically in the text.

Chapter 6

Forsaken Justice:
Thomas Shadwell's *The Libertine* and the
Earl of Rochester's *Lucina's Rape Or the*
Tragedy of Vallentinian

Motifs used by dramatists of the horror plays expose underlying scepticism about the existence of moral absolutes. This final chapter will explore how expressions of materialism are used in these plays to bring into question the validity of Christian dogma, such as the immortality of the soul. More importantly, it will explore the doubts these expressions raise about the doctrine of the nature of God – His traditional attributes of justice, mercy and wisdom – and His relationship with man. *The Libertine* (Duke's 1675) by Thomas Shadwell and *Lucina's Rape Or the Tragedy of Vallentinian* (written for the King's 1675/76 but not produced until 1684) by John Wilmot, the Earl of Rochester, epitomise this trend. Both plays were fashioned from earlier works. Although the adaptations maintain essentially the same plots, by expanding some scenes, adding new characters and significantly altering others, the revised works project views in stark contrast to those of the original authors. In the earlier works, the audience expectation that there will be a simple cause-and-effect relationship between crime and punishment and virtue and reward is upheld. The most telling change in the adaptations is that, although evil behaviour is eventually punished by death, the evildoers remain defiant – death brings no remorse or repentance. And virtuous behaviour brings neither mercy nor justice, despite desperate pleas to a higher power. Both plays discount the existence of a sentient supernatural force amenable to human supplication – a view at the heart of atheism.

Atheism and materialism were highly subversive and topical issues in the 1670s. The 'sins' of both were regularly conflated by critics of the period; thus philosophers such as Hobbes, Epicurus and Lucretius (and even Seneca) were grouped together as atheists because of their non-teleological, mechanistic and materialistic view of nature. Contemporary discoveries in mathematics and science prompted a growing interest in a materialist view of the universe. In the middle of the seventeenth century, the French philosopher and scientist Pierre Gassendi had re-established interest in the ancient theory of atomic physics. Although he did not agree with Lucretian chance, he wrote numerous treatises and commentaries on atomism and on its ancient proponent, Epicurus. Gassendi's work was translated into English by Thomas Stanley and incorporated into the third volume of Stanley's *The History of Philosophy* in 1660. The scrutiny of Epicurean philosophy generated an interest in the work of Epicurus's most prominent disciple, the Roman philosopher Lucretius. Lucretius's legacy is an epic poem, *De rerum natura*, which reconstructs Epicurean thought. A portion of the poem was first translated into English in 1656; the first Latin edition published on English soil was in 1675.[1] According to Lucretius, Epicurean atomic physics dictates that the nature of reality can be explained in terms of infinitesimally small, indestructible atoms of matter moving randomly within infinite empty space; that the world was formed not by design but by chance; and the randomness and vain motion of atoms preclude any higher order: "the nature of the universe has by no means been made for us through divine power: so great are the faults it stands endowed with" (II.178–81).[2] And, for Lucretius, no ordained and fixed order in nature means there is no divine intervention in men's lives:

> For the very nature of divinity must necessarily
> enjoy immortal life in the deepest peace, far removed
> and separated from our affairs [...]
> needing us not at all, it is neither
> propitiated with services nor touched by wrath. (II.646–51)

For the ancient atomists, the human soul is corporeal, not immortal; consequently, there is no afterlife. In *De rerum natura*, Lucretius opposes the use of tales of eternal punishment by priests and poets as weapons to make man fear death:[3] "Cerberus [...] and the Furies and the withholding of / light, and Tartarus belching horrible fires from his / throat – these neither exist anywhere nor in truth can / exist" (III.1011–14).

It is not difficult to imagine why Lucretius's materialistic doctrine of atomism, with its corporeal soul and its infinite nature indifferent to human needs, could be seen as akin to atheism in the seventeenth century. Certainly Gassendi and other scientists, such as Robert Boyle, who were interested in the science of atomism were conscious of the implications of their studies and sought, in their writing, to combine the theory with Christian doctrine. Those who dealt with Lucretius's work as a literary subject also sought to distance themselves from Epicurean atheism. Lucretius's poem was finally translated into English by Thomas Creech in 1682. In his Dedicatory Epistle to George Pit, Creech refers to "the absurd fancy of a Material Soul." He speaks in glowing terms of the Christian religion, contrasting it with a "Contempt" for atheists ("the only conviction such Animals deserve"). In spite of its subject, Creech justifies his desire to translate the poem: "I have heard that the best Method to overthrow the Epicurean Hypothesis (I mean as it stands opposite to Religion) is to expose a full system of it to publick view." His key weapon is Lucretius's sublime verse: "any man [...] may perceive that he is elegant in his kind, curious and exact in his images, [...] of a brisk and ready Witt, pointed in Satyrs, severe in taunts, grave in precepts, quick and vivacious in his discourses, and every way fitted for his bold attempt."[4]

Thomas Hobbes, who was at Charles II's court in the early 1670s, also viewed the universe as materialistic and non-teleological, and he certainly believed that seeing a universe in scientific terms could banish superstition and a fear of the unknown; but his similarities to the ancient atomists ended here, and he was not directly inspired by either Epicurus or Lucretius. He was, however, considered by his contemporaries to be chiefly responsible for the Epicurean and Lucretian revival of the seventeenth century. Creech, for example, makes the connection explicit in his preface:

> the admirers of Mr. Hobbes may easily discern that his Politicks are but Lucretius enlarg'd; His state of Nature is sung by our Poet; the rise of Laws; the beginning of Societies; the Criteria of Just and Unjust exactly the same, and natural Consequents of the Epicurean Origine of Man; no new adventures.

It was the consequences that Hobbes deduced from materialist thought that caused much of the controversy surrounding his work. For the ancient atomists, divine gods existed: they simply lived far removed from man. In Hobbes's view of the universe, there are no exceptions to the rule – everything is material, nothing is absolute. Hobbes never explicitly denied the existence of God, but his God is a material God. By stripping God of his divinity, Hobbes threw into question the attributes traditionally associated with Him – holiness, justice, wisdom, mercy and goodness. As an extension of this argument, Hobbes contends there can be no immutable 'natural law' – no absolute standards of morality drawing authority from a just and reasonable God. Words themselves, in fact, have no absolute meaning: "[f]or these words of Good, Evill, and Contemptible, are ever used with relation to the person that useth them: There being nothing simply and absolutely so; nor any common Rule of Good and Evill [...]."[5]

Along with his doctrine of ethical relativism, Hobbes upheld a determinist position and argued, in contrast to the atomists, that man has no free will. In his study on *Leviathan*, Samuel Mintz explains why Hobbes's materialism terrified the religious establishment in particular:

> [...] [it] undermined the spiritual basis of religious belief. It led naturally to a determinist position, and determinism made a mockery of moral responsibility. Robbed of his freedom to choose between good and evil, man would deserve neither reward nor punishment; his piety, his prayers, the whole apparatus of worship would then become meaningless; justice, heaven, hell would then be empty words; and the whole edifice of religion must tumble down.[6]

Anti-materialist treatises and sermons proliferated in the 1670s. For Robert South atheism was "the growing rampant Sin of the Times."[7] He believed its impetus derived from Hobbes:

> [...] the great prevalence of that Atheistical Doctrine of the Leviathan; and the unhappy Propogation of Erastianism [...] [have] loosed the Bands of Conscience, and eaten out the very Heart and Sense of Christianity amongst us [...] [W]ere it not for this sole Obstacle, Religion is not now so much in danger of being divided, and torn piece-meal by Sects and Factions, as of being at once devour'd by Atheism. Which being so, let none wonder that Irreligion is accounted Policy, when it is grown even to a fashion; and passes for Wit, with some, as well as for Wisdom with others.[8]

In *The Catching of Leviathan*, Bishop Bramhall described materialism as "that main root of Atheisme, from which so many lesser branches are daily sprouting up."[9] Bishop John Wilkins concurred in his 1675 treatise *Of the Principles and Duties of Natural Religion* when he described "this degenerate Age, which hath been so miserably over-run with Scepticisme and Infidelity [...] the pernicious Doctrines of [...] Libertine-Enthusiasts."[10] In his sermon before the king in 1676, William Cave charts the progress of this "present evil" from its inception, when the "first approaches of impiety are modest and bashful," to its growth into "a more stubborn and positive infidelity":

> And then how ordinary is it to hear such Men, more than whisper their Sentiments to this effect; that all Religion is but a trick of Art, a notion started by the fears of Men, hatch'd at first by some jealous Mind, or contrived by some crafty Statesman, to keep the World in peace and order; that the existence of a supreme Being is but a dreadful and melancholy fancy, and the invisible terrours of another World are but painted flames, kindled in the warm brain of some devout and pious Preacher; that a future state is but a precarious notion, and that there is no reason to believe what is at so vast a distance from us.[11]

As already argued, while churchmen virulently criticised Hobbes's works, a version of his philosophy, combined with adulterated versions of Epicureanism and Lucretianism, was championed by some in literary and court circles. The Earl of Rochester and his group of 'Libertine-Wits' are the most notorious followers of a materialist/determinist philosophy that questioned a teleological universe, the existence of moral absolutes and the concept of free will. Thomas Shadwell was a part of this group. It is clear that he was familiar with Hobbes's writings – he willed a copy of Hobbes's works to his son.[12] Shadwell was also familiar with Lucretius's work, as is made evident by reference to that philosopher in several of his plays. In *The Virtuoso*, produced at Dorset Garden in 1676, Bruce – "a gentlem[a]n of wit" – refers to Lucretius as "Thou profound Oracle of Wit and Sence! [...] [who] reconcil'st Philosophy with Verse, and dost, almost alone, demonstrate that Poetry and Good Sence may go together" (I.i.6). Bruce then reads from *De rerum natura*, expressing Lucretius's denial of divine intervention:

> The gods, by right of nature, must possess
> An everlasting age of perfect peace;
> Far off removed from us and our affairs;
> Neither approached by dangers, or by cares;
> Rich in themselves, to whom we cannot add;
> Not pleased by good deeds, nor provoked by bad.[13]

However, it is particularly in his profoundly popular play *The Libertine* – a version of the Don Juan legend – that Shadwell expounds on aspects of Lucretian and Hobbesian materialism.

Don Juan made his first foray into England with *The Libertine*. The legend of Don Juan as it has come down to us is based on the mythical figure of the amorous trickster and on the Spanish folk tale of a Double Invitation to dinner with a dead man.[14] The latter is a tale of avenging death. In early representations, a man finds a skull on the road and kicks it. Death then comes after him because of his lack of respect for the dead. In other versions, a man treats a statue of a dead man with amused contempt – often by tweaking his beard. The man invites the statue to dinner. The statue offers a counter-invitation, and the contemptuous man is taken down to Hell.[15] In 1616, Tirso de Molina took both elements and incorporated them into a play for the first time: *El Burlador de Sevilla y Convidado de piedra*. A version of the play was performed as part of the Italian commedia dell' arte repertoire and then picked up in France, where there were four different versions written in the 1660s. Two minor playwrights, Villiers and Dorimon, wrote versions of the play before Molière produced his much more celebrated *Dom Juan, ou Le Festin de Pierre* (1665). After Molière's death, the French actor Claude La Rose, Sieur de Rosimond wrote another adaptation of the play for the Théâtre du Marais entitled *Le nouveau Festin de Pierre, ou L'Athée foudroyé* (1669). This is the play that Shadwell chose as his model for *The Libertine*. Rosimond made several fundamental changes to the story which Shadwell used and, in many cases, exaggerated.

Rosimond influenced Shadwell's depiction of Don John as more philosophical and less misogynistic, but also as more violent and criminal than he is in any of the earlier plays. He is no longer the 'burlador' of Tirso de Molina who finds his pleasure in tricking women into bed, or the seducer of Molière who finds satisfaction in savaging the virtue of his female victims:

> [...] to combat by Transports, Sighs, and Tears the innocent Virtue of a Soul, which can hardly prevail with itself to yield; to demolish Inch by Inch all the little Resistances that oppose us; to vanquish the Scruples on which she prides herself, and to lead her gently whither we would have her go. (I.ii) [16]

Rosimond's and Shadwell's 'Don Juans' are not interested in games or even in cheating and humiliating women – they rape and murder to satisfy their insatiable appetites for sex and violence. They have no remorse or conscience. In their deterministic view, man has no free will so cannot make the choice between good and evil: he cannot be held responsible for 'evil' actions because he is simply following his nature. A fundamental difference between the two characters, however, is that Rosimond's Don Juan is explicitly a pagan, so his sins can be attributed to his ignorance of Christian morals. Shadwell does not use this distancing technique, and his Don John is more dangerous not only because he is a more prodigious (and, at times, random) rapist and murderer but also because he is a Christian: he does not hide his philosophy or his actions behind the façade of unenlightened paganism.[17]

In the early plays, Don Juan acts out his crimes alone, but Rosimond adds two impious rogues to the story. They accompany Don Juan and provide a malevolent influence over him as the valet Carille details:

> [...] sans eux vous seriez un fort homme de bien.
> Vous n'auriez jamais eu tant d'habitude aux crimes,

> Si vous n'aviez suivy leurs coupables maxims;
> Mais, depuis qu'ils se sont attachez près de vous,
> Tousjours on vous a vu faire de méchans coups. (I.iv)[18]

In *The Libertine*, Shadwell retains the two partners-in-crime (Don Lopez and Don Antonio) but delegates them to Don John's followers or hangers-on. In the first scene of the play, we discover that all three men have committed heinous crimes. Don Lopez has murdered his brother to retain his estate, and Don Antonio has raped and impregnated his sisters. Neither can outdo Don John, however, according to his valet Jacomo: "you are both Saints to my hopeful Master; / I'll turn him loose to Belzebub himself; / He shall outdo him at his own Weapons" (I.i).[19] Jacomo lists Don John's crimes: he has killed his own father and murdered Don Pedro, the Governor of Seville, in order to rape his sister. He has scaled the walls of monasteries: "Two Nuns, I know, you ravish'd, and a third you dangerously wounded for her violent resistance" (I.i). In short, he has committed "[s]ome thirty Murders, Rapes innumerable, frequent Sacrilege, Parricide [...] not one in all the Catalogue of Sins have scap'd you" (I.i). Don Antonio says he will "imitate" the patterns of these crimes. Don Lopez calls Don John "our Oracle" whose philosophy has "[d]ispelled the Fumes which once clouded our Brains" (I.i). Don John's "philosophy" is amoral materialism.

> Thus far without a bound we have enjoy'd
> Our prosp'rous pleasures, which dull Fools call Sins,
> Laugh'd at old feeble Judges, and weak Laws,
> And at the fond, fantastic thing call'd Conscience
> Which serves for nothing but to make men Cowards,
> An idle fear of future misery. (I.i)

Don John is an unabashed murderer and rapist. Shadwell, however, draws him as a somewhat admirable figure – an aristocratic, handsome and eloquent villain touched neither by fear nor guilt: consistent and heroic in his determination. He is attractive to women and loyal to his friends. It is inaccurate to describe him as "wholly without charm" and to suggest that, in Shadwell's Don John, "the anti-hero is stripped of all his would-be charm, atheism, irreverence, wit and liberty."[20] In fact, Shadwell inverts early representations of Don Juan as the hypocrite and the valet as his 'conscience'; the valet becomes the hypocrite and a foil to Don John, giving greater credence to the Don's philosophy. In earlier versions, Don Juan is a hypocrite by choice:

> Pour vivre il faut scavoir l'art d'éblouir les hommes,
> [...] Couvrir ses actions d'une belle apparence,
> Se masquer de vertu pour perdre l'innocence,
> Estre bon dans les yeux et méchant dans le coeur [...]. (*Le nouveau Festin* I.v)

His blasphemy and hypocrisy are juxtaposed with the (comic) piety of his servant. Even as a sometimes weak or frightened figure of comedy, the valet strives to convince Don Juan to change his ways, for his own good:

CATALINÓN.   You and the others like you who cheat and seduce women will pay for your pleasure with your lives. (*El Burlador* I.iv) [21]

SGANARELLE. [...] whoever has no Law lives as a brute Beast; and, in consequence, you shall be damn'd to all the Devils [...] I always had Hopes of your Salvation, but now I despair of it [...]. (Dom Juan V.iii, iv)

CARILLE.   Quittez, Monsieur, quittez cette maudite envie; Cette témérité vous coustera la vie. (*Le nouveau Festin* V.v)

In *The Libertine*, however, the servant Jacomo is appalled by what his master does, not because of any inherent evil in the deed but because of his fear that it will endanger his own life. When he discovers Don John and his cronies have torched a nunnery, Jacomo is concerned only with how the event will affect him:

[...] they have done the deed. There is no flying; now
the place will be full of People, and wicked Lights that
will discover me if I fly. (V.i)

When the play opens, Don John speaks of his disdain for (religious) hypocrites:

that would persuade us
To I know not what, which they call Piety,
[And] Have in reserve private delicious Sins,
Great as the happy Libertine enjoys,
With which, in corners, wantonly they roll. (I.i)

Later in the same scene, Jacomo finds himself alone with Leonora, one of Don John's rejected lovers. She swoons when she finds out Don John no longer loves her. Jacomo's response exemplifies the hypocrite that Don John has identified moments earlier:

Ha! The place is
Private – if I should make use of a Natural Receit to
refresh her, and bring her to life again, 'twould be a
great pleasure to me, and no trouble to her. Hum!
'tis very private, and I dare sin in private. (I.i)

When Don John and his group plan to rape some shepherdesses, Don John insists that Jacomo ravish the women as they do. Jacomo responds that he cannot do it – not because the deed is despicable but because his "Courage lies not that way [...]" (IV.ii). Throughout the play, Jacomo's cowardice and obsequiousness are juxtaposed with the dons' bravery and assertiveness. Shadwell's radical alteration from the valet's role of 'conscience' for the philandering Don John to a weak, cowardly hypocrite accentuates the fearlessness and consistency of Don John.

Shadwell uses the character of the hermit in much the same way. The early French versions of the play by Dorimon and Villiers introduce Don Juan to a pilgrim or a hermit. The character does not appear in Molière or Rosimond, but he resurfaces in Shadwell's play to confront the dons with what becomes a debate on free will and religious hypocrisy. The new scene allows Don John to exhibit another attribute – his ability to articulate and to debate. When the dons survive a shipwreck and land on shore, they meet the hermit – "a fellow of mighty Beard and Sanctity" – who is immediately set up as a figure of ridicule by Don John:[22]

> A good civil old Hypocrite […]
> I know not what Sanctity he may have, but he has Beard
> enough to make an Owl's Nest, or stuff a Saddle with. (III.ii)

When the men ask the hermit where they can find a whore, the debate begins:

HERMIT.   Oh Monsters of impiety! are you so lately scap'd the wrath of Heaven, thus to provoke it?

DON ANTONIO. How! by following the Dictates of Nature. Who can do otherwise?

DON LOPEZ.   All our actions are necessitated, none command their own wills.

HERMIT.   Oh horrid blasphemy! would you lay your dreadful and unheard of Vices upon Heaven? No, ill men, that has given you free-will to good.

DON JOHN.   I find thou retir'st here, and never read'st or think'st.
                 Can that blind faculty the Will be free
                 When it depends upon the Understanding?
                 Which argues first before the Will can choose;
                 And the last Dictate of the Judgment sways
                 The Will, as in a Balance, the last Weight
                 Put in the scale, lifts up the other end,
                 And with the same Necessity […]

HERMIT.   The Understanding yet is free, and might persuade 'em better.

DON JOHN.   The Understanding never can be free;
                 For what we understand, spite of ourselves we do:
                 All objects are ready form'd and plac'd
                 To our hands; and these the Senses to the Mind convey,
                 And as those represent them, this must judge:
                 How can the Will be free, when the understanding,
                 On which the Will depends, cannot be so. (III.ii)

The hermit has no retort for Don John. He merely demands that Don John "[l]ay by your devillish Philosophy, and change the dangerous and destructive course of your lewd lives" (III.ii).

This exchange parodies the debates that comprised many of the anti-materialist and anti-Hobbesian sermons and pamphlets of the 1670s, which often took the form of a catechism. Sir Charles Wolseley's *The Unreasonableness of Atheism made manifest* (1669) and Thomas Tenison's *The Creed of Mr. Hobbes examined* (1671) are two examples of how the technique was used to argue that Hobbes and materialism are unnatural and evil. The Earl of Rochester also parodies these debates in his work. In *A Satyr against Reason and Mankind* (written c. 1674/75), Rochester sets up a debate between a witty protagonist and his orthodox (clerical) adversary – "some formal band and beard" (46) – who will, "[s]earch heaven and hell, find out what's acted there, / And give the world true grounds of hope and fear" (70–71).[23] Gillian Manning argues that the *Satyr*'s speaker is written in a manner

> especially calculated to exasperate the orthodox. He personifies [...] the churchmen's oft-expressed notion of a witty, atheistic scoffer, yet [...] he answers the church party's demands for more considered and rational arguments by presenting a powerfully phrased, coherently organised and closely argued case, wholly subversive of orthodox views on reason and mankind.[24]

Shadwell, in *The Libertine*, challenges the orthodox view in a similar way by constructing eloquent debaters on behalf of the heterodox, who produce a series of rational arguments. And, as Barbara Simerka argues, "the character who performs and voices defiance of religious norms is far more attractive than the forces that seek to contain him."[25] The hermit is reduced to a figure of ridicule who cannot sustain his side of the argument. The dons also have the last word:

DON LOPEZ. What we are, we are by Nature; our reason tells us we must follow that.

DON JOHN. Our Constitutions tell us one thing, and yours another; and which must we obey? If we be bad, 'tis Nature's fault that made us so.

The hermit can only end with the impotent: "Farewell. I dare no longer hear your impious discourse. Such hardened Wretches I ne'r heard of yet." Don John's victory is conclusive: "Thus Sots condemn what they can never answer" (III.ii).

In *The Libertine*, Shadwell presents a scenario where nature is cast as God's transcendent aspect – impersonal and eternal – but where there is no evidence of a personal God: a righteous, merciful superhuman being accessible to man through supplication. There are numerous examples throughout the play of characters taking oaths and making vows to God as witness that are dismissed as no more than empty phrases. When Don John abandons Leonora, she is as astonished as she is anguished by the betrayal: "all my Innocence believed your solemn Contract, when you invok'd all the Pow'rs above to testify your Vows." To which Don John replies, "'tis nothing but a way of speaking"; and, later, "Oaths! Snares to catch conceited Women with" (II.i). Jacomo and the hermit, two characters seemingly imbued with religious fervour, frequently – almost automatically – appeal to God for help or retribution. But their prayers, prompted more by indignation or fear than by sanctity, go unanswered.

Shadwell also introduces a character whose primary goal is to vow that she will avenge the crimes perpetrated by Don John against her family. As in the earlier plays, Don John dresses up in his rival's clothes to seduce a woman, but, when he is discovered, he kills her lover and her brother. The woman, Maria, then becomes Don John's nemesis, and her determination and valid motivation for revenge make her a formidable enemy. She is resourceful and assumes the identity of a young man in order to follow Don John without arousing suspicion. Throughout Maria's pursuit she regularly vows her vengeance: "I'll be reveng'd on thee yet ere I die" (II.ii). She asks Heaven to assist her "in that just cause" (III.ii), but she wants to see her revenge: she wants it to be exacted in this world. Maria pursues Don John onto the ship that sinks in a storm. When she escapes and reaches land, her only wish is that "the Villain I pursue has scap'd. I would not be revenged by Heaven, but my own hand; or if not by that, by the Hangman's" (III. ii). Maria, however, is never able to exact her revenge – Heaven does not appear to hear her oaths. As she watches Don John escape punishment from yet another heinous crime, Maria finally realises that no one is listening to her:

> Whither shall injur'd Innocence fly for succour.
> [...] if this foul unnatural murther be not reveng'd,
> there is no Justice left [...]. (IV.i)

Shadwell draws Maria in parallel with one of Shakespeare's charismatic female protagonists, Viola from *Twelfth Night*. Viola also finds herself alone in the world after she survives a shipwreck. She too must use her intelligence and resources, and she disguises herself as a man in order to survive in a strange land. Ultimately her determination and bravery pay off – she is successful and finds love as well as her long-lost brother. An audience familiar with Shakespeare's play would expect a formidable and central character such as Maria also to be successful in her quest. But Shadwell ends Maria's quest, and her life, ignominiously. Not only does Maria never exact any vengeance against Don John for his crimes against her family but also he takes her life. She dies unknown and unmourned – her death a mere stage direction: [They fight. Maria and Don Francisco are killed, the two Bridegrooms are hurt, Jacomo runs away.]

In Shadwell's play, the absence of divine intervention in human affairs diminishes to casuistry the ideas of salvation and damnation. A seventeenth-century audience watching a Don Juan play has one guarantee – that the main character will descend to a fiery Hell in the final scene. Shadwell's play adheres to this principle in theory, but Shadwell makes important changes in the final scene that raise questions about the existence of Hell. In Tirso's play, Don Juan is conscious that he must repent or pay the price, but he consistently puts it off, repeating that there is "[p]lenty of time for that" (*El Burlador* I.v). He never denies the existence of providential justice; he simply feels that he has much more time to get away with his tricks. Molière's Don Juan similarly acknowledges that he must repent sometime in the future: "Yes, Faith, we must reform; we'll live thus for twenty or thirty Years longer, and then we'll take care of ourselves" (*Dom Juan* IV.vii). When their time comes to descend to Hell with the statue, both Tirso and Molière's Don Juans demonstrate profound fear – and there is little question that Hell is a tangible reality:

> Ai, I'm burning alive! Burning, burning! [...]
> let my hand go! [DON JUAN *draws his dagger with his free hand.*]
> I'll stab you to death. ...
> Useless! I'm stabbing the empty air! (*El Burlador* V.vii)

> O Heav'ns, what do I feel! An invisible Flame consumes me;
> I can bear it no longer; all my Body is a burning Firebrand. Oh –
> [*Thunder and Lightning, with a great noise, fall upon* DON JOHN, *the Earth opens and swallows him up and Great Flames rise* ...]. (*Dom Juan* V.vi)

The most startling aspect of Rosimond's play (and something that clearly attracted Shadwell to that adaptation) is that he breaks from this tradition and depicts Don Juan as brave, unrepentant and, most importantly, defiant to the end. Shadwell translates Don Juan's final defiant speech directly from Rosimond:

> These things I see with wonder, but no fear.
> Were all the Elements to be confounded,
> And shuffl'd all into their former Chaos,
> Were Seas of Sulphur flaming round about me,
> And all Mankind roaring within those fires,
> I could not fear or feel the least remorse.
> To the last instant I would dare thy power.
> Here I stand firm, and all thy threats contemn;
> Thy Murderer stands here; now do thy worst. (V.ii)

Earlier in the play, Shadwell had used analogous imagery when the dons battled bravely against the prodigious storm:

> DON JOHN. Let the Clouds roar on and vomit all their Sulphur out; they ne'r
> shall fright me [...] Can you that have stood so many Cannons,
> be frighted at the farting and the belching of a Cloud? [...] Let the
> Heav'ns do their worst, 'tis but drowning at last [...]

> DON LOPEZ. A Man and fear: 'tis but dying at last. (III.i)

This contrasts sharply with the captain of the ship, who clearly has extensive experience of the sea yet is terrified: "I am quite unmann'd" (III.i). Jacomo's fearful words as the ship begins to sink – "Oh! Oh! We burn, we drown, we sink. Oh! We perish, we are lost, we are lost. Oh, Oh, Oh" (III.i) – echo those of the earlier Don Juans as they are taken into Hell.

The ultimate fear and breakdown of resolve for the early Don Juans when approaching Hell is allied, in *The Libertine*, with a despicable, hypocritical character like Jacomo. And Shadwell goes further. Throughout Rosimond's play, Don Juan never denies the existence of God or of Hell; he simply repeats his philosophy that there is little use in fearing death, as it is inevitable. Shadwell, however, defines a new breed of 'Don Juan' who explicitly denies any existence of Heaven or Hell. When Jacomo tells Don John that he will go to the Devil, Don John's materialist response is: "[l]eave off your idle tales, found out by Priests to keep the Rabble in awe" (II.i). Don John's words echo Seneca's *Troades* (Act II, Chorus), translated by Rochester:

> For hell and the foul fiend that rules
> God's everlasting fiery jails
> (Devised by rogues, dreaded by fools),
> With his grim, grisly dog that keeps the door,
> Are senseless stories, idle tales,
> Dreams, whimseys, and no more.[26]

In Rosimond's play, Don Juan's sidekicks are taken to Hell as a warning a day before Don Juan is to die. This gives Don Juan 24 hours to reflect on what he has seen. During this time the ghosts of his two partners-in-crime visit and try to convince him to repent. Shadwell does not use this scene. Instead, in *The Libertine*, the three dons descend to Hell together. Their descent and the statue's final words "Thus perish all / Those men who by their words and actions dare / Against the will and power of Heav'n declare" (V.ii) make it appear as though Shadwell is delivering a moral closing to his story of outrage. But the dons are the philosophical partners of Don John and the only characters Don John might believe. By removing the scene in which the dons speak from Hell, Shadwell effectively removes the only concrete evidence for the characters that Hell exists. Although Shadwell chose to adapt a fable that dictates that the protagonists go to Hell, he used the opportunity to suggest, in an echo of Hobbes and Lucretius, that Hell and other supernatural concepts exist only in the minds of the superstitious or gullible. The final scene is stacked with the numerous ghosts of Don John's victims, but they do not exist in any realistic way. Their role is simply to be part of a gruesome and spectacular pyrotechnic finale, rather than to offer any hope of retribution after death. In addition, the statue that takes the men to Hell is a ghost. Christopher Wheatley argues that, "the fact that the ghost is the instrument of divine vengeance would tend to undercut even this weak version of a divine guarantee of justice [...] there isn't really any room in Protestant theology for ghosts."[27] Ultimately, Don John defies these 'ghosts' and will not believe in Hell. *The Libertine*, with its overdrawn characters in extreme situations, makes no attempt at believability; and Hell, Shadwell suggests, is part of the fabrication.

Influenced by Lucretian and Hobbesian philosophy, Shadwell seeks to uncover and satirise the hypocrisy and fear upon which some Christian dogmas rely; and ultimately, he rejects the probability of divine intervention in man's life. Taking up the theme, Rochester's play *Lucina's Rape or the Tragedy of Vallentinian* depicts a world where divine intervention, if it exists at all, favours the powerful. *Lucina's Rape* is an adaptation of John Fletcher's *The Tragedy of Valentinian*. The first known production of Rochester's play took place in February 1684, several years after Rochester's death. It was a success, according to John Downes's account in *Roscius Anglicanus*: "The well performance, and the vast Interest the Author made in Town, Crown'd the Play, with great Gain of Reputation; and Profit to the *Actors*" (83). It appears, however, that Rochester wrote the manuscript for the play early in 1675.[28] Larry Carver argues that the cast given in Rochester's manuscript "suggests that it was intended for the 1675–76, possibly the 1676–77, season."[29] Although the manuscript was left unfinished, the alterations Rochester made to Fletcher's play are extensive[30] and give an insight into a disillusioned, bleak materialist view of the world not unfamiliar in Rochester's poetry of the time.

Lucina's Rape and Fletcher's *The Tragedy of Valentinian* are based on historical events from Procopius's *History of the Wars*: specifically, an account of the Emperor Valentinian III and his raping of senator Petronius Maximus's chaste wife after winning a ring from her husband at draughts.[31] Rochester rewrites history by making fundamental changes to key characters and events. The focus of his play, made clear in the title, is the rape of Lucina rather than the tragic downfall of Vallentinian and Maximus's revenge. Rochester's main characters are emblematic of either innocence or corruption, and he sets the two sides up in a moral struggle which reaches its climax in the rape of pious innocence.

In Fletcher's play, Maximus starts out as a noble senator but ends as a Machiavellian intriguer. He lusts after power, engineers the death of his friend Aecius, becomes Emperor and attempts to force the widowed Empress Eudoxa into marriage. When Maximus drunkenly tells her that he contrived the death of Vallentinian because of his love for her and that he was a conspirer in his own wife's rape, Eudoxa poisons him. Both Maximus and Vallentinian share the same end. Although Fletcher's version is much more true to Procopius, Rochester removes this aspect of the story and ends his play at Vallentinian's death. Consequently, in Rochester's hands, Maximus's characterisation, although not historically accurate, is much more consistent: he begins the play as a noble senator who is the victim of the emperor's lust and ends the play as a noble victim. He is also more admirable: he does not conspire in Aecius's death, and he remains faithful to his wife. Rather than being corrupted by ambition after his wife's death, Rochester casts Maximus into "a theological abyss"[32] aligning him with the rape victim.

Rochester paints the court and Vallentinian, however, as much more corrupt and debauched than they are in Fletcher's version. Rochester accentuates Vallentinian's lasciviousness in his overt sexual encounters with the Eunuch Lycias (in this case, as they are "discover'd on a Couch"):

> Oh let me presse those balmy lips all day,
> And bath my Love-scorch't Soule in thy moist kisses;
> Now by my joyes thou art all sweete and soft,
> And thou shalt be the Alter of my Love. (V.v.1–4)

The emperor's wantonness at the expense of affairs of state is excoriated by Vallentinian's stalwart and trustworthy general Aecius:[33]

> Thinke how hee may by force of worth and virtue
> Maintaine the right of his imperiall Crowne
> Which he neglects for Garlands made of Roses

> Whilst in disdeigne of his ill guided youth
> Whole Provinces fall off and scorne to have
> Him for their Prince who is his Pleasures Slave. (I.i.22–7)

Aecius's condemnations of Vallentinian make implicit comparisons with Charles II and the common anxiety, expressed in contemporary writing and satirical verse, that Charles's immoderate sexual desires were taking him away from important matters of state. And, as Love suggests, this comparison between the two rulers and their courts extends into Rochester's portrayals of Vallentinian's palace, which are also descriptive of the palace of Whitehall.[34]

Vallentinian's lust for Lucina is affiliated with his tyranny in *Lucina's Rape*.[35] As with Nathaniel Lee's Nero and Alexander, Rochester's emperor consciously constructs himself as an absolute monarch, living in unparalleled proximity to the gods. When Lucina refuses his advances, Rochester's Vallentinian pronounces his absolutism:

> Can you believe your husbands right to you
> Other than what from mee hee does derive
> Who justly may recall my owne at pleasure?
> Am I not Emperour? this World my owne
> Giv'n mee without a partner by the Gods?
> Each man, each Beast, even to the smallest fly,
> Noe mortall Creature dare call his – but I […]. (I.i.218–24)

Rochester adds several complex scenes between Lucina and Vallentinian which examine their understanding of and relationship to the gods. Lucina believes in providence. She makes supplication to the gods and tells Vallentinian:

> Had Heav'n design'd for mee so great a fate
> As Cesars Love I shoud have ben preserv'd
> By carefull providence for him alone
> Not offer'd up at first to Maximus. (I.i.241–4)

Vallentinian, in contrast, issues a warning to the gods: "Incense noe longer to those Gods shall burne / Unless they strive to serve mee in their turne" (I.i.297–8). It is Vallentinian's petition to the gods that is successful: his rash threats appear to reach an audience that Lucina's pious supplications do not. Lucina is left with none of her former trust in "the Powers above / Those wise and carefull Guardians of the good" (III.i.39–40).

In contrast to her role in the Fletcher play, Rochester's play delineates and draws in on aspects of Lucina's character, in particular her piety and chastity.[36] Rochester also increases the importance of Lucina's role by creating several new scenes for her. It is clear that Rochester wanted an established actress to play the role. The MS cast list for the King's Company records Rebecca Marshall as Lucina. When the play was first performed in 1684, Elizabeth Barry took on the role, which indicates that it was considered a strong woman's part, "requiring an experienced dramatic actress rather than an ingénue."[37]

Rochester also extends the role of the eunuch Lycias to create a foil for Lucina, and their contrasting relationships with the emperor reflect on and illuminate the character of Vallentinian. In Fletcher's play, Lycias is a minor, asexual character. In Rochester's treatment, he takes on the more important role of the emperor's lover. The epitome of moral baseness, he is easily seduced by offers of worldly goods and uses his sexuality for self-promotion. When Lycias is first requested to meet with the emperor in "his closett," he sees it as "a Summons to Prosperity" (III.i.67). Lucina, in contrast, will not indulge in the depravity of the court. The courtiers and bawds describe her as "beyond all Temptation" (II.ii.121). Rochester emphasises that it is Lucina's sanctity that fires Vallentinian's desire: "to possesse her chast and uncorrupted! / There lyes the joy and Glory of my Love" (II.ii.164–5). At least one critic feels that Rochester's portrayal of Lucina is irritatingly puritanical.[38] Lucina's extreme sanctity and Lycias's extreme corruption, however, are personifications of abstract concepts of good and evil.

Rochester plays the two off against each other in juxtaposed scenes where the lasciviousness repeatedly insinuates itself into virtue's sphere. The scenes build up images of a godless world where moral baseness is the victor over piety. After Vallentinian's bawds tell him they have been unable to procure Lucina, Vallentinian's response has deep Hobbesian echoes:

> Wretches! whose vitious Lives when I withdraw
> The Absolute protection of my Favour
> Will dragge you into all the Miseries
> That your owne Terrours, Universall hate
> And Law with whips and jayles can bring upon you. (II.ii.142–6)

The emperor works himself up to a sexual frenzy thinking of Lucina's chastity, adding "flaming fury to my fire" (II.ii.157). He immediately demands his bawd, Chilax, fetch him the "sweet fac'd Eunuch" Lycias. Chilax then ends the act with a prolonged and graphic description of Lycias's sexual gifts:

> Tis a soft Rogue this Licias,
> And rightly understood
> Hee's worth a thousand Women's Nicenesses.
> [...] a deare Boyes disinterested flame,
> Gives Pleasure, and for meer Love gathers Paine:
> In him alone fondnes sinceere does prove
> And the kind, tender, naked boy, is Love. (II.ii.178–80, 185–8)

Immediately afterwards, Lucina enters the stage alone. The scene shifts from the depravity of court to "sollitary Groves where Peace does dwell / Sweet Harbours of pure Love and Innocence" (III.i.1–2). Rochester composes a monologue for Lucina in which she describes the beauty and harmony of her surroundings, away from "the contentious Court or clamorous Camp" (III.i.17). But once more this peaceful space is soon ruptured by Lycias, with news that Lucina's husband has been called to court by the emperor. Lucina's reverie is immediately broken:

"The Emperour! Unwonted horrour seizes mee all o're" (III.i.30–31). Then, as Lucina tries to sleep, Lycias conspicuously remains onstage to read aloud a letter he has received from court:

Thou art the most fortunate of men!
Riches and honours come upon thee full sayle [...]
The Emperour loves thee, Longs for thy company [...]
What an Opportunity has thou to destroy thy enemyes,
delude thy friends, enrich thy self, enslave the World, raise thy kindred,
humble thy Master and Governe him. (III.i.57–63)

He exits the stage in haste to meet his fortune, while Lucina's peaceful sleep is broken by a nightmarish dream of her rape.

The rape itself is the climax of the play: the action towards which everything advances. It is the point where any sense of absolute mercy or justice is destroyed and the faithful characters lose their trust and belief in providence. When Lucina is deceived into coming to court believing that Maximus is there, heavenly allusions abound. She and her waiting-women are met by sniggering remarks from the court bawds: "The fair Lucina here! nay then I finde / Our Slander'd Court has not sinn'd up so high / To fright all the good Angels from its Care" (IV.ii.35–7). When her waiting-woman, troubled by Lucina's frightened countenance, anxiously asks "are there not Gods and Angels?" to protect her, Lucina's response gives evidence of her incipient despair: "None in this place I feare but Evil ones! / Heav'n pitty mee" (IV.ii.90–91). Short, fast-paced, incongruous scenes then build up to the climactic rape scene. The emperor has brought in masquers to create a diversion and direct attention from the rape.

EMPEROR. And if (by chance) odd noises shoud bee heard,
          As womens shricks or soe, say tis a play
          Is practicing within.

LYCINUS. The Rape of Lucrece
          Or some such merry pranck [...]. (IV.ii.193–6)

Vallentinian clarifies his design as his right by nature: "Tis nobler like a Lion to invade / Where appetite directs, and seize my prey / Then to wait tamely like a begging Dogg" (IV.ii.197–9). And once more he derides the gods: "I scorne those Gods who seek to cross my wishes / [...] – Force / Of all the powers is the most Generous (IV.ii.201–3).

At the end of this disturbing revelation, "five or six Dancing-Masters" are discovered practising. The manifestly inept dancers are fumbling around, unable to 'hit' the right step. As they begin their dance, the farce is broken by the violence of Lycinius's entrance:

Blesse me! the Lowd shricks and horrid out cryes
Of the poor Lady! Ravishing d'yee call it?
She roares as if she were upon the racke! (IV.iii.9–11)

When he realises the dancers do not hear the screams, he starts some casual banter with them – "Good morrow Gentlemen / What, is all perfect?" (IV.iii.18–19) – while the screams and torture are unabated: the dance and the rape continue. Although the audience does not see the rape take place, the violence is explicit and unsettling. And the next scene opens in Vallentinian's chamber, with the graphic image of "Lucina newly unbound by the Emperour."³⁹

After the rape, Lucina still wants to "cry for Justice," but Vallentinian tells her simply: "Justice will never hear you, I am Justice" (IV.iv.5–6). She finally comes to the realisation that there is no recourse for injured innocence:

> Is this the end of goodness! this the price
> Of all my Early Prayers to protect mee?
> Why then I see there is noe God but power
> Nor virtue now alive that cares for us. (IV.iv.112–15)

Maximus's response to the rape of his wife is markedly different in Rochester's version of the story. When Fletcher's Maximus is beginning the Machiavellian machinations for his insidious rise to power, Rochester's Maximus is soliloquising over the loss of justice. He asks the gods "How wou'd you have your mercy understood?" (IV.iv.303);

> How cou'd you ever have produce'd such ill?
> Had your eternall mindes been bent to good,
> Cou'd humane happiness have prov'd so Lame?
> Rapine, Revenge, Injustice, thirst of Bloud
> Griefe, Anguish, Horrour, want, despair, nor shame
> Had never found a being nor a name. (IV.iv.310–15)

Vallentinian is eventually murdered by his soldiers, so it could be argued that Maximus does have revenge on the emperor for Lucina's rape; but, at the same time, Maximus ultimately loses more. No longer believing in moral certainties, he has lost the ability to navigate through his world.

> If there bee noe such thing as right or wrong
> But force alone must Swallow all possession
> Then to what purpose for soe long descents
> Were Roman Laws observ'd or Heav'n obey'd? (V.v.152–5)

Maximus gets little of value in Vallentinian's response to his anguished question. Certain of his death, there is a brief moment when it appears as if Vallentinian will follow the traditional route of 'evildoers' in tragedy and acknowledge or even repent of his crimes. Instead, Vallentinian is defiant: he justifies his right to do what he chooses, implying he has been vindicated by the gods: "I am satisfy'd that thou did'st ever hate mee: / Thy wife's Rape therefore was an effect of Justice" (V.v.195–6).

Like Don John, Vallentinian shows no repentance and no remorse. In fact, as Don John tortures the statue with images of his daughter's rape, Vallentinian goads Maximus by assuring him that, given the opportunity, he would commit the crime again: "Would the Gods raise Lucina from the grave / And fetter thee but while I might enjoy her / Before thy face I'd ravish her againe" (V.v.240–42). When Lucina realises that justice will not help her in this life, one of her final cries (similar to Maria's in *The Libertine*) is that the gods revenge her against Vallentinian after her death:

> Vengeance and Horrour circle thee – the Empire
> In which thou livest a strong continued surfeit
> Like poyson will disgorge thee, good men raze thee
> From ever being read againe. (IV.iv.14–17)

Vallentinian repudiates this judgement. Implying that there is no ultimate judgement or retribution, Vallentinian informs Maximus that, on the contrary, he will have eternal life – living on in men's minds: "Altars shall be rais'd / To my great Name; while your more vile inscriptions / Time rots and mould'ring Clay is all your portion" (V.v.250–52). After Vallentinian is killed, Maximus does become a 'successful' usurper in the sense that the act of regicide is not punished; but he is a leader who is ambivalent about the future. The play ends bleakly, with little faith that Maximus – or anyone else – can salvage what was lost: "Lead me to Death or Empire which you please / For both are equall to a Ruin'd man" (V.v.253–4).

   Lucina's Rape and *The Libertine* give vivid accounts of a world where providence is a fantasy. In *The Libertine* vice holds the stage. Don John and his colleagues represent a version of 'natural man,' driven completely by physical desires and urges. He is devoid of altruism, callous, cruel and unrestrained by any laws, earthly or heavenly. As such he is free to indulge in any and all vices, without any deleterious consequences to himself. While evil characters remain powerful even after death, virtuous characters get short shrift. In *The Libertine*, the horror, humiliation and death the victims suffer at the hands of the dons is, for the most part, given little emphasis. In contrast, *Lucina's Rape* emphasizes the despair, sense of betrayal and outrage felt by the virtuous, begging in vain for surcease of their pain or, at the very least, some sign of deliverance as a mark of their piety. In these plays, natural law is not immutable. Following a Hobbesian dictum, Shadwell and Rochester provide no evidence in their plays of absolute standards of morality drawing authority from a just and reasonable God. Goodness is mocked, magnanimity is taken advantage of, chastity is ridiculed and solemn vows are derided. Both playwrights present a bleak view of human nature, but equally their materialist standpoint suggests there is no higher justice to turn to: no God to hand down laws from heaven or to redress wrongs. Heaven and Hell are empty words; and justice, in these plays, is ultimately what the most powerful person says it is.

Endnotes

[1]   John Evelyn, *An Essay on the first book T. Lucretius Carus De Rerum Natura* (London, 1656). As the title suggests, Evelyn only translated Book 1 of Lucretius's poem. In 1675 and 1686, John Hayes of Cambridge reprinted Tanaquil Faber's 1662 Latin Saumur edition, *De Rerum Natura Libri Sex*. In 1682, Thomas Creech edited the first complete English translation: *Titus Lucretius Carus. The Epicurean Philosopher, His Six Books De Natura Rerum Done into English Verse with Notes* (Oxford, 1682). Creech's translation was influential and reprinted twice in 1683.

[2]   *De Rerum Natura*, trans. W.H.D Rouse (Cambridge: Harvard UP, 1975). The following quotations from *De Rerum Natura* are taken from Rouse's translation and are hereafter cited parenthetically in the text. Because of the publishing history of Lucretius's poem in the seventeenth century, I have chosen a twentieth-century translation from the Latin. As indicated above, the only English translation of the poem before the period of study was Evelyn's translation of Book 1, published 20 years previously. Lucy Hutchinson's translation was never published, so could have had little influence. The only editions of the poem available to writers and philosophers of the early to mid-Restoration would have been in Latin, likely an edition either of Denys Lambin or Lambinus (1563/64; 1570; 1583) or Daniel Paré or Pareus (1631). The only other translation possibly available would be M. de Marolles's edition in Latin and French (published in Paris, 1650 and 1659).

[3]   When translating "religionibus atque minis obsistere vatum" into "the superstitions and threatenings of the priests" (I.109), W.H.D. Rouse notes that Lucretius's use of 'vatum' "refers to all professional supporters of traditional religion and mythology, both priests and poets" (Rouse 11n).

[4]   Lucretius, *The Epicurean Philosopher, His Six Books De Natura Rerum*, trans. Thomas Creech (Oxford, 1682) preface.

[5]   Hobbes, *Leviathan*, ed. Tuck 39.

[6]   Mintz 153.

[7]   Robert South, "A Sermon Preach'd at Lambeth-Chappel 25 November, 1678," *Twelve Sermons Preached upon Several Occasions* 240.

[8]   Robert South, "A Sermon Preached at Westminster-Abbey 1676" *Twelve Sermons Preached upon Several Occasions* 439.

[9]   John Bramhall, *The Works of the Most Reverend Father in God, John Bramhall ...*, tome 3 (Dublin, 1676) 873.

[10]   In the preface to *Of the Principles and Duties of Natural Religion* (London, 1675). An example of identifying Epicurus's thought with Hobbes is Samuel Parker's *Demonstration of the Divine Authority of the Law of Nature* (London, 1681).

[11]   William Cave, *A sermon preached before the King at Whitehall*, 5–6.

[12]   Although he warned his son John "to have a care of some ill opinions of [Hobbes] concerning government," Shadwell went on to suggest that John "may make use of what is good in him." *The Works of Thomas Shadwell*, ed. Montague Summers, vol. 3 (London, Fortune, 1927) cxxx–cxxxi. Also quoted in Stroup, "Shadwell's Use of Hobbes" *Studies in Philology* 35: 3 (1938): 407.

[13]   *De Rerum Natura* I. 44–9. In Shadwell's play, Bruce reads the quotation in Latin (*The Works of Thomas Shadwell*, ed. Summers 3:105). I use Rochester's poignant translation of these lines from *The Complete Poems of John Wilmot*, ed. Vieth 35.

¹⁴   Anthony Kaufman traces Don Juan's development from the ancient figure of the trickster: "He is pancultural, appearing in the legends of North American Indians and, in his European version, stemming from the ambiguous figure of Hermes [...] His story seems always to suggest doubleness: he fools others and is fooled; he triumphs and is defeated; he exults and suffers" ("The Shadow of the Burlador," ed. A. R. Braunmuller and J.C. Bulmans, *Comedy from Shakespeare to Sheridan* [Newark: U of Delaware, 1986] 237). See also Paul Radin, *The Trickster* (New York: Schocken, repr. 1973); and Edith Kern, *The Absolute Comic* (New York: Columbia UP, 1980).

¹⁵   Oscar Mandal examines variants of the Spanish folktale of the Statue and the Double Invitation. He argues that the perplexing and macabre nature of the invitation and counter-invitation to a meal must have come down to us as "a mitigation of a grim and yet intelligible motif, that of the eating of the dead, possibly as a religious rite" [*The Theatre of Don Juan* (Lincoln: U of Nebraska P, 1963)]. See also Dorothy MacKay, *The Double Invitation in the Legend of Don Juan* (Palo Alto: Stanford UP, 1943).

¹⁶   All references to Molière's "Dom Juan ou Le Festin de Pierre," trans. John Ozell, are from Mandel, *The Theatre of Don Juan*, and are hereafter cited parenthetically in the text.

¹⁷   Wolfgang Fleischmann argues that seventeenth- and eighteenth-century editors of *De Rerum Natura* excuse Lucretius for his denial of divine providence and of the immortality of the soul because he was an unenlightened pagan (*Lucretius and English Literature 1680–1740* [Paris: A.G. Nizet, 1964] 83).

¹⁸   All references to Claude La Rose, Sieur de Rosimond's "Le Nouveau Festin de Pierre ou l'Athée foudroyé" are from V. Fournel, ed., *Les Contemporains de Molière*, vol. 3 (Paris, 1875), and are hereafter cited parenthetically in the text.

¹⁹   ¹⁹ All references to Shadwell's "The Libertine" are from Mandal, *The Theatre of Don Juan*, and are hereafter cited parenthetically in the text.

²⁰   Aaron Jaffe, "Seditious Appetites and Creeds" *Restoration: Studies in English Literary Culture, 1660–1700*, 24:2 (2000): 57, 69–70.

²¹   All references to Tirso de Molina's "El Burlador de Sevilla," trans. Adrienne M. Schizzano, are from Mandal, *The Theatre of Don Juan*, and are hereafter cited parenthetically in the text.

²²   According to E. Cobham Brewer, there are several insults traditionally attached to the beard. To make one's beard (Chaucer) or 'faire la barbe a quelqu'un' means "to have him wholly at your mercy"; to beard one is "to defy him, to contradict him flatly, to insult by plucking the beard"; and to laugh at one's beard is "[t]o attempt to make a fool of a person" (*The Dictionary of Phrase and Fable* [Hertfordshire: Wordsworth, repr. 1993] 109–10).

²³   "A Satyr against Reason and Mankind," *The Complete Poems of John Wilmot*, ed. Vieth 96.

²⁴   Gillian Manning, "Rochester's Satyr Against Reason and Mankind and Contemporary Religious Debate" *The Seventeenth Century* 8:1 (Spring 1993): 111.

²⁵   Barbara A. Simerka, "Eros and Atheism," *Echoes and Inscriptions*, ed. Barbara A. Simerka and Christopher B. Weimer (Lewisburg: Bucknell UP, 2000) 223.

²⁶   *The Complete Poems of John Wilmot*, ed. Vieth 151.

²⁷   Christopher J. Wheatley, *Without God or Reason* (Lewisburg: Bucknell UP, 1993) 90–91.

²⁸   Larry Carver, "Rochester's Valentinian" *Restoration and Eighteenth-Century Research* 4 (1989): 26, and Harold Love, *The Works of John Wilmot*, ed. Love 450 concur with this date.

²⁹ Carver 26; Judith Milhous and Robert D. Hume believe the MS cast suggests "performance or intended performance by the King's Company ca. 1675–76" (Downes, *Roscius Anglicanus* 83n).

³⁰ Useful accounts of the changes made are also given in Carver, Love, Arthur Colby Sprague, *Beaumont and Fletcher on the Restoration Stage* (New York and London: Benjamin Bloom, repr. 1965); and Warren Chernaik, "Sex, Tyranny, and the Problem of Allegiance; Political Drama During the Restoration," *Theatre and Culture in Early Modern England, 1650–1737: From Leviathan to Licensing Act*, ed. Catie Gill (Farnham: Ashgate, 2010) 75–86.

³¹ Procopius of Caesarea. *History of the Wars: Book III*, trans. H.B. Dewing (London: William Heinemann, 1968) 2:4–5. The story had also been told in the second part of Honore Durfey's *L'Astree*, 1610.

³² Sandra Clark, "Sex and Tyranny Revisited: Waller's The Maid's Tragedy and Rochester's Valentinian" *Theatre and Culture in Early Modern England, 1650–1737*, ed. Catie Gill 86.

³³ Nathaniel Lee uses the old general Clytus for similar purposes in *The Rival Queens*. It is interesting to note that because of echoes in Lee's *The princess of Cleve*, Harold Love believes Lee must have read Rochester's play in manuscript (*The Works of John Wilmot*, ed. Love 454n). *The Rival Queens* was produced in 1676 after Rochester would have written his manuscript, so Lee's effective portrayal of the relationship between Clytus and Alexander the Great could have been influenced by Rochester.

³⁴ Harold Love, "Was Lucina betrayed at Whitehall?" *That Second Bottle: Essays on John Wilmot, Earl of Rochester*, ed. Nicholas Fisher (Manchester: Manchester UP, 2000) 179–90. See, for example, II.ii.176; III.ii.52–3; IV.ii.74–5.

³⁵ Warren Chernaik argues that the "rape of a chaste woman by a tyrant in Jacobean and Restoration drama is always an assertion of the power of the unbounded will … A tyrant's rape is an example of overreaching, ignoring Machiavelli's advice that a ruler should never allow himself to be despised by his subjects" ("Sex, Tyranny, and the Problem of Allegiance" *Theatre and Culture in Early Modern England, 1650–1737*, ed. Catie Gill 103).

³⁶ It is interesting that even in Procopius the character is unnamed.

³⁷ *The Works of John Wilmot*, ed. Love 451n.

³⁸ Sprague 170.

³⁹ This is not the first evidence of physical violence in the play (see, for example, I.i.284, where Vallentinian "lays hold" of Lucina; or IV.ii.136, where Vallentinian draws Lucina in). The description of the rape has its counterparts in other horror tragedies of the mid-1670s, such as Nathaniel Lee's *Gloriana* (IV.i) and Elkanah Settle's *The Empress of Morocco* (IV.iii).

Conclusion

In March 1681, the third and final Exclusion bill was defeated in parliament: Charles and the court party had won the battle to ensure the rightful succession of his brother James. By this time, Rochester, Milton, Hobbes and Marvell were all dead; but Aphra Behn, Thomas Shadwell, Elkanah Settle, Nathaniel Lee and Thomas Otway were poised to write some of their most famous work. In the new political climate, plays became openly propagandist. Behn and Dryden wrote propaganda for the crown: Behn wrote no more tragedy, but several of her comedies attacked the Whigs; Otway was increasingly associated with the court and Tory politics, his most famous play of civil discontent, *Venice Preserv'd*, was produced in 1682; and Settle and Shadwell wrote on behalf of the Whig exclusionists. Settle produced pamphlets and satires. Shadwell's *The Lancashire Witches* (Duke's 1681) was cut by the censor because of the anti-Catholic satire, and he did not write for the theatre again until 1688. The previous year Lee's republican play, *Lucius Junius Brutus* (Duke's 1680), had been banned after several performances, and the production of Dryden and Lee's *The Duke of Guise* (Drury Lane 1682) had been prohibited for several months by the Lord Chamberlain. Although these later plays retained elements of the earlier horror plays, their tone and focus were necessarily different during this time of change. This was no longer a time of hidden anxieties: the outbreak of the Popish Plot and parliament's active drive to exclude James from the throne had forced underlying fears onto the table. The dramatists, responding to a changing environment and reflecting shifting emphases, became not more political but, rather, more overtly partisan in the politics they espoused.

For the remainder of seventeenth century, nothing quite like the horror plays of the 1670s returned to the stage. After the Exclusion Crisis, the next major political upheaval for England was the Glorious Revolution of 1688, which forced James II off the throne. The subsequent Bill of Rights barred future Catholic succession to the throne and circumscribed the monarch's powers – two key issues that were an enormous cause of anxiety in the 1670s. A decade after this revolution, playwrights such as Mary Pix, Delariviere Manley, Catherine Trotter and John Banks began to delve again into horror. Robert Hume classifies these later plays as part of the "pathetic" genre in the "heroics and horrors style," arguing they derive from the plays of the 1670s. As in the horror plays, none of the characters in this later drama is exemplary: in fact, all the characters (good and bad) are deficient in something; good actions are not necessarily rewarded, nor can evil forces always be contained. As Hume suggests, however, these plays generally allow a "high, even religious moral" to infiltrate them in order to "recommend and to encourage Vertue."[1]

Gruesome elements certainly exist. In Delariviere Manley's *The Royal Mischief*, for example, an unfaithful lover gets shot from a cannon in the final scene, as punishment for his personal and political betrayal. After the cannon is shot, an officer tells the audience that the betrayed wife, Princess Selima,

> [...] ranges the fatal Plain, Gathering the smoaking Relicks of her Lord, Which
> singe, as she grasps them; now on the Horrid Pile, her self had heap'd, I left
> her Stretcht along, bestowing burning Kisses And Embraces on every fatal
> piece. (V.i)[2]

As violent and disturbing as these images are (reminiscent of those in Seneca and
the horror plays), they are conjured up solely in the audience's imagination, unlike
plays such as *Oedipus*, *Caesar Borgia* or *The Empress of Morocco*, where the
audience is required to behold, first hand, extreme spectacles of violence. Although
they can be and have been analysed as political plays, pathos for couples thwarted
in love is a central focus, and, as in the Jacobean drama, revenge looms large.
These plays question expected moral responses to extreme situations, and they
investigate relationships between power and justice; but several characteristics
integral to the horror plays, such as the deep disillusionment, the scepticism over
moral absolutes and the lack of final hope, are missing.

The Restoration horror plays possess a definable set of traits and motifs which
distinguish them from the other serious drama of the era: from the earlier heroic
plays on the one hand, and from later sentimental tragedy on the other. Taken
together, these plays written in the years between 1670/71 and 1680/81 come very
close to being characterised not as exempla, for there are no moral lessons to
be learned, but as vivid explications of the Seven Deadly Sins: Pride, Avarice,
Lust, Envy, Gluttony, Anger and Sloth. In this respect, they can truly be labelled
"horror" plays, dealing as they do with some of the most egregious human traits.
And in the plays, the traits are ascribed most often to duly consecrated, legitimate
rulers rather than to sinister outsiders. The evil that infiltrates these plays is
often motiveless: revenge as an inducement to violence is rarely depicted. Moral
structure has broken down to the extent that, while innocent victims beg in vain
for justice from a higher power, revengers and murderers can go free; at the very
least, criminals die defiantly, without repentance or remorse.

Paternal authority in these plays is destructive and perverse. Kings, the heads of
family and state, are corrupt and vacillating: their actions undermine the stability
of the state. They are depicted either in the middle of psychological disintegration
or as perverting intra-family relationships through incest and jealousy. All are
debilitatingly self-important and self-obsessed. The traditional notion of the
patriarch as a wise steward of his family (and, in the case of the sovereign, his
subjects) is consistently undermined: their diseased minds spread destruction.
There is a dangerous antipathy between father and son: most often, the fathers
endeavour to exile or kill off their own sons. Suspicious and fearful, they cling to
the present, viewing their sons not as precious heirs whose job is "to continue the
name and traditions of authority and meaning in a patriarchal society" but, rather,
as rivals: "the sign of [their own] mortality."[3]

There are no heroes in these plays. Those characters who are expected to
provide leadership or stability are nowhere to be found. The would-be heroes are
deeply flawed – heirs only to an unhealthy legacy of depravity, they are unable to
fulfil their expected roles. They have no acumen, provide no moral example, induce

no admiration, and are, ultimately, ineffectual – impotent victims either to lustful women or to men more powerful than they. Familial loyalty and maternal love are mocked. Menacing, histrionic women reject the moral expectations and obligations implicit in their traditionally assigned roles. Female power is feared; monstrous queens threaten legitimate descent and commit the most unnatural of crimes.

At the conclusion of each of the horror plays, there is no sense of a renewed hope or faith that there will be any improvement in the condition of the people or the state. In many instances, tyrants have been disposed of, but those who are left are as impaired as the tyrants they helped to destroy. Most disturbingly, no characters seem to have learned from the mistakes made, and the plays imply that there will be a continual repetition of the same errors. Providential justice and any sense of moral absolutes – of central importance in the earlier Restoration plays as well as in the Jacobean drama – are absent in the horror plays. They are replaced by an active questioning of the nature of God and the validity of Christian dogma. The identification of power with justice is rejected. In fact, the devastating lack of accountability of kings to their subjects is a recurring theme.

The horror plays are a direct result of, and a reaction to, the particular circumstances in which the English found themselves in the middle years of the Restoration of Charles II. As detailed, the period was a time of scepticism in literary, scientific and philosophical fields – about absolute power, God's justice, the existence of absolutes, and man's relationship to God. Above all, it was a time of misgiving and unease: unease drawn from disappointment with the re-establishment of a king who did not possess his people's and his parliament's trust; apprehension over a betrayal to the Catholics and a repetition of the events that had led to civil strife 30 years previously. The horror plays respond to the particular climate of retrospective fear, forced forgetting and uncertainty about the future, through images of monstrosity, diseases of the mind and body, repellent sexual aberrations and defiant agnosticism.

The plays were of great interest to a population that was active in expressing disquiet, yet shrank from actual commitment to change. The satisfying, fantastical catharsis of the theatre was re-created, in the streets, by the real burning of imaginary popes. After Charles was made to enforce the recusancy laws in 1673, there were more bonfires and more popes being burnt in effigy than there had been for 30 years. According to one pamphlet: "the Citizens rejoyceing, seemed to swel the banks last *Wednesday* Night, where you might have seen the broad Streets of *London* so thick with Bonfires, as if they had been but one Hearth."[4]

The horror plays appear to have provided a similarly cathartic experience for their audiences, enacting, as they did, primal taboos in innovative theatrical spaces that were able to support audience fascination with and desire for extreme visual display. They were incredibly well attended and popular. In *Roscius Anglicanus*, John Downes contends that *Oedipus* "was Admirably well Acted […] it took prodigiously, being Acted 10 Days together" (79). On *Don Carlos*, Downes reflects, "all the Parts being admirably Acted, it lasted successively 10 days; it got more Money than any preceding Modern Tragedy" (76).[5] *The Libertine*, according to

Downes again, was "very well Acted, and got the Company great Reputation" (78). According to Judith Milhous, Behn's *Abdelazer* provided a £25 dividend for the Duke's Company Stockholders.[6] It was also popular enough to be revived at the end of the century. The popularity of *The Empress of Morocco, The Rival Queens* and *The Tragedy of Nero* quickly spawned imitations – Durfey's burlesque *The Empress of Morocco, The Rival Kings* and *Piso's Conspiracy*, a restaging of the 1624 *Nero*. Productions of *The Empress of Morocco* and *The Rival Queens* were regularly reprised, the latter being presented for the queen's birthday celebration in November 1681, played again before the king and queen in December 1685, at court in October 1686 and again at Drury Lane in January 1690.[7] I would suggest these plays were so popular precisely because they engaged with contemporary feelings of social, personal and political disaffection. They mirrored the profound unease of a society fighting to understand and assimilate changes in its rapidly changing world.

In their exploration of human iniquity, the horror plays are not unique to dramatic or literary history: they share similarities with other periods and other genres. When reflecting on the Gothic tales of Poe and Hoffman, Angela Carter's analysis could just as easily be employed to characterise the English horror plays of the 1670s:

> The Gothic tradition in which Poe writes grandly ignores the value systems of our institutions; it deals entirely with the profane. Its great themes are incest and cannibalism. Character and events are exaggerated beyond reality, to become symbols, ideas, passions. Its style will tend to be ornate, unnatural – and thus operate against the perennial human desire to believe the word as fact. Its only humour is black humour. It retains a singular moral function – that of provoking unease.[8]

The horror plays also hark back to the unsettling tone and the cynical depictions of power and evil in the tragedies of Seneca. Seneca, who was writing at a particularly dark time in Roman history under the reign of Nero, sees man's innate fallibility at the centre of man's tragedy. The struggle of searching for and finding justice in a world with no evidence of a divine intervening power impels both Seneca and the horror dramatists to stare at the bleak reality of earthly power. Man, in these plays, is deeply flawed and susceptible to corruption.

The momentum in Senecan tragedy, as Gordon Braden argues, leads towards "uncompromised individual power."

> In the wake of the apocalypse men discover what they are; and where the shaken survivors of the Greek stage can regain a sense of community in their helplessness, the victims in Seneca face their conquerors, not each other, and discover only the absoluteness of the power that has destroyed them. This power is absolute and immitigable because it is totally human, and in that knowledge the world is unimaginably bleak [...].[9]

In a similar way, the bleakness that permeates the horror plays is tied to the understanding that in this world the fount of justice and absolute power is human; and, given human fallibility, men cannot offer absolute justice and cannot sustain absolute power without corruption. In times of deep political or psychological uncertainty, effective literature reflects the dislocation in society. The horror plays reflect deep societal schisms, but they do not offer answers to their audiences, nor do they endeavour to edify. They provoke unease. They give deep-seated and repressed anxieties a metaphoric reality that can be reflected upon. They resonate with the pessimistic questioning of (a set of) belief systems that had served generations: ultimately, they express a loss of faith in the future.

Endnotes

[1]   Robert Hume, *The Development of English Drama*, 403, 422–4.

[2]   *The Royal Mischief*, ed. Margarete Rubik and Eva Mueller- Zettlemann, vol. 1, D. Hughes, et al., eds., *Eighteenth-Century Women Playwrights* (London: Pickering & Chatto, 2001) 102.

[3]   Jessica Munns, *Restoration Politics* 32.

[4]   Anon., *The Burning of the Whore of Babylon* 2.

[5]   Milhous and Hume note an interesting comment from Barton Booth in a letter to Aaron Hill in 1732: "Mr. Betterton observ'd to me many Years ago, that Don Carlos succeeded much better than either Venice Preserv'd or the Orphan, and was infinitely more applauded and follow'd for many Years" (*A Collection of Letters ... written ... To the Late Aaron Hill, Esq.* [London, 1751] 82; quoted in Downes, *Roscius Anglicanus* 76, n230).

[6]   Milhous, "The Duke's Company's Profits, 1675–1677" 81.

[7]   *The Works of Nathaniel Lee*, ed. Stroup and Cooke 213.

[8]   Angela Carter, *Fireworks: Nine Profane Pieces* (London: Quartet, 1974) 122.

[9]   Braden, *Renaissance Tragedy and the Senecan Tradition* 58.

Bibliography

Primary Texts and Editions of Plays

A Letter From a Person of Quality to his Friend in the Country. London, 1675.

A Letter to Mr. S. A Romish Priest Concerning the Impossibility of the Publick Establishment of Popery Here in England. London, 1672.

A True and Perfect Relation of Three Inhumane Murders, Committed By William Blisse alias Watts ... With the wonderful discovery of the Murtherer. London, 1672.

Anon. *An Exact Narrative of the Bloody Murder and Robbery Committed by Stephen Eaton, Sarah Swift, George Rhodes and Henry Prichard upon the Person of Mr. John Talbot, Minister*. London, 1669.

Anon. *The Tragedie of Nero*. London, 1624.

Anon. *Piso's Conspiracy, A Tragedy*. London, 1676.

Anon. *The Voice of the Nation or, An humble Address to the High and Honourable Court of Parliament ...* London, 1675.

Anon. *The Burning of the whore of Babylon*. London, 1673.

Aristotle, *The Art of Rhetoric*. Ed. and trans. John Henry Freese. London: William Heinemann Ltd., 1926.

Aubrey, John. *Aubrey's Brief Lives*. Ed. Oliver Lawson Dick. London: Secker and Warburg, 1949.

Bacon, Francis. *The Works of Francis Bacon*. Ed. J. Spedding, R.L. Ellis, D.D. Heath. 14 vols. Edinburgh 1857–74.

Banks, John. *Cyrus the Great*. London, 1696.

Barroughs, Philip. *The Method of Physick*. London, 1652.

Bayfield, Robert. *A Treatise de Morborum Capitis Essentiis & Prognosticis*. London, 1663.

Beaumont, Francis, and John Fletcher. *The Dramatic Works in the Beaumont and Fletcher Canon*. Ed. Fredson Bowers. 10 vols. Cambridge: Cambridge University Press, 1966–96.

Behn, Aphra. *The Works of Aphra Behn*. Ed. Janet Todd. 7 vols. London: William Pickering, 1996.

Blount, Sir Henry. *A Voyage into the Levant*. 8th ed. London, 1671.

Bramhall, John. *The Works of the Most Reverend Father in God, John Bramhall ...* 4 tomes. Dublin, 1676.

Burbury, John. *A Relation of a Journey of ... my Lord Henry Howard from London to Vienna, and thence to Constantinople*. London, 1671.

Burnet, Gilbert. *Bishop Burnet's history of his own time*. 2nd ed. 6 vols. Oxford, 1833.

———. *Some Passages in the Lif...*. London, 1680.

Burton, Robert. *The Anatomy of Melancholy*. Ed. Thomas C. Faulkner, Nicholas K. Kiessling and Rhonda L. Blair. 6 vols. Oxford: Clarendon Press, 1989–2000.

Calendar of State Papers, Domestic Series, of the Reign of Charles II. Ed. Mary Anne Everett Green, et al., 28 vols. (London, 1860–1968).

Carkesse, James. *Lucida Intervalla*. Ed. M.V. DePorte. Los Angeles: University of California Press, 1979.

Cartwright, Thomas, Bishop of Chester. *A sermon preached before the king at Whitehall, January 9, 1675/6*. London, 1676.

Carus, T. Lucretius. *The Epicurean Philosopher, His Six Books De Natura Rerum*. Trans. Thomas Creech. Oxford, 1682.

———. *De Rerum Natura*. Trans. W.H.D Rouse. Cambridge, Mass.: Harvard University Press, 1975.

Cave, William. *A sermon preached before the King at Whitehall*, January 22, 1675/6.

The Character of a Coffee-House, with the Symptomes of a Town Wit London, 1673.

Clarke, Samuel. *A True and Full Narrative of those two never to be forgotten Deliverances*. London, 1671.

———. *A general martyrologie, containing a collection of all the greatest persecutions which have befallen the church of Christ, from the creation to our present times*. 3rd ed. London, 1677.

Clowes, William. *A briefe and Necessary Treatise, Touching the Cure of the disease now usually called Lves Venerea*. London, 1596.

Cobbett, W. *The Parliamentary History of England*. 36 vols. London, 1806–20.

Cobbett's Complete Collection of State Trials and Proceedings for High Treason from the Earliest Period to the Present Time. 33 vols. London, 1809–26.

Collop, John. *Itur Saytiricum*. London, 1660.

Commons Debates 1621. Ed. Wallace Notestein and Frances Helen Relf, mHartley Simpson. 7 vols. New Haven: Yale University Press, 1935.

Commons Debates 1629. Ed. Wallace Notestein et al. Minneapolis: University of Minnesota, 1921.

Corneille, Pierre. *Théâtre complet*. Ed. Alain Niderst. 3 vols. Rouen: Publications de l'Université de Rouen, 1984–87.

Crowne, John. *Caligula: a tragedy, as it is acted at the Theatre Royal, by His Majesty's servants*. London, 1698.

Dalton, Michael. *The Countrey Justice: Containing the Practice of the Justices of the Peace As well in as out of their Sessions*. London, 1666.

Danchin, Pierre, ed. *The prologues and epilogues of the Restoration 1660–1700*. 7 vols. Nancy: Publications de l'Universite de Nancy, 1981–88.

Davenant, Charles. *Circe: a tragedy as it is acted at His Royal Highness the Duke of York's Theatre*. London, 1677.

Davenant, William. *Macbeth: a tragedy: with all the alterations, amendments, additions, and new songs*. London, 1674.

Dekker, Thomas. *The Dramatic Works of Thomas Dekker*. Ed. Fredson Bowers. 4 vols. Cambridge: Cambridge University Press, 1953–61.

Denton, William. *The Burnt Child Dreads the Fire*. London, 1675.

Discours merveilleux de la vie, action et deportements de Catherine de Medicis, Royne-Mere. Ed. Nicole Cazauran. Geneva: Librairie Droz S.A., 1995.

Donne, John. *Complete Poetry and Selected Prose.* Ed. John Hayward. London: The Nonesuch Press, 1962.

Downes, John. *Roscius Anglicanus.* Ed. J. Milhous and Robert D. Hume. London: The Society for Theatre Research, 1987.

Drage, William. *Physical Nosonomy: Or, A New and True Description of The law of God (called Nature) in The Body of Man.* London, 1665.

Dryden, John. *The Works of John Dryden.* ed. H.T. Swedenberg, Jr., et al. 20 vols. Berkeley and Los Angeles: University of California Press, 1956–2000.

Eachard, J. *Some Opinions of Mr. Hobbs Considered.* London, 1673.

Egane, Anthony. *The Book of Rates now used in the Sin Custom-house of the Church of Rome.* London, 1673.

Erasmus. *The Colloquies of Erasmus.* Trans. Craig R. Thompson. Chicago and London: University of Chicago Press, 1965.

Evelyn, John. *The Diary of John Evelyn.* Ed. E.S. de Beer. 6 vols. Oxford: Oxford University Press, 1955.

Ferguson, Robert. *A Sober Inquiry into the nature, measure and principle of moral virtue.* London, 1673.

Filmer, Sir Robert. *Patriarcha and Other Political Works.* Ed. Peter Laslett. Oxford: Basil Blackwell, 1949.

Fletcher, John. "The Tragedie of Valentinian" *The Works of Francis Beaumont and John Fletcher.* Ed. Arnold Glover and A.R. Waller. 10 vols. Cambridge: Cambridge University Press, 1905–12.

Foulis, Henry. *The History of Romish Treasons and Usurpations.* London, 1671.

Fournel, V., ed. *Les Contemporains de Molière.* Paris, 1875.

Fox, George. *George Fox: The Journal.* Ed. Nigel Smith. London: Penguin, 1998.

Foxe, John. *The Book of Martyrs.* London, 1676.

Fracastoro, Girolamo. *Fracastor: Syphilis or the French Disease.* Trans. Heneage Wynne-Finch. London: William Heinemann Medical Books Ltd., 1935.

Franklin, Robert. *A Murderer Punished; and Pardoned. Or, A True Relation of theWicked Life, and Shameful-happy Death of Thomas Savage; Imprisoned, Justlycondemned, and Twice Executed at Ratcliff, for his Bloody Fact in Killing his Fellow-servant, on Wednesday Octob. 28. 1668.* 12th ed. London, 1669.

Glidon, Charles. *A Comparison Between Two Stages.* New York and London: Garland Publishing, Inc., 1973.

Goodman, Christopher. *How Superior Powers Ought to be Obeyed of their Subjects.* London, 1558.

Graham, Richard Viscount Preston. *Angliae Speculum Morale: The Moral State of England.* London, 1670.

Graunt, John. *Natural and Political Observations Made upon the Bills of Morality 1662.* Ed. Peter Laslett. Germany: Gregg International Publishers, Ltd., 1973.

Grey, Anchitel. *Debates in the House of Commons 1667–1694.* 10 vols. London, 1763.

Harvey, Gideon. *Great Venus unmasked Or a more Exact Discovery of the Venereal Evil, or French Disease.* 2nd ed. London, 1672.

———. *Little Venus Unmask'd Or, a perfect Discovery of the French Pox.* London, 1670.

The Histories of the Gunpowder-Treason and the Massacre at Paris: Together with a Discourse concerning the Original of the Powder Plot .... London, 1676.

Hobbes, Thomas. *Leviathan.* Ed. Richard Tuck. Cambridge: Cambridge University Press, 1996.

Hyde, Edward, Earl of Clarendon. *A Brief View and Survey of ... Leviathan.* Oxford, 1676.

———. *The Life of Edward, Earl of Clarendon.* 3 vols. Oxford, 1759.

Joyner, William. *The Roman Empress.* London, 1671.

Knox, John. *The First Blast of the Trumpet against the monstrous regiment of Women.* Geneva, 1558.

Langbaine, Gerard. *An Account of the English Dramatick Poets.* New York and London: Garland Publishing Inc., 1973.

The last speech and confession of the Whore of Babylon, at her place of execution, on the fifth of November last .... London, 1673.

Lee, Nathaniel. *The Works of Nathaniel Lee.* Ed. Thomas B. Stroup and Arthur L. Cooke. 2 vols. New Brunswick, N.J.: The Scarecrow Press, 1955.

L'Estrange, Roger. *An Account of the Growth of Knavery, Under the Pretended Fears of Arbitrary Government and Popery.* London, 1678.

Locke, John. *Locke's Travels in France.* Ed. John Lough. Cambridge: Cambridge University Press, 1953.

L.S. *A letter from a gentleman of the Lord Ambassador Howard's retinue, to his friend in London.* London, 1670.

Luigini, Luigi. *De Morbo Gallica....* 2 vols. Venice, 1566–67.

Luttrell, Narcissus. *A Brief Historical Relation of State Affairs.* 6 vols. Oxford: Oxford University Press, 1857. Republished by Gregg International Publishers Ltd., Farnborough, 1969.

Maclean, Gerald, ed. *The Return of the King: An Anthology of English Poems Commemorating the Restoration of Charles II.* Electronic Text Center, University of Virginia Library. http://wyllie.lib.virginia.edu:8086/perl/toccer-new?id=MacKing.xml&images=images/modeng&data=/texts/english/modeng/parsed&tag=public&part=all.

Maidment, James, ed. *The Dramatic Works of John Crowne.* 4 vols. New York, Blom, repr. 1967.

Marvell, Andrew. *An Account of the Growth of Popery and Arbitrary Government.* Amsterdam, 1677.

———. *A Collection of Poems on Affairs of State by A.M. and other eminent wits....* London, 1689.

———. *The Poems and Letters of Andrew Marvell.* Ed. H.M. Margoliouth. 3rd ed. 2 vols. Oxford: Clarendon Press, 1971.

Milton, John. *Complete Prose Works of John Milton.* Ed. Don M. Wolfe. 8 vols. New Haven and London: Yale University Press, 1953–82.

————. *The Poems of John Milton*. Ed. John Carey and Alastair Fowler. London and Harlow: Longmans, Green and Co. Ltd., 1968.

Miscellany Poems. London, 1684.

Nedham, Marchamont. *A Pacquet of Advices and Animadversions Sent From London to the Men of Shaftesbury*. London, 1676.

————. *Medela Medicinae*. London, 1665.

Otway, Thomas. *The Works of Thomas Otway*. Ed. J.C. Ghosh. 2 vols. Oxford: Clarendon Press, repr. 1968.

Parker, Samuel. *A Discourse of Ecclesiastical Politie*. 3rd ed. London, 1671.

————. *Demonstration of the Divine Authority of the Law of Nature*. London, 1681.

Payne, Henry Nevil. *The Fatal Jealousy*. London, 1673.

————. *The Morning Ramble*. London, 1673.

————. *The Siege of Constantinople*. London, 1675.

Pepys, Samuel. *The Diary of Samuel Pepys*. Ed. Robert Latham and William Matthews. 11 vols. London: G. Bell and Sons Ltd., 1970–83.

Plutarch. *The Age of Alexander: Nine Greek Lives by Plutarch*. Ed. Ian Scott-Kilvert. Hamondsworth: Penguin Books, 1973.

Procopius of Caesarea. *History of the Wars*. Trans. H.B.Dewing. 7 vols. London: William Heinemann Ltd., repr. 1968.

Reynolds, John. *Blood for Blood*. London, 1661.

————. *The Triumph of Gods Revenge Against Murther*. London, 1670.

Rochester, John Wilmot, Earl of *The Complete Poems of John Wilmot, Earl of Rochester*. Ed. David M. Vieth. New Haven and London: Yale University Press, 1968.

————. *The Works of John Wilmot, Earl of Rochester*. Ed. Harold Love. Oxford: Oxford University Press, 1999.

Rymer, Thomas. *The Critical Works of Thomas Rymer*. Ed. Curt A. Zimansky. New Haven: Yale University Press, 1956.

Scott, John. *The Christian Life*. London, 1681.

Seneca. *Seneca: The Tragedies*. Ed. and trans. David R. Slavitt, et al. 2 vols. Baltimore and London: The Johns Hopkins University Press, 1992.

————. *Seneca: Four Tragedies and Octavia*. Ed. E.F. Watling. London: Harmondsworth, repr. 1972.

Settle, Elkanah. *Cambyses, King of Persia*. London, 1671.

————. *The Empress of Morocco, A Tragedy with Sculptures*. London 1673.

————. *The Female Prelate: being the History of the Life and Death of Pope Joan*. London 1680.

————. *Ibrahim the Illustrious Bassa: a tragedy acted at the Duke's Theatre*. London, 1677.

————. *Love and Revenge: a tragedy acted at the Duke's Theatre*. London, 1675.

Shadwell, Thomas. *Psyche: a tragedy*. London, 1675.

————. *The Works of Thomas Shadwell*. Ed. Montague Summers. 5 vols. London: Fortune Press, 1927.

Sharrock, Robert. *The Ends of Christian Religion*. Oxford, 1673.

Shipman, Thomas. *Henry III of France, Stabb'd by a Fryer, with the Fall of the Guise*. London, 1672.

Sophocles. *The Three Theban Plays*. Trans. Robert Fagles. New York: Penguin Books, 1982.

South, Robert. *Twelve Sermons Preached upon Several Occasions*. London, 1692.

Spenser, Edmund. *The Faerie Queene*. Ed. A.C. Hamilton. London: Longman, 2001.

Tenison, Thomas. *The Creed of Mr. Hobbes examined*. 2nd ed. London, 1671.

Tryon, Thomas. *A Discourse of the Causes, Natures and Cure of Phrensie, Madness or Distraction*. London, 1689.

W.H., *London drollery, or, The wits academy*. London, 1673.

Wilkins, Bishop John. *Of the Principles and Duties of Natural Religion*. London, 1675.

Willis, Thomas. *Two Discourses concerning the soul of brutes, Which is that of the Brutal and Sensitive of Man*. London, 1683.

Wiseman, Richard. *Several Chirurgicall Treatises*. London, 1676.

Wolseley, Sir Charles. *The Reasonableness of Scripture-Belief*. London, 1672.

———. *The Unreasonableness of Atheism made manifest*. 2nd ed. London, 1669.

Wood, Anthony A. *Athenae Oxonienses*. Ed. P. Bliss. 3rd ed. London, 1813.

Wycherley, William. *The Complete Works of William Wycherley. Ed. Montague Summers*. 3 vols. New York: Russell & Russell, Inc., 1964.

Secondary Texts

Allard, James Robert, and Mathew R. Martin, eds. *Staging Pain 1580–1800: Violence and Trauma in British Theater*. Ashgate: Farnham, 2009.

Anselment, Raymond A. "Seventeenth-Century Pox: The Medical and Literary Realities of Venereal Disease." *Seventeenth Century* 4 (1989): 189–211.

Armistead, J. M. *Nathaniel Lee*. Boston: G.K. Hall, 1979.

———. "Nathaniel Lee and Family: The Will of Richard Lee, D.D." *Notes & Queries* 24 (1977): 130–31.

———. "Nathaniel Lee" *Oxford Dictionary of National Biography*. Oxford: Oxford University Press, 2004.

Arrizabalaga, Jon, John Henderson, and Roger French. *The Great Pox: The French Disease in Renaissance Europe*. New Haven: Yale University Press, 1997.

Ashcraft, Richard. *Revolutionary Politics and Locke's 'Two Treatises of Government.'* Princeton: Princeton University Press, 1986.

Avery, Emmett L. "The Restoration Audience." *Philological Quarterly* 45 (1966): 54–61.

Barbour, F. "The Unconventional Heroic Plays of Nathaniel Lee." *University of Texas Studies in English* 20 (1940): 109–16.

Barlow, Frank. "The King's Evil." *English Historical Review* 95:374 (1980): 3–27.

Barthelemy, Anthony Gerard. *Black Face Maligned Race: The Representation of Blacks in English Drama from Shakespeare to Southerne*. Baton Rouge and London: Louisiana State University Press, 1987.

Beattie, J.M. *Crime and the Courts in England 1660–1800*. Princeton, N.J.: Princeton University Press, 1986.

———. *Policing and Punishment in London 1660–1750*. Oxford: Oxford University Press, 2001.

Bedvold, Louis I. *The Intellectual Milieu of John Dryden: Studies in Some Aspects of Seventeenth-Century Thought*. Ann Arbor: University of Michigan Press, 1934.

Behrens, B. "The Whig Theory of the Constitution in the Reign of Charles II." *Cambridge Historical Journal* 7:1 (1941): 42–71.

Bell, H.E. *An Introduction to the History and Records of the Court of Wards and Liveries*. Cambridge: Cambridge University Press, 1953.

Bennett, Joan. "God, Satan, and King Charles: Milton's Royal Portraits." *Perodicals of the Modern Language Association* 92 (1977): 441–57.

Bentley, Greg. "Melancholy, Madness, and Syphilis in Hamlet." *Hamlet Studies* 6:1–2 (1984): 75–80.

———. *Shakespeare and the New Disease: The Dramatic Function of Syphilis in Troilus and Cressida, Measure for Measure and Timon of Athens*. Diss., U of California, Davis, 1985.

Berman, David. *A History of Atheism in Britain: From Hobbes to Russell*. London and New York: Routledge, 1988.

Black, Jeremy, and Jeremy Gregory, eds. *Culture, Politics and Society in Britain, 1660–1800*. Manchester: Manchester University Press, 1991.

Boehrer, Bruce Thomas. *Monarchy and Incest in Renaissance England*. Philadelphia: University of Pennsylvania Press, 1992.

Boose, Lynda E., and Betty S. Flowers, eds. *Daughters and Fathers*. Baltimore and London: The Johns Hopkins University Press, 1989.

Booth, Stephen. *An Essay on Shakespeare's Sonnets*. New Haven and London: Yale University Press, 1969.

Borgman, Albert S. *Thomas Shadwell: His Life and Comedies*. New York: Benjamin Blom, 1969.

Boswell, Eleanore. *The Restoration Court Stage 1660–1672*. London: George Allen & Unwin Ltd., 1932.

Braden, Gordon. *Renaissance Tragedy and the Senecan Tradition*. New Haven and London: Yale University Press, 1985.

Brant, Clare, and Diane Purkiss. *Women, Texts and Histories 1575–1760*. London and New York: Routledge, 1992.

Braude, Ronald. "Revenge and Revenge Tragedy in Renaissance England." *Renaissance Quarterly* 28 (1975): 38–58.

Braunmuller, A.R., and J.C. Bulmans, eds. *Comedy from Shakespeare to Sheridan: Change and Continuity in the English and European Dramatic Tradition*. Newark: University of Delaware Press, 1986.

Braverman, R. *Plots and Counterplots: Sexual Politics and the Body Politic in English Literature 1660–1730*. Cambridge: Cambridge University Press, 1993.

Brewer, E. Cobham. *The Dictionary of Phrase and Fable*. Hertfordshire: Wordsworth Editions Ltd., repr. 1993.

Brooks, Harold F. "English Verse Satire, 1640–1660: Prolegomena." *Seventeenth Century* 3 (1989): 17–46.

Brown, Frank C. *Elkanah Settle: His Life and Works*. Chicago: The University of Chicago Press, 1910.

Brown, Laura S. *English Dramatic Form 1660–1760: An Essay in Generic History*. New Haven and London: Yale University Press, 1981.

———. "The Defenseless Woman and the Development of English Tragedy." *Studies in English Literature* 22 (1982): 429–43.

Brown, Richard E. "Nathaniel Lee's Political Dramas 1679–1683." *Restoration: Studies in English Literary Culture, 1660- 1700* 10 (1986): 41–52.

———. "The Dryden-Lee Collaboration: Oedipus and The Duke of Guise." *Restoration: Studies in English Literary Culture, 1660–1700* 9 (1985): 12–25.

———. "Heroics Satirized by 'Mad Nat. Lee.'" *Papers on Language and Literature* 19 (1983): 385–401.

Bruneau, Marie-Florine. "The Epistle 'To The King' and Alexandre le Grand: The Death of Tragedy! Long Live History." *Proceedings of the Annual Meeting ofWestern Society for French History* 13 (1986): 114–20.

Butler, Martin. *Theatre and Crisis 1632–1642*. Cambridge: Cambridge University Press, 1984.

Byrd, Max. *Visits to Bedlam: Madness and Literature in the Eighteenth Century*. Columbia: University of South Carolina Press, 1974.

Canfield, J. Douglas. "Dramatic Shifts: Writing an Ideological History of Late Stuart Drama." *Restoration and Eighteenth Century Theatre Research* 6:1 (1991): 1–9.

———. *Heroes and States: On the Ideology of Restoration Tragedy*. Lexington: The University Press of Kentucky, 2000.

———. "The Ideology of Restoration Tragicomedy." *English Literary History* 51 (Fall, 1984): 447–64.

———. "Mother as Other: The Eruption of Feminine Desire in Some Late Restoration Incest Plays." *Eighteenth Century* 39:3 (1998): 207–19.

———. "The Significance of the Restoration Rhymed Heroic Play." *Eighteenth-Century Studies* 13 (1979): 49–62.

Canfield, J. Douglas, and Deborah C. Payne, eds. *Cultural Readings in Restoration and Eighteenth-Century English Theatre*. Athens and London: The University of Georgia Press, 1995.

Cannan, Paul D. "New Directions in Serious Drama on the London Stage, 1675–1678." *Philological Quarterly* 73 (1994): 219–42.

Carter, Angela. *Fireworks: Nine Profane Pieces*. London: Quartet Books, 1974.

Carver, Larry. "Rochester's Valentinian." *Restoration and Eighteenth-Century Research* 4 (1989): 25–38.

Charney, Maurice. "The Persuasiveness of Violence in Elizabethan Plays." *Renaissance Drama* 2 (1969): 59–70.

Chernaik, Warren. *The Poet's Time: Politics and Religion in the Work of Andrew Marvell*. Cambridge: Cambridge University Press, 1983.

———. *Sexual Freedom in Restoration Literature*. Cambridge: Cambridge University Press, 1995.

————. "Unhappy Families: The Family and the State in Otway, Lee, Filmer and Dryden." *Restoration and 18th Century Theatre Research* 22 (Summer 2007): 72–90.

Chew, Samuel. *The Crescent and the Rose: Islam and England during the Renaissance*. New York: Octagon Books, 1974.

Clark, Sandra. *Women and Crime in the Street Literature of Early Modern England*. Basingstoke: Palgrave Macmillan, 2003.

Claydon, Tony and Thomas N. Corns, eds. *Religion, Culture and National Community in the 1670s*. Cardiff: University of Wales Press, 2011.

Condren, C., and A. Cousins, eds. *The Political Identity of Andrew Marvell*. Aldershot: Scolar Press, 1990.

Connerton, Paul. *How Societies Remember*. Cambridge: Cambridge University Press, 1989.

Costa, C.D.N., ed. *Seneca*. London and Boston: Routledge & Kegan Paul, 1974.

Crawford, Katherine. *Perilous Performances: Gender and Regency in Early Modern France*. Cambridge, Mass.: Harvard University Press, 2004.

Creed, Barbara. "Horror and the Monstrous-Feminine: An Imaginary Abjection." *Screen* 27:1 (1986): 44–71.

Cressy, David. *Bonfires and Bells: National Memory and the Protestant Calendar in Elizabethan and Stuart England*. London: Weidenfeld & Nicholson, 1989.

————. *Travesties and Transgressions in Tudor and Stuart England*. Oxford: Oxford University Press, 2000.

Cudar-Dominguez, Pilar. "The Islamization of Spain in William Rowley and Mary Pix: The Politics of Nation and Gender." *Comparative Drama* 36:3–4 (2002/03): 321–36.

Daly, James. *Sir Robert Filmer and English political thought*. Toronto: University of Toronto Press, 1979.

Davenport-Hines, Richard. *Sex, Death and Punishment*. London: Collins, 1990.

DePorte, Michael V. *Nightmares and Hobbyhorses: Swift, Stern, and Augustan Ideas of Madness*. San Marino: The Huntington Library, 1974.

Dolan, Frances E. "Gentlemen, I have one more thing to say": Women on scaffolds in England, 1563–1680" *Modern Philology* 92.2 (1994): 157–78.

Dollimore, Jonathan. *Radical Tragedy: Religion, Ideology and Power in the Drama of Shakespeare and his Contemporaries*. 2nd ed. London and New York: Harvester Wheatsheaf, 1989.

Evans, David R. "Private Greatness: The Feminine Ideal in Dryden's Early Heroic Drama." *Restoration: Studies in English Literary Culture, 1660–1700* 16 (1992) 2–19.

Fabricius, Johannes. *Syphilis in Shakespeare's England*. London and Pennsylvania: Jessica Kingsley Publishers, 1994.

Faller, Lincoln B. *Turned to account: The forms and functions of criminal biography in late seventeenth- and early eighteenth-century England*. Cambridge: Cambridge University Press, 1987.

Felstein, Ivor. *Sexual Pollution: The Fall and Rise of Venereal Diseases*. Newton Abbot: David and Charles, 1974.

Fessler, A. "The Management of Lunacy in Seventeenth Century England." *Proceedings of the Royal Society of Medicine* 49 (1956): 901–7.

Finlayson, Michael G. *Historians, Puritanism, and the English Revolution: the Religious Factor in English Politics before and after the Interregnum.* Toronto, Buffalo and London: University of Toronto Press, 1983.

Fisk, Deborah Payne, ed. *The Cambridge Companion to English Restoration Theatre.* Cambridge: Cambridge University Press, 2000.

Fleischmann, Wolfgang Bernard. *Lucretius and English Literature 1680–1740.* Paris: A.G. Nizet, 1964.

Flores, Stephan P. "Patriarchal Politics Under Cultural Stress: Nathaniel Lee's Passion Plays." *Restoration and Eighteenth Century Theatre Review* 8:2 (1993): 1–28.

Folkenflik, Robert, ed. *The English Hero, 1660–1800.* Newark: University of Delaware Press, 1982.

Forest, Emma. "Iconography: The Mary Bell tolls for you." *Guardian.* 4 May 1998:8.

Foucault, Michel. *Discipline and Punish: The Birth of the Prison.* Trans. Alan Sheridan. New York: Vintage Books, 1979.

———. *Madness and Civilization: A History of Insanity in the Age of Reason.* Trans. Richard Howard. New York: Pantheon Books, 1965.

French, Roger, and Jon Arrizabalaga, Andrew Cunningham, and Luis Garcia-Ballester, eds. *Medicine from the Black Death to the French Disease.* Aldershot: Ashgate Publishing Ltd., 1998.

Gabriel, Roger, and A. Neal. "Post-traumatic stress disorder." *British Medical Journal* 324:7333 (9 February 2002): 340. 8 March 2002. http://bmj.com/cgi/content/full/324/7333/340?lookupType=volpage?eaf.

Gatrell, V.A.C. *The Hanging Tree: Execution and the English People 1770- 1868.* Oxford: Oxford University Press, 1994.

Gill, Catie, ed. *Theatre and Culture in Early Modern England, 1650–1737: From Leviathan to the Licensing Act,* Farnham: Ashgate, 2010.

Gill, Pat. "Pathetic Passions: Incestuous Desire in Plays by Otway and Lee." *Eighteenth Century* 39:3 (1998): 192–208.

Goldberg, Jonathan. *James I and the Politics of Literature.* Baltimore: Johns Hopkins University Press, 1983.

Greaves, Richard L. *Deliver Us From Evil: The Radical Underground in Britain, 1660–1663.* Oxford: Oxford University Press, 1986.

———. *Enemies under his Feet: Radicals and Conformists in Britain, 1664–1677.* Stanford: Stanford University Press, 1990.

Greenberg, Mitchell. "Racine, Oedipus, and Absolute Fantasies." *Diacritics* 28:3 (1998): 40–61.

Gregg, Pauline. *King Charles I.* London: J.M. Dent & Sons Ltd., 1981.

Haley, K.H.D. *The First Earl of Shaftesbury.* Oxford: Clarendon Press, 1968.

———. *Politics in the Reign of Charles II.* Oxford: Blackwell Press, 1985.

Haller, William. *Foxe's Book of Martyrs and the Elect Nation.* London: Jonathan Cape, 1963.

Hallett, Charles A., and Elaine S. Hallett. *The Revenger's Madness: A Study of Revenge Tragedy Motifs*. Lincoln and London: University of Nebraska Press, 1980.

Ham, Roswell Grey. *Otway and Lee: Biography from a Baroque Age*. New Haven, Conn.: Yale University Press, 1931.

Hare, Robert D. *Without Conscience: The Disturbing World of the Psychopaths Among Us*. London: Little, Brown and Company, 1993.

Hare, R.D., and D. Schalling, eds. *Psychopathic Behavior: Approaches to Research*. Chichester and New York: John Wiley & Sons, 1978.

Harris, Tim. *London Crowds in the Reign of Charles II: Propaganda and Politics from the Restoration to the Exclusion Crisis*. Cambridge: Cambridge University Press, 1987.

———. *Pen for a Party: Dryden's Tory Propaganda in its Contexts*. Princeton: Princeton University Press, 1993.

———. *Restoration: Charles II and His Kingdoms 1660–1685*. London: Allen Lane, 2005.

Harris, Tim, Paul Seaward, and Mark Goldie, eds. *The Politics of Religion in Restoration England*. Oxford: Blackwell Press, 1990.

Hartle, Robert W. "Le Brun's Histoire d'Alexandre and Racine's Alexandre Le Grand." *The Romanic Review* 48 (1957): 90–103.

Hartman, Geoffrey H. "On Traumatic Knowledge and Literary Studies." *New Literary History* 26 (1995): 537–63.

Hauser, David R. "Otway Preserved: Theme and Form in Venice Preserv'd." *Studies in Philology* 55 (1958): 481–93.

Hay, Douglas, Peter Linebaugh et al., eds. *Albion's Fatal Tree: Crime and Society in Eighteenth-Century England*. New York: Pantheon Books, 1975.

Heinemann, Margot. *Puritanism and Theatre: Thomas Middleton and Opposition Drama under the Early Stuarts*. Cambridge: Cambridge University Press, 1980.

Hill, Christopher. *The Collected Essays of Christopher Hill*. 3 vols. Brighton: Harvester, 1985–86.

———. *Some Intellectual Consequences of the English Revolution*. London: Weidenfeld & Nicolson, 1980.

———. *The World Turned Upside Down: Radical Ideas during the English Revolution*. New York: The Viking Press, 1972.

Holland, Peter. *The Ornament of Action: Text and Performance in Restoration Comedy*. Cambridge: Cambridge University Press, 1979.

Hotson, Leslie. *The Commonwealth and Restoration Stage*. Cambridge: Harvard University Press, 1928.

Howe, Elizabeth. *The First English Actresses: Women and Drama 1660–1700*. Cambridge: Cambridge University Press, 1992.

Hughes, Derek. *English Drama 1660–1700*. Oxford: Clarendon Press, 1996.

———. *Dryden's Heroic Plays*. London: The MacMillan Press Ltd., 1981.

———. "Providential Justice and English Comedy 1660–1700: A Review of the External Evidence." *Modern Language Review* 81:2 (1986): 273–92.

Hughes, Derek, and Janet Todd, eds. *The Cambridge Companion to Aphra Behn.* Cambridge: Cambridge University Press, 2004.

Hughes, D. et al., eds. *Eighteenth-Century Women Playwrights.* 6 vols. London: Pickering & Chatto, 2001.

Huizinga, Johan. *The Waning of the Middle Ages.* Trans. F. Hopman. Harmondsworth: Penguin Books, repr. 1976.

Hume, Robert D. *The Development of English Drama in the Late Seventeenth Century.* Oxford: Clarendon Press, 1976.

———. "The Maid's Tragedy and Censorship in the Restoration Theatre." *Philological Quarterly* 61:4 (1982): 484–90.

———. *The Rakish Stage, Studies in English Drama, 1660–1800.* Carbondale: Southern Illinois University Press, 1983.

———. "Texts Within Contexts: Notes Towards an Historical Method." *Philological Quarterly* 71 (1992): 69–100.

———. ed. *The London Theatre World 1660–1800.* Carbondale: Southern Illinois University Press, 1980.

Hunt, Lynn, ed. *Eroticism and the Body Politic.* Baltimore: The Johns Hopkins University Press, 1991.

Hunt, Russell Arthur. "Nathaniel Lee: A Critical Study." Diss. Northwestern University, 1969.

Hunter, Michael, and David Wootton, eds. *Atheism from the Reformation to the Enlightenment.* Oxford: Oxford University Press, 1992.

Hunter, Richard, and Ida Macalpine, eds. *Three Hundred Years of Psychiatry, 1535–1860.* Oxford and London: Oxford University Press, 1963.

Hutton, Ronald. *Charles the Second: King of England, Scotland, and Ireland.* Oxford: Clarendon Press, 1989.

———. *The Restoration: A Political and Religious History of England and Wales 1658–1667.* Oxford: Oxford University Press, 1985.

Icard, Curtis B. "Venereal Iconography in the Poetry of John Wilmot, Earl of Rochester." Diss. University of Rochester 1997.

Jaffe, Aaron. "Seditious Appetites and Creeds: Shadwell's Libertine and Hobbes's Foole." *Restoration: Studies in English Literary Culture, 1660–1700* 24:2 (2000): 55–74.

Jones, Edgar et al., "Post-combat syndromes from the Boer war to the Gulf war: a cluster analysis of their nature and attribution" *British Medical Journal* 324:7333 (9 February 2002): 321. 8 March 2002. http://bmj.com/cgi/content/full/324/7333/321?eaf.

Jones, J.R. *Country and Court: England, 1658–1714.* Cambridge, Mass.: Harvard University Press, 1978.

Jooma, Minaz. "The Alimentary Structures of Incest in *Paradise Lost*." *English Literary History* 63 (1996): 25–43.

Jose, Nicholas. *Ideas of the Restoration in English Literature 1660–71.* Cambridge, Mass.: Harvard University Press, 1984.

Kastan, D.S. "Nero and the Politics of Nathaniel Lee." *Papers in Language and Literature* 13 (1977): 125–35.

Keeble, N.H. *The Literary Culture of Non-Conformity in Later Seventeenth-Century England.* Leicester: Leicester University Press, 1987.

Kenny, Shirley Strum, ed. *British Theatre and Other Arts, 1660–1800.* London: Associated University Presses Inc., 1984.

Kenyon, J.P. *The Popish Plot.* London: Heinemann, 1972.

Kernan, Alvin. *The Cankered Muse: Satire of the English Renaissance.* New Haven: Yale University Press, 1959.

Kerrigan, John. *Revenge Tragedy: Aeschylus to Armageddon.* Oxford: Clarendon Press, 1996.

———. "Revenge Tragedy Revisited: Politics, Providence and Drama, 1649–1683." *The Seventeenth Century* 12:2 (1997): 207–29.

Kerrigan William. *The Sacred Complex: On the Psychogenesis of Paradise Lost.* Cambridge, Mass: Harvard University Press, 1983.

Kingdon, Robert M. *Myths about the St. Bartholomew's Day Massacres 1572–1576.* Cambridge, Mass. and London: Harvard University Press, 1988.

Kirsch, Arthur C. *Dryden's Heroic Drama.* Princeton: Princeton University Press, 1965.

Kitchin, George. *Sir Roger L'Estrange.* London: Kegan Paul, Trench, Trubner & Co. Ltd., 1913.

Knecht, R.J. *Catherine de' Medici.* London and New York: Longman, 1998.

Knight, G. Wilson. *The Golden Labyrinth: A Study of British Drama.* London: Phoenix House, Ltd., 1962.

Knoppers, Laura Lunger. *Historicizing Milton: Spectacle, Power, and Poetry in Restoration England.* Athens and London: The University of Georgia Press, 1994.

Knoppers, Laura Lunger, and Joan B. Landes, eds. *Monstrous Bodies/Political Monstrosities in Early Modern Europe.* Ithaca and London: Cornell University Press, 2004.

LaCapra, Dominick. *Writing History, Writing Trauma.* Baltimore and London: The Johns Hopkins University Press, 2001.

Leacock, Dawn. "Computer Analysis of Restoration Staging, II: 1671–1682." *Theatre Notebook* 47:3 (1993) 141–56.

Lindley, David, ed. *Court Masques: Jacobean and Caroline Entertainments 1605–1640.* Oxford: Oxford University Press, 1995.

Loewenstein, David. *Milton and the Drama of History: Historical Vision, Iconoclasm, and the Literary Imagination.* Cambridge: Cambridge University Press, 1990.

Loftis, John. *The Politics of Drama in Augustan England.* Oxford: Clarendon Press, 1963.

Lord, George deF et al., eds. *Poems on Affairs of State: Augustan Satirical Verse, 1660–1714.* 7 vols. New Haven and London: Yale University Press, 1963–75.

Love, Harold, "State Affairs on the Restoration Stage." *Restoration and Eighteenth Century Theatre Review* 14 (1975): 1–9.

———. "Who were the Restoration Audience?" *Yearbook of English Studies* 10 (1980): 21–44.

————, ed. *Restoration Literature: Critical Approaches*. London: Methuen & Co. Ltd., 1972.

Lowenstein, David. *Milton and the Drama of History*. Cambridge: Cambridge University Press, 1990.

Luis-Martinez, Zenon, and Jorge Figueroa-Dorrego, eds. *Re- Shaping the Genres: Restoration Women Writers*. Bern: Peter Lang, 2003.

MacDonald, Michael. *Mystical Bedlam: Madness, Anxiety and Healing in Seventeenth-Century England*. Cambridge: Cambridge University Press, 1981.

MacKay, Dorothy. *The Double Invitation in the Legend of Don Juan*. Palo Alto: Stanford University Press, 1943.

Maclean, Gerald. *Time's Witness: Historical Representation in English Poetry, 1603–1660*. Madison: The University of Wisconsin Press, 1990.

————, ed. *Culture and Society in the Stuart Restoration: Literature, Drama, History.* Cambridge: Cambridge University Press, 1995.

————, ed. *The Return of the King: An Anthology of English Poems Commemorating the Restoration of Charles II*. Electronic Text Center, University of Virginia Library. http://wyllie.lib.virginia.edu:8086/perl/ toccernew?id=MacKing.xml&images=images/modeng&data=/texts/english/ modeng/parsed&tag=public&part=all.

Maguire, Nancy Klein. *Regicide and Restoration: English Tragicomedy 1660–1671*. Cambridge: Cambridge University Press, 1992.

————. "Regicide and Reparation: The Autobiographical Drama of Roger Boyle, Earl of Orrery." *English Literary Renaissance* 21 (1991): 257–82.

Mandel, Oscar, ed. *The Theatre of Don Juan*. Lincoln: University of Nebraska Press, 1963.

Manning, Gillian. "Rochester's Satyr Against Reason and Mankind and Contemporary Religious Debate." *The Seventeenth Century*, 8:1 (1993 Spring): 99–121.

Marsden, Jean I., ed. *The Appropriation of Shakespeare: Post- Renaissance Reconstructions of the Works and the Myth*. London: Harvester Wheatsheaf, 1991.

Matar, N.I. "The Renegade in English Seventeenth Century Imagination." *Studies in English Literature* 33 (1993): 489–505.

————. "Islam in Interregnum and Restoration England." *The Seventeenth Century* 6:1 (1991): 57–71.

Maus, Katharine Eisaman. "Playhouse Flesh and Blood: Sexual Ideology and the Restoration Actress." *English Literary History* 46 (1979): 595–619.

————, ed. *Four Revenge Tragedies*. Oxford: Oxford University Press, 1995.

McCabe, Richard. *Incest, Drama and Nature's Law, 1550–1700*. Cambridge: Cambridge University Press, 1993.

McIlwain, Charles Howard, ed. *The Political Works of James I*. New York: Russell & Russell Inc., 1965.

McKeon, Michael. *Politics and Poetry in Restoration England: The Case of Dryden's Annus Mirabilis*. Cambridge, Mass and London: Harvard University Press, 1975.

McLeod, A.L. "Nathaniel Lee's Birth Date." *Modern Language Notes* 69:3 (1954): 167–70.

Merians, Linda E., ed. *The Secret Malady: Venereal Disease in Eighteenth-Century Britain and France.* Lexington: The University Press of Kentucky: 1996.

Milhous, Judith. "The Duke's Company's Profits, 1675–1677." *Theatre Notebook* 32 (1978): 76–88.

———. "The Multimedia Spectacular on the Restoration Stage." *British Theatre and the Other Arts, 1660–1800*, ed. Shirley Strum Kenny. London and Toronto: Associated University Presses, 1984.

Milhous, J., and Robert D. Hume. "Dating Play Premieres from Publication Data, 1660–1700." *Harvard Library Bulletin* 22 (1974): 374–405.

Miller, John. *Charles II.* London: Weidenfeld and Nicolson, 1991.

———. *Popery and Politics in England 1660–1688.* Cambridge: Cambridge University Press, 1973.

Miner, Earl, ed. *Literary Uses of Typology from the Late Middle Ages to the Present.* Princeton, N.J.: Princeton University Press, 1977.

Mintz, Samuel I. *The Hunting of Leviathan.* Cambridge: Cambridge University Press, 1962.

Munns, Jessica. *Restoration Politics and Drama: The Plays of Thomas Otway, 1675–1683.* Newark: University of Delaware Press, 1995.

Murray, Meg McGavran, ed. *Face to Face: Fathers, Mothers, Masters, Monsters – Essays for a Nonsexist Future.* Westport, Conn, and London: Greenwood Press, 1983.

Neelakanta, Vanita. "Exile and Restoration in John Crowne's *The Destruction of Jerusalem by Titus Vespasian.*" *Philological Quarterly* 89:2–3 (2010): 185–207.

Neely, Carol Thomas. "'Documents in Madness': Reading Madness and Gender in Shakespeare's Tragedies and Early Modern Culture." *Shakespeare Quarterly* 42:3 (Autumn 1991): 315–38.

Nevo, Ruth. *The Dial of Virtue: A Study of Poems on Affairs of State in the Seventeenth Century.* Princeton, N.J.: Princeton University Press, 1963.

Nichols Jr., James H. *Epicurean Political Philosophy: The De rerum natura of Lucretius.* Ithaca and London: Cornell University Press, 1972.

Nicoll, Allardyce. *A History of English Drama 1660–1900.* 4 vols. Cambridge: Cambridge University Press, rev. 1952.

———. "Political Plays of the Restoration." *Modern Language Review* 16 (1921): 224–42.

Norbrook, David. *Poetry and Politics in the English Renaissance.* Oxford: Oxford University Press, revised 2002.

Novak, Maximillian E., ed. *The Empress of Morocco and Its Critics.* Los Angeles: University of California Press, 1968.

———. "Margery Pinchwife's 'London Disease': Restoration Comedy and the Libertine Offensive of the 1670's." *Studies in Literary Imagination* 10 (1977): 1–23.

Nussbaum, Felicity. "'Real, Beautiful Women': Actresses and *The Rival Queens.*" *Eighteenth-Century Life* 32:2 (Spring 2008): 138–58.

Ogg, David. *England in the Reign of Charles II*. 2nd ed. 2 vols. Oxford: Clarendon Press, 1955.

Orgel, Stephen. *The Illusion of Power: Political Theater in the English Renaissance*. Berkeley: University of California Press, 1975.

Ornstein, Robert. *The Moral Vision of Jacobean Tragedy*. Westport, Conn.: Greenwood Press, 1975.

Owen, Susan J., ed. *A Companion to Restoration Drama*. Oxford, Blackwell Publishers Ltd., 2001.

———. "'He that should guard my virtue has betrayed it': The Dramatization of Rape in the Exclusion Crisis." *Restoration and Eighteenth Century Theatre Review* 9 (1994): 59–68.

———. "Interpreting the Politics of Restoration Drama." *Seventeenth Century* 8 (1993): 67–97.

———. *Restoration Theatre and Crisis*. Oxford: Clarendon Press, 1996.

Patterson, Annabel. *Marvell and the Civic Crown*. Princeton: Princeton University Press, 1978.

Pearson, Jacqueline. *The Prostituted Muse: Images of Women and Women Dramatists 1642–1737*. London: Harvester Wheatsheaf, 1988.

Peterson, Dale, ed. *A Mad People's History of Madness*. Pittsburgh: University of Pittsburgh Press, 1982.

Picard, Liza. *Restoration London*. London: Weidenfeld & Nicolson, 1997.

Pocock, Gordon. *Boileau and the Nature of Neo-classicism*. Cambridge: Cambridge University Press, 1980.

Pocock, J.G.A. *Virtue, Commerce and History: Essays on Political Thought and History*. Cambridge: Cambridge University Press, 1985.

Porter, Roy. *Mind-Forg'd Manacles: A History of Madness in England from the Restoration to the Regency*. London: Athlone Press, 1987.

———. *A Social History of Madness: Stories of the Insane*. London: Weidenfeld and Nicolson, 1987.

Porter, R., W.F. Bynam and Michael Shepherd, eds. *The Anatomy of Madness*. 3 vols. London and New York: Tavistock Publications, 1985.

Posner, Donald. "Charles Lebrun's Triumphs of Alexander." *The Art Bulletin* 41 (1959): 237–48.

Potter, Lois. *Secret Rites and Secret Writing: Royalist Literature 1641–1660*. Cambridge: Cambridge University Press, 1989.

Powell, J. *Restoration Theatre Production*. London: Routledge & Kegan Paul, 1984.

Quetel, Claude. *History of Syphilis*. Trans. Judith Braddock and Brian Pike. Cambridge: Polity Press, 1990.

Quinsey, Katherine M. *Broken Boundaries: Women and Feminism in Restoration Drama*. Lexington: The University Press of Kentucky, 1996.

Rabbi, Stella Gargantini. "D'un Alexandre a l'Autre: Le mythe d'Alexandre le Grand sous Louis XIV." *Transhumances culturelles: Mélanges*. Pisa: Libreria Goliardica, 1985.

Rank, Otto. *The Don Juan Legend.* Trans. and Ed. David G. Winter. Princeton: Princeton University Press, 1975.

Reed, Robert. *Bedlam on the Jacobean Stage.* New York: Octagon Books, repr. 1970.

Rierson, Don. "Foundations of the English *Oedipus*: An Examination of the translations of Sophocles's *Oedipus Tyrannus* by John Dryden and Nathaniel Lee, and Lewis Theobold." Diss. The Florida State University, 1984.

Righer [Barton], Anne. "Heroic Tragedy." *Restoration Theatre*, eds. John Russell Brown and Bernard Harris. London: Edward Arnold Publishers Ltd., 1965.

Roberts, D. *The Ladies: Female Patronage of Restoration Drama 1660–1700.* Oxford: Clarendon Press, 1989.

Robinson, John Martin. *The Dukes of Norfolk.* Oxford: Oxford University Press, 1982.

Romanowski, Sylvie, and Monique Bilezikian, eds. *Homage to Paul Benichou.* Birmingham, Ala.: Summa Publications, Inc., 1994.

Rothstein, Eric. *Restoration Tragedy: Form and the Process of Change.* Westport, Connecticut: Greenwood Press, 1967.

Russell Brown, John and Bernard Harris, eds. *Restoration Theatre.* London: Edward Arnold Publishers Ltd., 1965.

Sage, Victor. *Horror Fiction in the Protestant Tradition.* London: Macmillan Press, 1988.

Salgado, Gamini ed. *Three Jacobean Tragedies.* Harmonsdworth: Penguin Books, 1965.

Sampson, H. Grant. "Some Bibliographical Evidence concerning Restoration Attitudes towards Drama." *Journal of Rutgers University Libraries* 38 (1976): 98–108.

Sawday, Jonathan. "Re-writing a Revolution: History, Symbol, and Text In the Restoration." *The Seventeenth Century* 7 (1992): 171–99.

Schille, Candy B.K. "At the Crossroads: Gendered Desire, Political Occasion, and Dryden and Lee's *Oedipus.*" *Papers on Language and Literature* 40:3 (Summer 2004): 305–28.

Schochet, Gordon. *Patriarchalism in Political Thought: The Authoritarian Family and Political Speculation and Attitudes Especially in Seventeenth-Century England.* New York: Basic Books, 1975.

Schwoebel, Robert. *The Shadow of the Crescent: The Renaissance Image of the Turk (1453–1517).* Nieuwkoop: B. de Graaf, 1967.

Scott, Jonathan. *Algernon Sidney and the English Republic 1623–1677.* Cambridge: Cambridge University Press, 1988.

———. *Algernon Sidney and the Restoration Crisis 1677–1683.* Cambridge: Cambridge University Press, 1991.

———. *England's Troubles.* Cambridge: Cambridge University Press, 2000.

Share, Don, ed. *Seneca in English.* London: Penguin Books, 1998.

Sharp, Buchanan. "Popular Political Opinion in England 1660–1685." *History of European Ideas* 10:1 (1989) 13–29.

Sharpe, J.A. "'Last Dying Speeches': Religion, Ideology and Public Execution in Seventeenth-Century England." *Past and Present* 107 (1985): 144–67.

———. *Crime in Early Modern England 1550–1750.* 2nd ed. London and New York: Longman, 1999.

Shepherd, S. *Amazons and Warrior Women: Varieties of Feminism in Seventeenth-Century Drama.* New York: St. Martin's Press, 1981.

Showalter, Elaine. *Hystories: Hysterical Epidemics and Modern Culture.* New York: Columbia University Press, 1997.

Simerka, Barbara A., and Christopher B. Weimer, eds. *Echoes and Inscriptions: Comparative Approaches to Early Modern Spanish Literatures.* Lewisburg: Bucknell UP, 2000.

Simkin, Stevie, ed. *Revenge Tragedy.* Basingstoke: Palgrave, 2001.

Singh, Sarup. *The Theory of Drama in the Restoration Period.* Bombay: Orient Longmans, 1963.

Skinner, Quentin. *The Foundations of Modern Political Thought.* 2 vols. Cambridge: Cambridge University Press, 1978–79.

———. "The Ideological Context of Hobbes's Political Thought." *Historical Journal* 9:3 (1966): 286–317.

Skrine, Peter N. "Blood, Bombast, and Deaf Gods: The Tragedies of Lee and Lohenstein." *German Life and Letters* 24 (1971): 14–30.

Smith, Molly Easo. "Spectacles of Torment in 'Titus Andronicus.'" *Studies in English Literature* 36:2 (Spring 1996): 315–31.

Smith, Nigel. *Literature and Revolution in England, 1640–1660.* New Haven and London: Yale University Press, 1994.

Spierenburg, Pieter. *The Spectacle of Suffering.* Cambridge: Cambridge University Press, 1984.

Sprague, Arthur Colby. *Beaumont and Fletcher on the Restoration Stage.* New York and London: Benjamin Bloom, repr. 1965.

Spring, J.R. "Platforms and Picture Frames: A Conjectural Reconstruction of the Duke of York's Theatre, Dorset Gardens, 1669–1709." *Theatre Notebook* 31:3 (1977): 6–19.

Spurr, John. *England in the 1670s.* Oxford: Blackwell Publishers, 2000.

Staves, Susan. *Players' Scepters: Fictions of Authority in the Restoration.* Lincoln and London: University of Nebraska Press, 1979.

Stephenson, Carl, and Frederick George Marcham, eds. *Sources of English Constitutional History.* New York and London: Harper & Row Publishers, 1937.

Stone, Laurence. *The Family, Sex and Marriage in England, 1500–1800.* New York: Harper and Row, 1979.

Straub, Susan C. *Nature's Cruel Stepdames: Murderous Women in the Street Literature of Seventeenth Century England.* Pittsburgh: Duquesne University Press, 2005.

Straulman, Ann. "Zempoalla, Lyndaraxa, and Nourmahal: Dryden's Heroic Female Villains." *English Studies in Canada* 1:1 (1975): 31–45.

Stroup, Thomas B. "Shadwell's Use of Hobbes." *Studies in Philology* 35:3 (1938): 405–32.

Swedenberg, T. *Essential Articles for the Study of John Dryden*. Hamden, Conn.: Archon, 1966.

Tanner, J.R. *English Constitutional Conflicts of the Seventeenth Century 1603–1689*. Cambridge: Cambridge University Press, repr. 1937.

Teeter, Louis. "The Dramatic Use of Hobbes's Political Ideas." *English Literary History* 3 (1936): 140–169.

Taylor, Mark. *Shakespeare's Darker Purpose*. New York: AMS Press, Inc., 1982.

Thomas, Susie. "This Thing of Darkness I Acknowledge Mine: Aphra Behn's Abdelazer, or The Moor's Revenge." *Restoration: Studies in English Literary Culture, 1660–1700* 22:1 (1998): 18–39.

Thompson, Roger. *Unfit for Modest Ears: A Study of Pornographic, Obscene and Bawdy Works Written or Published in England in the Second Half of the Seventeenth Century*. London: The MacMillan Press Ltd., 1979.

Tilley, Morris Palmer. *A Dictionary of the Proverbs in England in the 16th and 17th Centuries*. Ann Arbor: University of Michigan Press, 1950.

Todd, Janet. *The Secret Life of Aphra Behn*. London: Andre Deutsch, 1996.

———. ed. *Aphra Behn Studies*. Cambridge: Cambridge University Press: 1995.

Tokson, Elliot H. *The Popular Image of the Black Man in English Drama, 1550–1688*. Boston: G.J.Hall and Co., 1982.

Trevor-Roper, Hugh. *From the Counter-Reformation to the Glorious Revolution*. London: Secker & Warburg, 1992.

Tuck, Richard. "A New Date for Filmer's Patriarcha." *Historical Journal* 29:1 (1986): 183–86.

———. "Power and Authority in Seventeenth Century England." *Historical Journal* 17 (1974): 43–61.

Underdown, David. *Revel, Riot and Rebellion: Popular Politics and Culture in England 1603–1660*. New York: Oxford University Press, 1985.

Van Lennep, W., E. Avery and A. Scouten, eds. *The London Stage 1660–1800*. 5 vols. Carbondale, Ill.: Southern Illinois University Press, 1965–68.

Vieth, David M. "Nathaniel Lee's The Rival Queens and the Psychology of Assassination." *Restoration: Studies in English Literary Culture, 1660–1700* 2 (1978): 10–13.

Waith, Eugene M. *The Herculean Hero in Marlowe, Chapman, Shakespeare and Dryden*. London: Chatto & Windus, 1962.

———. *Ideas of Greatness: Heroic Drama in England*. New York: Barnes and Noble, Inc., 1971.

Walker, D.P. *The Decline of Hell: Seventeenth-Century Discussions of Eternal Torment*. London: Routledge & Kegan Paul, 1964.

Walker, J. "The Censorship of the Press during the Reign of Charles II." *History* (October 1950): 219–38.

Wallace, John M., ed. *The Golden and The Brazen World: Papers in Literature and History, 1650–1800*. Berkeley and London: University of California Press, 1985.

Wasserman, Earl R. "The Pleasures of Tragedy." *English Literary History* 14:4 (1947): 283–307.

Wever, Harold M. *The Restoration Rake-Hero: Transformations in Sexual Understanding in Seventeenth-Century England.* Madison: University of Wisconsin Press, 1986.

Wheatley, Christopher. *Without God or Reason: The plays of Thomas Shadwell and secular ethics in the Restoration.* Lewisburg: Bucknell UP, 1993.

White, Arthur F. "Office of the Revels and Dramatic Censorship during the Restoration Period." *Western Reserve University Bulletin* 34 (1931): 5–45.

Wikander, Matthew H. "The Spitted Infant: Scenic Emblem and Exclusionist Politics in Restoration Adaptations of Shakespeare." *Shakespeare Quarterly* 37 (1986): 340–358.

Wilcox, Helen. *Women and Literature in Britain, 1500–1700.* Cambridge: Cambridge University Press, 1996.

Wilson, John Harold. *All the King's Ladies: Actresses of the Restoration.* Chicago: The University of Chicago Press, 1958.

————. *A Preface to Restoration Drama.* Cambridge, Mass.: Harvard University Press, 1965.

Winn, J. *John Dryden and His World.* New Haven and London: Yale University Press, 1987.

Winter, Jay. *Sites of Memory, Sites of Mourning: The Great War in European Cultural History.* Cambridge: Cambridge University Press, 1995.

Winterbottom, John. "The Development of the Hero in Dryden's Tragedies." *Journal of English and Germanic Philology* 52 (1953): 161–73.

Wong, Erwin John. "Ideas of Madness in the Drama of Nathaniel Lee. " Diss. State University of New York at Stony Brook, 1983.

Zimbardo, Rose A. "At Zero Point: Discourse, Politics, and Satire in Restoration England." *English Literary History* 59 (1992): 785–98.

Zwicker, Steven. "Is There Such a Thing as Restoration Literature?" *Huntingdon Library Quarterly*, 69:3 (September 2006): 425–50.

————. *The Language of Politics in the Age of Dryden.* Princeton: Princeton University Press, 1984.

————. *Lines of Authority: Politics and English Literary Culture, 1649–1689.* Ithaca and London: Cornell University Press, 1993.

Index

Printed in Great Britain
by Amazon

22232095R00110